AF370484

OUR STORIES, OUR STRUGGLE

Violence and the Lives of Women

Narratives and Poetry by South Asian Women

Edited by **Mitali Chakravarty** and **Ratnottama Sengupta**

SPEAKING TIGER BOOKS LLP
125A, Ground Floor, Shahpur Jat, near Asiad Village,
New Delhi 110049

First published by Speaking Tiger Books 2024

Anthology copyright © Speaking Tiger Books 2024
Preface copyright © Mitali Chakravarty 2024
Introduction copyright © Subhashini Ali 2024

The copyright for individual essays and excerpts vests in the respective
authors, proprietors and translators or their heirs/estates.

Page 305 is an extension of the copyright page.

ISBN: 978-93-5447-107-0
eISBN: 978-93-5447-099-8

10 9 8 7 6 5 4 3 2 1

All rights reserved.
No part of this publication may be reproduced, transmitted, or stored in
a retrieval system, in any form or by any means, electronic,
mechanical, photocopying, recording or otherwise,
without the prior permission of the publisher.

This book is sold subject to the condition that it shall not, by way of
trade or otherwise, be lent, resold, hired out, or otherwise
circulated, without the publisher's prior consent, in any
form of binding or cover other than
that in which it is published.

Mitali Chakravarty writes and edits with a vision of fostering a more equitable world that transcends manmade barriers, aiming for a happier future. In that spirit, she founded the online journal, *borderlessjournal.com*, and edited its first anthology, *Monalisa No Longer Smiles: An Anthology of Writings from Across the World* (Om Books International, 2022). Her writings have been widely published and anthologised. Her most recent book is *Flight of Angsana Orioles: Poems* (Hawakal Books, 2023). Mitali lives with her family on a tropical island.

Ratnottama Sengupta transitioned to directing with *And They Made Classics* (2017), exploring the unique collaboration between screenwriter Nabendu Ghosh and director Bimal Roy. Her extensive involvement in the arts includes writing books on cinema and art, programming film festivals, and curating art exhibitions. Sengupta has authored works such as *Krishna's Cosmos: The Creativity of an Artist, Sculptor & Teacher* (Mapin Publishing, 2003) and edited notable collections like *That Bird Called Happiness* (Speaking Tiger, 2018). She has also contributed to the *Encyclopaedia Britannica* on Hindi cinema, served on the Central Board for Film Certification, and was a member of the National Film Awards jury, earning a National Award herself. Formerly the Arts Editor of *The Times of India,* she is also a member of the National Film Development Corporation's script committee. Her other edited, translated and authored volumes include *Me and I* (translated by Devottam Sengupta, Hachette India, 2017), *Chuninda Kahaniyaan: Nabendu Ghosh* (Roshnai Prakashan, 2009) and *Kadam Kadam* (Bhaishilpi, 2016).

CONTENTS

PART THREE: Verse of Resilience

PREFACE

Living in the safe haven of Singapore where golden orioles soar amidst yellow angsana blooms, one might wonder: why would an unfamiliar voice seek to unleash women's voices against violence in South Asia? Well, because I am a woman. I have travelled around the world for over thirty years and seen the freedom with which women dress and move around in many places, and I have always wondered why we don't do the same in South Asia, where I was born.

When Nirbhaya was gang raped in 2012, I heard her clothes being classed as inappropriate,[1] as was her being out at night with her boyfriend—but do these circumstances justify or excuse the act of rape?

In Suzhou, China, where I was in 2012 when Nirbhaya's death buried the world in grief for a daughter violated beyond comprehension, I recall an expat woman in our gated compound walking home at midnight, naked, intoxicated, with her husband carrying her clothes. Remarkably, she faced no immediate harm or danger. All that happened is that the following day, the property's security issued a warning to her against indecent exposure.

It is not that rapes are uncommon in other countries, but why would a woman be blamed for a man's criminal act?

This book started its journey when a young vet was raped in Hyderabad in broad daylight and burnt. It was torturous even to imagine what could happen to any woman at any time in India. It was incomprehensible. It was time to tell the rapists, the criminals, and the establishment that women are strong and resilient. Not only can we heal from violence but also get laws related to rape changed, as illustrated by the 'Nirbhaya' case, our launchpad in the book. But were these stricter laws enough to stop rapes and change mindsets?

Women shaken by crimes gathered around in sisterhood when I told them about my proposed venture to gather women from all walks of life who were willing to give voice to our united resilience and resistance against criminal acts committed against one-half of the world's population.

Our stories aim to spark a transformation in the South Asian social framework by highlighting the insufficient efforts to fully integrate women into the mainstream of humanity, historically dominated by men. The outspoken tales of resilience amid suffering in this book strike at the very heart of the patriarchal mindset in all its forms. We, as writers, are determined to sear the sky with the assertion that men and women are equally vital, equally indispensable for the survival of humanity. The topics covered cross the borders of India into Pakistan, Bangladesh, Nepal and Sri Lanka for precisely that reason. This collection includes stories, narratives, and chronicles of rape—familial rape, the rape of children—murder, hudood, honour killing, marital violence, dowry cases, forced disappearances, molestation, stalking, the egregious identitarian crimes committed upon tribal women and girls, and others for their caste and class status. They look back at the shadows cast by rape, neglect and abuse on the widows of the 1971 Bangladesh Liberation War and feature the untamed primordial urges in all these societies that underpin many crimes against women, such as those taking the form of Sati, the outrageous practice of acid attacks, and the ultimate humiliation—the rejection of a girl child by her family.

This book is a blend of non-fiction, fiction, and poetry that celebrates women's resilience and their capacity to transcend victimhood. It will inspire courage in victims of all kinds of violence.

We have endeavoured to unite under the commonality of suffering that transcends borders. We aim not to 'other' individuals but to embrace each other in creating transformative changes that will heal societies from self-propagated corruption. We hope our unified voices will have a meaningful impact and inspire enough people to prompt significant change.

* * *

Central to this anthology is Meenakshi Malhotra's powerful essay on 'Nirbhaya', whose case catalyzed critical changes to rape laws in India. The protests against the injustice and barbarity of that gang rape brought unprecedented international attention to the issue. Her tragedy exposed the fallacies in laws made by a patriarchal society, shedding light on the mindset that confines a woman in South Asian cultures to restrictions on movement, dress, and the pursuit of a dignified life. Malhotra, an academic and gender studies researcher, comments on how the victim and her parents 'broke the mould of victimhood' and instead 'of succumbing to notions of shame they, in a sense, were able to convey their outrage and sense of loss and devastation by garnering the informative/reverberative power of the media to reach people'.

But is that a reality for all South Asian women today? I am not so sure. Academic Hoineilhing Sitlhou provides an eye-opening account of heinous sexual crimes against women during the ongoing Kuki/Zo-Meitei conflict in Manipur. Teresa Rehman, an award-winning journalist from the Northeast known for her quiet grit, writes about a powerful tool that can defy the criminal patriarchal mindset justifying crimes against women: defiance. She uses the experience of the imas in her book, *Mothers of Manipur: Twelve Women Who Made History* to conclude: 'Women's defiance to different forms of power and domination can be a formidable instrument of social change.' Twelve women in their sixties and seventies had marched in 2004 to an army post and stripped naked to challenge the soldiers for raping and shooting young Manorama, supposedly picked up for questioning as they called her an insurgent. Speaking out boldly against the harassment women from the Northeast face is

Ngurang Reena's powerful essay, hinged on her own and others' experiences in metropolises, especially Delhi. Reena, who used to teach at Jawaharlal Nehru University, has taken up issues of racial discrimination and sexual harassment.

Farah Ahamed, a Pakistani lawyer and writer, bases her story on interviews with a young Christian woman in Lahore, wrongfully incarcerated under stern patriarchal laws. Capturing such darkness in words without getting lost in the overwhelming abundance of misery is a daunting task. But all the writers in this anthology rise above it, writing to illuminate hope through their gripping narratives.

Sohana Manzoor, a writer and an academic, gives us a compelling real-life case study from Bangladesh. Eli Prue Marma, a writer from the Chittagong Hill Tracts in Bangladesh, narrates the harrowing lives of Chakma women (who also live in Burma and India and often profess the Buddhist faith). In their stories, Manzoor and Eli Prue, the latter a member of the Marma community, grapple with themes of rape and death—reminiscent of Nirbhaya's ordeal, albeit within a different cultural context.

Anuradha Kumar, an established writer, approaches a case study on suicide stemming from familial rape in a manner that sends unsettling shivers down the spine. Multiple narratives of marital discord and violence, by academic Nishi Pulugurtha and poet Mallika Bhaumik (both from India), and Pakistani artist-writer Selma Tufail, underscore societies steeped in patriarchy in which only some dare to be different.

One of the most poignant and brave is the first-hand telling of sexual abuse by writer Ankita Banerjee. She concludes powerfully: '...I no longer care if anyone thinks I'm making things up. I have pulled up the carpet, and my truth is out there. Turn your face, shove it under a new carpet if the truth is uncomfortable, but I don't allow you to tell me I invited it. Not anymore.' Her defiance is the voice that has evolved from the yearning in Angelou's 'Caged Bird', which sings of freedom. The same defiance we saw in Nirbhaya and her family.

These real-life stories reverberate with the breaking of silence, seamlessly integrating voices from the past: none exemplifies it better than the translation from the Bengali of Sandhya Sinha's (she would have approached a hundred years of age had she lived) protest essay after Roop Kanwar's Sati in the 1980s. Her translator, and the co-editor of this anthology, established journalist Ratnottama Sengupta, journeys through the darkness towards light, illustrating how, instead of burning widows, in the twenty-first century, we find a group geared to encourage widow remarriage and the marriage of abandoned women. Sengupta supports strict regulation of crimes against women in her non-fiction works and holds that education—beyond schools and through carefully crafted stories disseminated via mass media—must bridge socio-economic gaps and generate meaningful employment opportunities for young men. This approach aims to foster respect for women's rights and prevent gender-based violence.

Caste, creed and gender have been explored in this collection with a powerful narrative centering around the Dalit rights activist from Telangana, Sathyavathi, by well-known lawyer and civil rights activist, Vasanth Kannabiran. Simran Chaddha, an academic, draws from poetry written by women in Sri Lanka during the height of the conflict in the country to highlight that women's emancipation takes a back seat when they are pulled and pushed by two opposite forces, each trying to marshal their support for a larger goal in which their emancipation is not the priority.

Sengupta has enriched this collection with compelling essays on two important themes. The first deals with acid attack, a terrible torture for anyone who faces it—and there are many. The stories of survivors-turned-activists are heart-warming and encouraging. Sengupta's intense essay on honour killing, which stems from her discussions with people she met during her long, illustrious career, enriches the timbre of this narrative. She writes: 'At the outset, let me clearly state: No part of this essay is fiction. If any incident or observation is not ascribed to a source, that is because my entire understanding of the subject comes from watching numerous films, conversations with filmmakers from Turkey, Egypt, Iraq, America, Kazakhstan, Pakistan and

India, reading, and reporting on the issue over a lifetime.' Our non-fiction highlights the Bilkis Bano case, which resurfaced recently: we are privileged that women's rights activist Subhashini Ali, who helped Bano seek—and attain—justice, has written the Introduction to this anthology. Kalpana Kannibaran's powerful essay on the State condoning such crimes also features in this collection.

* * *

The echoes of these stories reverberate in the fiction in this selection. I marvel at how the creators of these pieces could grasp the terror and the horror of each situation described. Sucharita Dutta-Asane's tribal woman, standing alone and tall after being widowed and raped, creates a sense of terror, of ominous power—one feels a Kali is born to avenge the demons of injustice and violence. No less ominous are the ghosts of the victims who fell to abuse in the real-life narratives. Aruna Chakravarti's poignant narrative of the loneliness, abuse and murder of an aged woman mingles with the story of her young granddaughter's coerced incestual relationship with her father, laying out the horror and pain we read about and often ignore in newspaper reports. Taking up the theme of marital violence are two stories from Sri Lanka by Radhia Rameez, whose fiction never fails to resonate with our non-fiction narratives, each account reaching out to touch the other over vast geographic distances.

Aysha Baqir, activist and writer, unfolds a powerful story about dowry in an affluent household in Pakistan where abuse begets abuse and the victim turns persecutor. The psychological distress and trauma caused by eternally underplayed stalking and molestation is retold with artistry by writer, columnist and activist Farah Ghuznavi, whose story recreates the lives of Bangladesh's well-to-do, evoking a sense of revulsion at the insensitivity of that world—the same insensitivity exhibited by Ankita Banerjee's family. In her fiction based on real life, social researcher and writer Dr Supriya Rakesh provides no respite from darkness except in disappearing. Child rape and molestation are further amplified in writer Tisa Muhaddes's story. The fiction section ends on a note of hope as S. Bari depicts rape in South Asia through the story of a courageous survivor who rebuilds her life, putting a disturbing past behind her.

* * *

Poetry in this collection presents a challenge: to inspire courage amid depictions of bleakness and victimization. It begins with the uplifting energy of Arundhathi Subramaniam's poem, capturing the spirit of this book. Sadaf Saaz's 'Birangona' follows, addressing the plight of widows. Dr Bipasha Haque, a multilingual poet and academic from Bangladesh, rebels against patriarchal norms in her verses, while the defiant tone peaks in Fulbright scholar Tamoha Siddiqui's poem. These narratives expressed powerfully, will stir turmoil within as they herald the construction of a more equitable society.

'Amphan Calls', written like an afterword that sums up the ancient lores used to justify patriarchal subjugation, advocates for a healthy partnership between genders to sustain life. It ends with a call to courage, urging readers to break out from their moulds of silence and catalyse change with the force of a hurricane.

We conclude with Deepti Naval's narrative in prose and verse, questioning the norms that perpetrate the gender imbalance in the social setting.

* * *

Every story, narrative, and poem in this book is curated with the purpose of stirring a sense of injustice and discomfort, with the ultimate goal of fostering equity, freedom and justice envisioning a better world. Man and woman are meant to live side by side, not as abuser and victim but as companions.

The ball is now in your court, dear reader, to read and respond.

MITALI CHAKRAVARTY
Singapore, May 2024

INTRODUCTION

This is a book of stories and testimonies that share heartbreaking narratives of the many griefs that beset a woman's life. The fact that much of what is depicted has been said and described many times before does not detract from the horrifying impact that this litany of the many tragic truths that are part of women's lives in India, Bangladesh and Pakistan leaves behind.

The book begins not with a testimony but with a detailed analytical account of the 'Nirbhaya' case of 2012, the different responses to it, the changes in the laws dealing with rape by the Verma Commission that the Government of India set up to assuage the anger that had been aroused, and the limits that a deeply patriarchal society imposes on steps taken to ensure gender justice. In this essay, 'The Engendering of Hurt', the author, Meenakshi Malhotra, deals with what is correctly called a 'critical event', an event that 'exerts pressure on people to take a stand, an event which shakes people out of their everyday torpor and catapults them into a situation where they become historical agents, with their agency exerting force in both determining events and their consequences and repercussions.'

Malhotra sees the unprecedented protests that erupted in Delhi and then spread to cities across India as the result of the expression of a sense of betrayal by large sections of urban youth who identified with Nirbhaya and her aspirations. Here was a modern, educated young woman who was preparing for a career, who had gone with a male friend to watch a non-mainstream film, *Life of Pi*, and had been subjected to the most brutal violence and left for dead in the heart of the capital. This attack was not some atrocity committed in a remote, rural area where such things did happen and went largely unreported and certainly unprotested because they were considered part of the backwardness of rural India. Instead, Nirbhaya's tragedy made upwardly mobile, confident young people suddenly aware of the dangers that every one of them was actually exposed to in a society of terrible inequalities that paid scant attention to the security of women since it believed for the most part that women were responsible for their own safety.

The recommendations for legal reforms made by the Verma Commission were comprehensive and framed within an astute understanding of the social sanction that violence against women enjoys in our society. Unfortunately, the laws that were actually enacted in 2013 were highly disappointing. People's representatives showed themselves unwilling to act against the prejudices that many of their voters held dear. The structural inequities of the legal system that 'put the burden of crime and its proof not on the perpetrator but the victim' were left relatively untouched. The fact that the proposal to criminalize marital rape brought howls of protest from Parliamentarians, who insisted that holy matrimony itself would be threatened, was proof not only of the strength of patriarchal thought but of definitions of what constituted holy matrimony itself.

This opening piece is followed by many others that are rich in diversity. True stories of violence and resistance, of helpless suffering and the horrific violence of acid attacks from different parts of India share space with similar renditions from our neighbours, Nepal, Pakistan, Bangladesh, and Sri Lanka. There are also in this anthology numerous pieces of fiction that go to the heart of terrible truths. Patriarchy is extremely strong in all these countries, and there is a commonality of sorrow, violence, injustice and maiming that it is responsible for women across borders.

It is truly tragic that there is so little common understanding of and common struggle against what is such an intrinsic part of women's lives and experiences in countries which are engaged in so much rhetoric, bluster and finger-pointing engineered by their governments that not only do not want these everyday acts of violence and discrimination to be understood and confronted but are responsible for ensuring that they go unpunished and undiminished.

Of course, there are dissimilarities, too, and many of the stories and testimonies illustrate both the commonality and the variances of what women in these countries experience. Hopefully, the narratives and stories from across the subcontinent will strike a chord with all its readers, including many in our neighbouring countries, and this may help to replace feelings of animosity with solidarity.

* * *

It is important to note two chapters on Manipur that illustrate the very contradictory roles that the very same group of women can play in both contesting and perpetrating violence. At a time when Manipur was witness to widespread State violence as a response to 'terrorism' and specially targeted women, which is, of course, very usual in such 'conflict zones', the women's organization Meira Paibis, 'Mothers of Manipur', played a heroic role. In one amazing act of courage, members of the organization stripped themselves in front of the Kangla Fort (a symbol of State power) and called out to the security forces to violate and kill them.

The other chapter on Manipur demonstrates how, since May 2023, members of the same Meira Paibis had become transformed into leaders of mobs that attacked and burned the homes of Kuki tribals and incited the most barbaric violence against Kuki women. The same organization that had used the naked bodies of its leaders to shame the State sponsors of gender violence participated in the violation of women's naked bodies by members of their own community in the most shameful display of identity politics and majoritarian impunity.

The role of the State as a perpetrator of violence and as a

protector of other perpetrators is also brought out in both these essays on Manipur. In 'The Defiant Woman' by Teresa Rehman, it is the State that, in the name of fighting militancy, subjects women to terrible violence. And in 'Manipur's Daughters?' by Hoineilhing Sitlhou, the State uses divisive and communal propaganda to divide the Meitei and Kuki populations, its police aid and abet those who strip, humiliate, and rape Kuki women, and it oversees the exodus of thousands of Kuki men, women and children from their homes in and around Imphal, and their confinement in refugee camps. It deprives their children of education. The Meitei people have also been injured and harmed in this conflict that has now gone on for more than a year, aided and abetted by State and central governments, both of the Bharatiya Janata Party (BJP).

The essay from Sri Lanka that speaks about the poems written by Sri Lankan women fighters on either side of the Sinhala-Tamil divide shows the extent to which identity politics can drive women to inflict terrible violence against each other. These poems glorify bloodshed and killing by women warriors even as they mourn the deaths of beloved sons and husbands. The poems they wrote do recognize the role of the vested interests behind the bloodshed and these deaths but do not denounce their motives.

In India, the role of the State in situations where the perpetrators of violence against women belong to the majority community and the victim is a Muslim woman and where the perpetrators belong to the caste higher in the social hierarchy than their Dalit women victims is discussed in 'Impunity Guaranteed' by Kalpana Kannabiran. Here, the Bilkis Bano case and the Khairlanji and Hathras cases are presented as illustrations. In Khairlanji and Hathras, Dalit women were raped and killed by men belonging to the Other Backward Classes and upper castes. In both cases, the state governments did everything to protect the perpetrators of violence and cast aspersions on the character of the victims. It is a fact that in most cases, the State, the administration and even the judiciary guarantee impunity to elite caste and majority community rapist-murderers or treat them with great lenience.

It is also a fact that what Muslim riot victims like Bilkis Bano suffer at the hands of the State, the collective victims of State-sponsored or State-abetted violence, are of a qualitative difference in a way that perhaps no essay can fully encompass. The Bilkis Bano case is a horrific example of how Muslim women victims of communal violence are able to access justice only after years of struggle. It is also a damning indictment of a State (in this case, the government of Gujarat and the central government) that goes to great lengths to protect rapist-murderers from being punished for their crimes, and then grants them remission after they have spent a few years in jail, and also ensures that they are greeted as heroes with garlands and sweets, and hailed as 'Sanskari Hindus' when they come out of jail.

This is not to detract from the reality of the unrelenting casteist violence that Dalit women suffer in most parts of India today. This kind of violence is intrinsic to the nature of the Varnashrama dharma, which is such a prominent feature of Indian society and something that the Hindutva-Manuvadi Sangh Parivar is committed to uphold. This kind of violence is also to be seen in the never-ending series of 'honour killings' in which those who enter into inter-caste marriages where the woman is of a higher caste than the man are regularly and remorselessly killed by her family members. The State acts reluctantly in such cases, and successive governments at the Centre have refused to pass a special comprehensive law to deal with all aspects of these crimes.

The growing strength of the Hindutva-Manuvadi forces after they acceded to power at the Centre and in many states has resulted in new forms of violence against women. Not only are Dalit women and Muslim women specially targeted, but women who do not conform to their norms of behaviour are subjected to violence of different kinds.

The very detailed opening chapter that deals with the Nirbhaya case mentions the numerous kinds of mobilizations that took place in its wake. One of them was how the date this horrible incident occurred was observed as 'Take Back the Night' in many cities and campuses across the country. These were exhilarating moments that large numbers of women experienced as they dared to go out and make the hours of darkness that had always been so threatening to their safety their own. Once the BJP government was formed in 2014, however, this observance came to a grinding halt as the participants, especially women students at Delhi University, were attacked by rowdies belonging to the ruling party's student wing, the ABVP. This kind of pushback was their way of announcing that women's assertions would not be tolerated and would be met with violence. The darkness of the night would once again mark the limits of women's freedom.

In addition to the domestic violence, sexual violence, violence of discrimination and violence of exploitation that much of the book deals with, these recent examples of Hindutva-Manuvadi violence have now become more and more frequent, all-pervasive, and those responsible enjoy a kind of impunity that is both new and terrifying.

The title of this collection is *Our Stories, Our Struggle.* Its contributors have helped us listen to many voices that remain silent or unheard. I hope many readers will be prodded into speaking with and for them and will rouse others to do so, too: speak and resist.

SUBHASHINI ALI
New Delhi/Kanpur
July 2024

PART ONE

Narratives from Life

NIRBHAYA: TWELVE YEARS AFTER

Meenakshi Malhotra

A girlhood betrayed. A hope denied. A family in grief. And a nation enraged.

The winter of Delhi's discontent, which we witnessed in 2019-20, was perhaps first seen in 2012 with large groups of students and women out on the streets marching, protesting, and holding candlelight vigils following the brutal gang rape and attack on a young physiotherapy intern on December 16 that year. The event elicited enormous rage and many public protests accompanied by outcries for speedy justice.

This essay explores and reflects upon some aspects of this critical event: first, the level of anger and outrage generated by the gang rape and second, the changes and legal reform that it led to. The time is perhaps ripe for an appraisal, a revisiting of some of the issues involved in the horrific event that aroused deep anger in the youth and women of India, particularly Delhi. There have been horrific events before and after, but this act, heinous as it was, came to be perceived as a nation's betrayal of its daughters. 'Nirbhaya' thus became 'India's daughter', mirroring the fate of many of its daughters in a country which is no place for women, a society which gives scant respect to them, where its daughters are often killed before they are born, or raped and mutilated afterwards. Or treated as second-class citizens, even among the upper classes and castes. Their thin integration into lineages of class and caste power, even within affluent sections of society, results in a saga of dispossession that continues well into the twenty-first century.

Given these ground realities, what was it about this case that made it assume the dimensions and magnitude of a critical event? Rapes had happened earlier, which, despite being brutal and horrifying, were, in many cases, perpetrated on the bodies of lower-class-caste Dalit women. Earlier, rapes of other upper-caste women often went unreported, as families would close their ranks against intrusion by the media and police. In Nirbhaya's case, the sheer brutality of the case was so obvious that it aroused the general public to protest and forced the State to take cognisance of the event. The case acquired the dimensions of a 'critical event', one which exerts pressure on people to take a stand, an event which shakes people out of their everyday torpor and catapults them into a situation where they become historical agents, with their agency exerting force in both determining events and their consequences and repercussions.[2]

A lot of the outcry generated had to do with the sheer senselessness and gratuitous brutality of the event. The case also directed attention to many of the loopholes beleaguering our legal system and limiting its scope and application. The laws around rape, in particular, had been a matter of contention and, for several decades, a focus of feminist critique. For the longest time, the onus of proving rape lay on the victim, who, feminists alleged, had to undergo the trauma of rape again and again, in the law court and the doctor's chamber, with the infamous two-finger test even after 2013 when the laws pertaining to rape/sexual assault were changed.

In the court, the 'character' of the victim was a major factor, and, very often, the case lost steam after the complainant was found to be a woman of 'loose morals' or 'easy virtue'. This was a factor that prevented convictions, the other problem with the law being the definition of rape and the age of consent. Another problem was to do with the idea of consent; the issue of rape was defined as an act that is 'against her (one's) will' and 'without her (one's) consent'. Several cases, like Tukaram versus State of Maharashtra in 1983, pointed out the difference between 'consent' and 'passive submission' and also that consent could be secured through coercion or intimidation. Either way, it was also extremely difficult to prove that sex had not been consensual since the complainant had to show evidence of injury. After the criminal law amendments spearheaded by the Justice JS Verma Committee, no injuries had to be proven to substantiate the accusation of rape.

In the Criminal Law Amendment Act that was put into place in 2013 because of ongoing protests to amend rape laws after the December gang rape, no undue focus was put on past behaviour, as many rapists utilized this loophole and cited loose morals to escape conviction.

Further, a major loophole was the definition of rape, which earlier only covered intercourse and penetration of the vagina by the penis. The definition was expanded to also include penetration by other objects after the ghastly December 2012 gang rape. According to a well-known lawyer working on women's rights, Flavia Agnes, the 'insertion of sharp-edged objects such as wooden splinters, iron rods, glass bottles, knives and swords can cause far more damage to the female anatomy but did not warrant the same punishment as it was not looked upon as a "fate worse than death".'[3]

People were horrified to learn that the innards—intestines and other organs—had spilled out of the victim's body because of the injuries inflicted by rods and other sharp objects. However, from a legal perspective, these actions were not deemed as grievous and injurious as vaginal penetration. Obviously, it is the patriarchal premise of 'vaginal purity' that colours this judgement, which does not view other kinds of assault like acid attacks, slashing of the face and insertion of objects—committed with murderous and malicious intent—as being as harmful and damaging as rape. Such acts of violence are not bracketed with rape but can be much worse, as pointed out by Agnes. The Justice Verma Committee took cognizance of these varied forms of sexual assault, recognizing that any form of violence to chastise and/or humiliate is objectionable, and this change reflected in the criminal law amendments of 2013.

The case also exposed the barely disguised misogyny and embedded patriarchal attitudes and mindsets of many Indian politicians, even in the twenty-first century. Some declared that Nirbhaya should have appealed to her rapists and addressed them as her brothers.

Some people raised eyebrows at the fact that she was out at 9 p.m. and that, too, with a male companion. It thus became a test case to gauge the retrogressive nature of Indian society, and the responses that came flying a dime a dozen exposed many of the crucial gaps, fissures, and fault lines of Indian society, its patriarchal mindset, and the loopholes in its legal system.

* * *

The fault lines of the legal system have come up for scrutiny time again, particularly in the wake of the postponement of capital punishment to the rapists, who sought to deploy every possible plea, ploy and loophole in the Indian legal system to put off the execution, until those involved were meted out justice.[4] Out of the six accused, one died in judicial custody on March 11, 2013. According to some published reports, the police said that Ram Singh had hanged himself, but the defence lawyers and his family challenged this view and alleged that he was murdered. Four of the five other accused—Pawan Kumar Gupta, Vinay Kumar Sharma, Akshay Singh Thakur and Mukesh Kumar Singh (Ram Singh's older brother)—were convicted for rape and murder and sentenced to death on September 10, 2013. There was an appeal, and in March 2014, the Delhi High Court upheld the guilty verdict and the death sentence. On December 18, 2019, the Supreme Court rejected the final appeals of the condemned, and the four adult accused were hanged on March 20, 2020. The fifth accused, a juvenile, was also given the maximum sentence of three years' imprisonment in a reform facility, per the Juvenile Justice (Care and Protection of Children) Act.

Many feminists are reiterating the crucial gaps in the capital punishment narrative, which is premised on the perhaps primitive and atavistic 'revenge' motive. However, Nirbhaya's family expressed their keenness on the implementation of capital punishment, arguing that it was not the desire for revenge but the desire for closure which impelled them to seek the death sentence for the rapists. The Nirbhaya case kept veering between the Scylla and Charybdis of both serving the cause of justice and arriving at a proper legal resolution that was acceptable to everybody and was not a knee-jerk reaction to what was widely perceived as an inhuman act. The question of bloodlust came up in the aftermath of another recent case where a young doctor, Dr Priyanka Reddy,[5] was similarly gang-raped and murdered in 2019. Very soon, the alleged rapists were killed in a police 'encounter'.

Feminist lawyers like Indira Jaising have questioned the validity of the death sentence, partly on the above premise: that the demand for death penalty rests on a notion of retributive justice. Lawyers against the death sentence argue that it does not necessarily or adequately address, in fact, obscures the pervasive and insidious nature of structural inequality and gender violence rampant in our societies. Apart from being short-sighted, the demand for capital punishment papers over the 'routineness of the violence that takes place in our societies, in our homes, in our private spaces and makes it seem like an aberration'.[6]

However, the State and judiciary pushed for the death penalty, which was finally carried out in March 2020 after the rapists had exhausted all legal/judicial avenues. While Nirbhaya's family experienced a sense of closure, there were voices for the other side also. People who knew the rapists and their families felt that there had been a 'trial by media', which had helped the labelling of the case as 'the rarest of rare cases'.

To a society inured to gender violence and blind to the impunity enjoyed by many criminals, what was it about this 'rarest of rare cases' that led to this level of public outcry? To what can we attribute the long shadow cast by the Nirbhaya case?

One way of understanding the case and its impact is to

study it as an expression of a new, resurgent India. The political mobilization in the period immediately after the Nirbhaya event was consciously organized around youth and feminist activism, which was evidenced in 'Take Back the Night' campaigns. Activist and dancer Maya Rao developed and choreographed a piece about a *flaneuse* who walks the city at night, claiming its spaces. The protesters did not only express anger and outrage but their actions were calibrated to convey a sense of reason wounded, a sense of rights and entitlements violated and transgressed upon. The protests also seemed to suggest that the root of the problem lay not just in violent individuals but in the patriarchal system, as also in the State, which had not delivered on its promise of granting democratic rights to everybody.

The media reported the simmering discontent and captured the outrage in the public sphere that put a certain level of pressure on the State and the judiciary. These protests were also remarkable in that they achieved a mass mobilization that was on an altogether different and unprecedented scale. Thus, in spite of the efforts of political parties, which sought to gain some mileage by appropriating the outrage and using it to subserve their own agendas, the case assumed a magnitude that pressed the government to set up a committee almost immediately.

* * *

As I have discussed in an earlier article, 'the gang rape and the response to it can be understood as a critical event—not only an event which generates a critical and mass opinion, which, in turn, forces change in terms of outlook, attitude, and legislation but also an event which defamiliarizes to an extent where past behaviour and attitudes are held up to scrutiny in such a way as to force a change'.

The mourning and outrage generated by the Nirbhaya case set off protests, which got exacerbated and reflected in international media as well, fitting in with the media's perception that India and South Asia are places which witness frequent violations of human rights and women's rights. The popular press latched on to the case, their response seeming to chime in with and answer to the view that 'suffering is the master subject of our 'mediatized times'. In the words of an *Economic and Political Weekly* editorial which came out in the immediate aftermath of the event:

> The popular protests, while they have successfully braved the repression of the government, have themselves contributed to building an atmosphere where, in some respects, repressive and regressive ideas have found fertile ground to grow.[7]

The discourse on rape in the South Asian context has been mired in and viewed through notions of shame and honour (especially family honour) and greeted with certain stereotypical responses, similar to the one expressed by a woman leader who spoke of the rape as leaving the young woman a living corpse, *'zinda laash'*.[8] Although the sentiment was expressed sympathetically, it demonstrates certain stereotypical and clichéd ways of thinking. A stock response of many leaders and parliamentarians in our country, it also betrays a mindset where all is lost when one is shamed and honour lost.

The twenty-two-year-old—'Nirbhaya' as she came to be called—who many wished could have survived the rape, revealed her wish to live fully during her brief spells of consciousness from her hospital bed. It almost seemed that she was preparing to live and face the consequences of rape and go forward in life. It is possible, given her fearless attitude, that she would have forged ahead on her chosen path without carrying the stigma or burden of constructed notions of guilt and shame, purity and pollution. Attributions of immorality which were attached to earlier rape survivors that exposed the limited understanding underlying earlier legislation and judgments on rape, probably did not occlude her vision. Referring to her in terms of an oxymoron—a living corpse—resonates with irony and sets up a contrast between her fearless mind and her brutalized and mutilated body. It reduces her to an object of pity and, at best, 'India's daughter', with all its attendant ironies. It also sets up a dichotomy between the mind and the body that has been commented upon by a feminist scholar. Discussing a similar dichotomy in the Sathin Bhanwari rape case, Taisha Abraham points out 'that the doublespeak and patriarchal mindset of the Centre/state machinery is visible in the splitting of mind and body, where the divide-and-rule macroscopic policy of patriarchy reveals its microcosmic form'. Through this mind-body split, patriarchal structures try to both 'disembody and silence women'.[9]

Extolling a single woman's spirit as 'fearless' is an evasive tactic that serves to paper over the cracks in the system—that of pervasive gender violence.

Regressive thinking was also evident in most responses which attributed the brutal rape to 'increasing Westernization' and claimed that cases of sexual harassment or rape occurred in India and not 'Bharat' (terms which stand for urban and rural India)—an allegation contrary to available statistical evidence. Any comment on the increasing number of rape cases as a fallout of increasing modernization or Westernization could be countered by the argument that it is not the number of cases that vary but the lacunae in reporting these cases that might explain the variation in numbers.

Further, the attribution of all ills to the incursion of 'Western modernity' points to a growing xenophobia and hypernationalism. Equally absurd was the attempt to place the onus of guilt on the raped woman by arguing that it was her resistant and defiant attitude that catalyzed the violence perpetrated upon her, thereby increasing the brutality of the assault.

Thus, apart from bringing about major changes in the rape laws of the country, the Nirbhaya case, in many ways, has been a test case that generated numerous debates on issues of sexual violence, both against women as well as against transgender people. It has given a platform to a plethora of voices brimming with discontent and claiming that their sentiments have been hurt.

There were several groups that put forward hurt claims, some genuine, some spurious. For groups of people working on women and the law, or child rights and issues of sexual harassment, the case became a sort of rallying cry to amend laws and bring new issues under their ambit. To that extent, the Justice Verma Committee demonstrated its awareness of the glaring gaps in Indian law about child abuse and set to work on them. As Brinda Karat reported, India has been among the few countries with no laws or protocols against child sexual abuse.[10] Similarly, this case gave some impetus to other pending laws and amendments, particularly on issues like sexual harassment at the workplace.

***

In this babel of voices, it is important to understand and gauge the validity and legitimacy of these hurt claims. One way of unravelling and understanding the public outcry and protest is through the lens of the disaffected groups seeking to articulate their hurt.

Whose sentiments were hurt? Which were the groups forwarding their wounded sentiments? At the broadest level, it was the urban youth who felt the most betrayed. Nirbhaya, by all accounts, was a student like them, confident in her chosen vocation of physiotherapy and working hard to fulfill her dream and better the quality of life of her parents, siblings and herself. Here, the subject—and not the victim—is one who, by all accounts, resisted objectification and was prepared to work hard and aspire for upward mobility in society.

Unlike the earlier cases of Rameeza Bee or Sathin Bhanwari, images and updates about this case circulated on social media. The citation and reiteration led to a situation where simmering public discontent and outrage came to a boil. This case, orchestrated by the power of social media, brought unprecedented numbers of young people out on the streets of Delhi—on midnight vigils and candlelight marches. Earlier, reporting of rapes, especially of lower-caste women, had received scant attention. It was always perceived as something that happened in the 'other India', feeding the narrative of two or more Indias, which exist cheek by jowl but are impervious to each other. The gut-wrenching saga of Nirbhaya shook people out of their sense of security and struck a chord with the urban youth and digital generation. There was a level of identification with the feeling that it could well have been any of the thousands of young women who migrate to cities in search of education, employment, or a better life. The ascribed identity of 'Nirbhaya' distinguished her from the many other unknown and unacknowledged victims/survivors of rape.

The 'urban connect' was inevitable as many young people found in her a mirror for their aspirations. Moreover, she was almost a role model in her community, where she lived and tutored children to supplement the family income.

It was this desire for a better life, for upward mobility, which may have struck a chord in the hearts of thousands of young people who read about her or followed her story. Her brutal gang rape that led to a painful death, therefore, constituted a betrayal of the hopes and aspirations of the multitude. She was not a silenced illiterate or subaltern but an embodiment of newly emerging Indian youth visiting malls and multiplexes while dreaming of a better life. The middle classes sought legitimacy through the media for their hurt sentiments that ran the gamut from issues of embedded misogyny to the question of women's safety.

Additionally, middle-class Indians bore witness to this tragic saga of a motivated young girl (as in the Priyanka Reddy case almost seven years later) and mourned her passing. Further, beyond sentimentalizing, it is important to understand how Nirbhaya and her parents broke the mould of victimhood. Instead of succumbing to notions of shame, they conveyed their outrage and sense of loss and devastation by employing the power of the media to reach people.

While these hurt claims being put forward can be seen as genuine, the case also, somewhat paradoxically, created a space for voicing what could be seen as spurious and false hurt claims. Thus, the case seemed to have licensed many rural patriarchal leaders to display and whip up xenophobic and jingoistic sentiments and circulate some blatant falsehoods. For instance, one such 'leader' advocated banning food[11] items like noodles that are allegedly supposed to induce raging hormones and, according to him and his ilk, have increased the occurrence of rapes.

While there is a religious, class, and caste ramification to almost every situation in which rape takes place, the focus in this particular case was not the fact that the rapists were from a lower socio-economic stratum but that they committed an act that was unpardonable and murderous.

'Modernities' in India are uneven, fractured and heterogeneous, and making laws that answer to a very stratified and diverse socio-economic spectrum is not easy. However, the 2013 criminal law amendments took a step in that direction by bringing to light many crimes and misdemeanours prevalent in Indian society. They also brought to the fore crimes that were enabled by internet availability, like pornography. The Nirbhaya case and the legislation it catalyzed have served as a consciousness-raising measure, although a lot still remains to be done. For instance, the 2013 criminal law amendments deviated considerably from the recommendations of the Justice Verma Committee and were regarded as shaped by the demands and contingencies of vote-bank politics.

One of the salient issues that came to the fore with the Nirbhaya case was the embedded misogyny that exists in Indian society, which normalizes violence at manifold levels, creating a context where sexual and other kinds of violence are seen as matters to be pushed under the carpet and relegated to silence. The second was the glaring structural inequalities, evident in everyday life and our laws, which have traditionally put the burden of crime and its proof not on the perpetrator but the victim. The case exposed the many anomalies in our society and our legal system and has become a reference point and touchstone for cases of sexual harassment/rape for many years to come. It was a cataclysmic event that constituted a coming-of-age moment for an entire nation.

IMPUNITY GUARANTEED: BRAZEN CONDONATIONS OF VIOLENCE AGAINST WOMEN

Kalpana Kannabiran

'It feels like a stone the size of a mountain has been lifted from my chest, and I can breathe again. This is what justice feels like...I have said before, and I say again today, journeys like mine can never be made alone...A year and half ago...I simply collapsed. I felt I had exhausted my reservoir of courage. Until a million solidarities came my way. Thousands of ordinary people and women of India came forward. They stood with me, spoke for me, and filed PIL (Public Interest Litigation) petitions in the Supreme Court: 6,000 people from all over, and 8,500 people from Mumbai wrote appeals, 10,000 people wrote an open letter, as did 40,000 people from twenty-nine districts of Karnataka. To each of these people, my gratitude for your precious solidarity and strength. You gave me the will to struggle, to rescue the idea of justice not just for me, but for every woman in India. I thank you...the dua that emerges from my heart today is simple—the rule of law, above all else and equality before law, for all.'

—Bilkis Bano, after remissions in her case were reversed by the Supreme Court of India.[12]

Violence against women has been a central concern of the women's movement in India since the mid-1970s when the discourse of women's rights first focused on issues of violence— State violence in the form of custodial rape in the aftermath of the Emergency in 1975, later moving on to raise the issue of domestic violence, particularly dowry-related violence and the murder of wives. Over the eighties and nineties, Indian feminist writing focused on understanding violence in the context of religious fundamentalism and identity politics, economic liberalization, caste violence, and the displacement of Adivasi communities. This process interlocked with human rights discourses that, too, began to focus increasingly on violence against women as a human rights issue, culminating in, but not stopping with a few more significant developments: The 'Women's Rights as Human Rights' formulation in the UN Conference on Human Rights in Vienna in 1993; the appointment of the UN Special Rapporteur on Violence against Women; Dalit feminists organizing and leading around CEDAW, the Convention on the Elimination of All Forms of Discrimination against Women, especially the 2007 and 2014 Alternative NGO Reports presented in New York and Geneva, respectively; and the World Conference against Racism in Durban in 2001. All these processes were shaped by the realities of violence and violation, particularly (not only) sexual violence, and the rights that women and LGBTQIA+ persons have claimed foregrounding violent practices—asserting the right to life in the most urgent and stark sense—graded by caste, tribe, religious community, and gender plurality. In India, it is within this recognition of denial, discrimination and overt, everyday violence that discourses on equality and non-discrimination are located. And it is against this backdrop that this essay reflects on women's experiences of sexual assault.

Sexual violence locks women of different classes, castes and communities into multiple intersecting axes of inequality and discrimination that spread out over a wide range—from social and economic life to political inequality—tying women of different classes together through the similarity of their experiences as women, and holding them apart in almost unbridgeable ways through the differences in their experiences as members of different social classes. The American sociologist Barrington Moore's words ring true six decades later: 'The prevailing order of society always grinds out its tragic toll of unnecessary death year after year.'[13]

Alongside the toll of deaths are the routine harms, injuries, and shrouds of silence. This politics of maiming, which Jasbir K Puar, a professor and Graduate Director of Women's and Gender studies at Rutgers University, USA, describes as 'a status unto itself, a status that triangulates the hierarchies of living and dying' and 'is exercised as a domain of sovereignty...enacted to target both bodies and infrastructure for debilitation'[14] spreads its deathly coils in India to articulate caste, community, conscience and gender in particularly essentialized ways.

* * *

Public discourse on sexual violence, in these virulently patriarchal contexts, may at times be characterized by a strong moral disapproval of perpetrators of violence. And yet, as Patricia Viseur Sellers, the international criminal lawyer, has argued, the problem is that this disapproval falls highly selectively—'the violence of normal times'[15] is neither equally condemned nor even equally recognized. It is because the greatest part of violence against women is the violence of normal times, which carries with it the guarantee of impunity—both civic and state—irrespective of penal, punitive, or constitutional safeguards. Sudden conflagrations of violence, or violent upsurges, must then be understood in the context of this steady, ever-present violence of normal times, and an understanding of the patterns of responses in a patriarchal society that are deeply discriminatory of women. Two illustrations of public and state responses to rape and sexual assault signpost the continuum of responses.

* * *

In December 2019, four men suspected of the rape and murder of the young veterinarian in Hyderabad were shot dead in Hyderabad, less than a week after the rape and murder. The Disha case triggered furious demands for speedy justice and the public lynching of rapists. On one level, there was genuine anguish that such a gruesome crime was even possible in the heart of a throbbing metropolis. It triggered memories of the similarly gruesome sexual assault leading to death of 'Nirbhaya' in Delhi in December 2012. In situations like this, demands for instantaneous retribution soar. For several families of victims, death of the accused feels like the only answer to the profound harms of rape. However, it must be remembered that public responses that equate judicial outcomes and 'justice' to immediate and quick retribution are not universal, nor are they just. Is retributive justice the way to go in a democratic country that prides itself in its unprecedented historical legacy of resisting violence in fundamentally non-retributive ways? The ends of justice are not served by wanton killing and retributive bloodlust. The course of justice cannot be determined by the grief and grieving of victims' families. Justice lies in supporting them in their moment of grief and pain *and* insisting on due process that brings suspects and accused to trial through a robust, stringent, and competent criminal investigation.

Let us juxtapose this to the case of the women wrestlers in 2023. We witnessed a month-long street protest by seven women wrestlers (all Hindu, all from rural agricultural families, who have won all international awards, including one an Olympic medal), against sexual harassment, stalking, groping, and the aggravated sexual assault against a wrestler who was a minor. A complaint to the Wrestling Federation of India (WFI) and another to the police yielded no action, which brought them onto the streets for a months-long dharna demanding action. The protesting wrestlers were arrested in a widely condemned police action and 109 FIRs (First Information Reports) were registered against them for protesting in a public place, rioting, breach of peace, and other sections in the penal code. The accused was then the chief of the

WFI, and a Member of Parliament from Uttar Pradesh belonging to the ruling party. We have seen no action yet against the accused, nor even censure from his political masters, but repeated re-victimization and trolling of the complainants.

* * *

The pervasive sexual harms and injustice specifically targeting Muslim, Dalit, and Adivasi women are symptomatic of a more pervasive majoritarian misogyny, and their sexual humiliation focuses in particular ways on the religious/caste 'Other' across gender. I reflect briefly on two cases of women—we could, of course, multiply them infinitely in the present time.

In Hathras in Uttar Pradesh, a nineteen-year-old Dalit woman was assaulted in the most brutal manner and killed by Thakurs from the same village known to her and her family. When her mother found her, she was naked, paralyzed with grave physical injuries, which included her tongue cut to silence her from testifying to the attack against her. Yet, despite the grave harms, violent humiliation and deep trauma, she made a statement naming the perpetrators. She, a young woman from a landless Valmiki Dalit family, whose only protection against chronic anticipated assault and humiliation by the Thakur perpetrators and their henchmen was to stay indoors, never be alone, and step out occasionally, always accompanied. Yet, even these did not guarantee her right to bare life. Incarceration by caste and annihilation by caste.

Can we even begin to understand Article 21 guarantees from the standpoint of this woman's experience? We know that 'Manisha' is not the first. The Bhotmange family in Khairlanji, Nisha in Kerala, the young girls in Badaun...the roads of this country are strewn with the bodies of Dalit women, young and old, and the bodies of Dalit men. Without multiplying examples—for that is a task impossible to complete given its sheer magnitude—our collective experience as a people sworn to the Constitution of India, in Hathras as elsewhere, has been one of *occupation* of Dalit, Adivasi and Muslim homes, neighbourhoods, and homelands; of violent death, collective violence, the desecration of places of worship, unimaginable suffering, humiliation as a condition of existence, the anticipation of violence and murder, and the trauma of silencing. The first expression of the 'right to maim' as Jasbir Puar poignantly calls it, is the brutal seizure of speech by the Thakur-State: slashing the tongue of the victim to obstruct her testimony, and arresting and incarcerating journalist Siddique Kappan under the draconian Unlawful Activities Prevention Act (UAPA) while he was on his way to cover this atrocity.[16]

In a country with people who gave themselves a constitution that affirms justice, equality, fraternity, freedom of faith, worship, and conscience, liberty, dignity, unity, integrity, we have a strident, violent, unabashedly partisan, elected government. We have officers of the government participating in and bolstering genocidal speech by curtailing the invocation of the Constitution—'pouring molten lead on the tongues' of Dalits, and ripping apart Article 17 guarantees. Witness the conduct of the District Magistrate and the police after the young woman's death in Hathras. Witness the fortification of the village against 'outsiders' reaching out to the victim's family, while the perpetrators and their families roamed free. The murderous sexual assault was held in place by the continuing assault on and humiliation of the family—by the dominant Thakurs and officers of government, no longer distinguishable in speech or conduct. This humiliation reached its unbearable limit in how her family was refused the right to her mortal remains, her body, though broken, wounded and lacerated, but what remained of her. This was an annihilation of the person, the body, and the claim to justice. 'No evidence of rape,' said the police without investigating the crimes that killed her. The right to preserve her body, and seek further investigation into the unspeakable injuries she suffered was denied, and the evidence she carried on her person was destroyed in the dead of night by the police.

⁂

We know by now that a forensic report is rarely a truthful record, especially when the case concerns crimes of dominance and crimes against humanity. We saw the Justice AK Muktadar Commission of Inquiry into the gang rape of Rameeza Bee in 1978 record that the medical and forensic reports had been tampered with to suit the police version of what had happened. In the case of the custodial death of Budhan Sabar, we saw the Calcutta High Court order a videographed second post mortem that revealed the cause of death as custodial violence and ordered a compensation to Budhan's wife. The disposal of the Hathras victim's body, therefore, was not merely disrespect to the dead person and disregard of the custom of her family in the matter of death rituals. Hathras Police were guilty of destruction of evidence. Threats, forced confinement to their homes, and fortification are forms of illegal custody that the family has been subjected to. There were armed police and other officers of state actively preventing the family from moving out and anyone from meeting them. They were incarcerated in their homes and threatened with greater harm if they did not change their testimonies.

She made a dying statement naming the perpetrators. The family was forced to cremate her in the dead of night under police watch. In March 2023, three of the four accused were acquitted, one person was convicted for culpable homicide not amounting to murder, and none were convicted for rape or gang rape. The judge of the Uttar Pradesh court observed that the victim (who died of grievous injuries) had probably been tutored by her family to record the offence of rape in her dying declaration.

* * *

What is required as a first step in reparation is the public acknowledgment by the court of the multiple ways in which the Constitution has been torn to shreds. How may courts, in their discharge of their duties under the Constitution, mend the social fabric comprehensively by calling the State to account and insisting on a continuing mandamus to force the government to bend to the Constitution by, in this case, imposing penalties for every excess committed? From the refusal to register an FIR, the refusal to arrest immediately on being informed of the crime, the delay in treatment, and the humiliation of the victim's family at every stage due to caste (barred under The Scheduled Caste and The Scheduled Tribes Prevention of Atrocities Act), the case runs the gamut of breaches. This accounting-for is the only route to the affirmation of the inherent human dignity, for the citizens of this country and the judiciary alike.

Clearly, the black letter understanding of the Constitution is woefully inadequate in our situation. If our routes to redress are blocked by caste and hate, what are courts going to do to affirm the 'triadic ethical foundation' of the Constitution—the Preamble, Fundamental Rights and Directive Principles of State Policy? Or will we sit back, fiddling with little reliefs, while constitutional derogation proceeds apace?

* * *

Bilkis Bano, a gang rape survivor of the 2002 anti-Muslim Gujarat pogrom, who was the sole eyewitness of the massacre of her entire family, including her three-year-old daughter, was back after two decades, petitioning the courts against the remission granted to the men (caste Hindus) pronounced guilty and convicted of gang rape and mass murder. The selective remission was granted in celebration of the 75th anniversary of Indian independence in August 2022.

Bilkis Bano waged a lonely twenty-year battle in defence of secular values for a democratic India, keeping hope and faith alive in the face of grave harms and profound suffering and loss. It is a testament to her faith in human dignity, life, liberty, justice, and a shared humanity and integrity that transcends narrow parochial constructions of belonging tethered to religion, excluding all else.[17] Here is a woman who suffered unimaginable cruelty, including aggravated sexual assault, survived, and stood steadfast as the sole witness to the murder of her extended family by men known to her in a hostile state. All those attacked were Muslim—and were attacked because they were Muslim. All the perpetrators were Hindu, who were hunting down Muslims in a pogrom that engulfed the entire state of Gujarat in February and March 2002.

Fourteen years after they were convicted of the crimes of mass rape and murder (among others), these men were set free in August 2022, and thereafter welcomed with garlands and sweets and the declaration by an elected MLA (Member of the Legislative Assembly) that they are Brahmin and, therefore, 'sanskari'. They were not acquitted of their crimes, nor was there a reversal of the finding of guilt against them. What, then, does this assertion by an elected legislator mean? The question of codes of conduct for elected representatives and consequences for those like this one must be debated threadbare regardless of everything else. When the death penalty was carried out in the case of other men convicted for rape and murder (as in the Nirbhaya case) or when the suspects in the Hyderabad case were 'encountered' (death penalty by other means), this writer's opposition to both was countered by well-known and well-regarded people for not taking the 'people's conscience' into account.

Bilkis Bano then reminds us why we must engage in conversation on the secular credentials of this country—and why a re-notation of the 'secular', and a resurrection of secular values in our everyday lifeworlds, is urgent. Zakia Jafri, Soni Sori, Irom Sharmila, Bhanwari Devi, Parveena Ahanger: Muslim-Adivasi, Kashmir, Manipur, Gujarat, Rajasthan, and the Armed Forces (Special Powers) Act, and more in similar vein. Women have been exemplars of secular citizenship and human rights defenders beyond compare—this we forget at our own peril.

In the remissions case, the Supreme Court delivered a stellar judgment that reversed the remissions granted to the persons convicted of mass crimes against Bilkis Bano and her family, and issued sharp reprimands of specific misinterpretations or 'usurpations' of the Constitution and rule of law by the Gujarat government.[18] A ray of hope. And yet, the worrying fact of the widespread majoritarian public sympathy for the convicted persons, and especially the soft and pliant approach of the State—from the magistracy and jail administration to the Union Home Ministry—points to the deep roots of the derogation of due process.

* * *

We could plot the paths of violence that uproot the idea of secular democracy. Every one of these is a case of crimes against humanity, of targeted violence on minorities, and women's resistance to them all has been steadfast and focused on interrogating the majoritarian state and community through courts and public engagement. They have been focused on resurrecting the idea of the secular by calling out the violent State and its brazen condonation of mass violence. And they have named the elephant in the room—repeatedly, unceasingly, without respite, and at enormous personal cost. These are victims and survivors of rape, witnesses to mass murder, survivors of torture by the State who have resisted impunity and struggled against the 'ethical loneliness'[19] that comes from abandonment after profound violence. They have repeatedly sought justice from courts and reminded the courts and governments of their constitutional duty. That is the power of the commitment to secular constitutional governance.

It is equally important that we think through the 'secular' as an attribute of being, thinking and doing, both individually and together, in the everyday, in our here and now, to rebuild and reclaim what we have been dispossessed of without our even realizing it. Instead of staying rivetted to the hubris of the rulers and terrorized by their foot soldiers, it is urgent to shred the shrouds that block our sense and sensibilities of convivial living, and the value of justice the Constitution opens with.

Who is the 'we' with which the Preamble to the Constitution of India begins? In what ways can we ensure justice, sororal queer fraternity, and the unequivocal affirmation of the dignity of the individual? For this is really at the heart of the secular life and convivial living.

When Indra Meghwal is killed for drinking water from a pot in school, or the Bhotmange family is raped and killed for daring to live on its own terms, or Bilkis Bano's assailants—all convicted of mass rape and murder by due process—are set free and given a celebratory and ceremonial welcome, what is the 'we' that we will constitute? Will it be a 'we' that affirms the idea of 'shared humanity' and inherent dignity at our own, small, individual levels? Or will it be a 'we' that will share a treacherous space of belonging with persons found guilty of inciting and committing mass crime, rape and murder, on communal terms—although we ourselves may in our own life choices and everyday transactions be non-violent and just? To allow the negation of the idea of the 'secular' and State action to descend into banal evil, dictating the terms of our lives, is to do ourselves the ultimate disservice.

The pathways of justice are not linear, nor without obstacles. But we have, as a people, chosen the route of democracy and the Constitution, so we really have no option but to school ourselves into constitutional morality. For, as Dr BR Ambedkar cautioned in anticipation: constitutional morality must replace public morality. It is not easy, because it is not a natural sentiment. But it is non-negotiable.

Note: *This short reflection draws on several essays I have written on this subject over the years, both academic and public writing, that have been published. I have provided citations wherever possible and a list of references at the end of this volume.*

MANIPUR'S DAUGHTERS? OR VICTIMS OF CONFLICT, TARGETS OF POLITICS

Hoineilhing Sitlhou

On July 19, 2023, a video showing a mob stripping and sexually assaulting two women in the Indian state of Manipur went viral, drawing global attention to the political turmoil and highlighting gender-based violence as a critical issue. The crisis in Manipur, sparked on May 3 of the same year, was ignited by unrest over the Meitei community's demand for Scheduled Tribe status, perceived as a threat to tribal groups' land rights.[20] Media coverage had documented the unfolding political crisis, while incidents of sexual assaults against women were reported subsequently. Nevertheless, the graphic nature of the viral video intensified the condemnation of these appalling acts both in India and internationally.

In the wake of this video, the other accounts of atrocities and sexual violence against Kuki-Zo women also gained attention, including horrific gang rapes, forcible abductions, physical assaults resulting in death or near-fatal injuries, immolations, shootings, and molestations. Each of these accounts revealed a consistent pattern to the violence against women in Manipur, illustrating how women experience unique impacts in zones of conflict, especially with their bodies reduced to sites for asserting power and advancing political agendas.

Primarily, the accounts of survivors and victims' families narrated how the perpetrators justified their brutal acts against women as revenge. For example: 'Your people have raped and killed our people in Lamka, and so we will do the same to you.' Lamka is another name for the hilly Churachandpur district, inhabited mainly by the Kuki-Zo and other tribal communities, while the majority of the numerically and socio-politically dominant Meitei community lives in the low-lying Imphal valley. But the alleged rapes in Churachandpur, which were weaponized to justify the rapes and assaults of Kuki-Zo women in Imphal, were proven to be misinformation—fake news—and repeatedly debunked, even by top police officials.[21] Despite these denials, those intent on extracting what they saw as retributive violence seemed undeterred. It appears that once individuals believed in these incidents, they acted upon them, disregarding contradictory accounts.

Another significant factor in the violence against women in Manipur was police complicity. A recent chargesheet from the Central Bureau of Investigation (CBI) revealed that both the women seen paraded naked in the viral video had managed to reach a police vehicle accompanied by two men. However, the police driver allegedly told them, 'There is no key,' and abandoned them to a 1,000-strong mob. The women and men then pleaded with the police to intervene and rescue a third man who was being attacked by the mob, but the charge sheet notes the testimony that the 'police did not help them'. The CBI has charged the accused under multiple sections of the Indian Penal Code, including those related to gang rape, murder, outraging the modesty of a woman, and criminal conspiracy.[22]

Thirdly, many survivor accounts reveal a troubling shift among the Meitei women's group, the Meira Paibis (or 'torch-bearers'). Once advocates for justice and human rights, they have now been accused of perpetrating violence against Kuki-Zo women and even inciting Meitei men to commit rape against them. Initially, in a dramatic display of solidarity, the Meira Paibis burned down the house of the first person arrested in connection with the viral video. However, their support waned quickly. When the seventh person linked to the video mob was arrested, the Meira Paibis organized a protest rally on July 28, 2023, with placards that read 'Stop Arresting Innocent People'.

Bangalore-based journalist Romal Laisram, speaking to BehanBox, a platform dedicated to gender perspectives, noted, 'People are able to make peace with themselves and the "fact" that these [are] acts of violence and aggression [because they] were committed during a "war" and are, therefore, "understandable".'[23]

The entire sequence of events in Manipur over the last fourteen months exposes how women's bodies from different ethnic communities are exploited in various ways. First and foremost, to shame, humiliate, dishonour, or dehumanize another community. Then, to delineate the socio-political boundaries that define who can belong as an 'insider' or 'outsider' in an imagined community. And finally, to view the 'other' as a detested enemy. As perceived outsiders, Kuki-Zo women were subjected to acts of retribution, expulsion, and disciplining, but these acts were really aimed at Kuki-Zo men, who were designated as the enemy. Once they were caught and frozen at the intersection of their gender and ethnic identities, as Kuki-Zo,[24] these women were paraded as symbols of their communal identity and subjected to brutality by individuals from the dominant Meitei community.[25]

When global condemnation of the viral video encouraged other survivors to speak out and file police reports, a thirty-seven-year-old Meitei woman also came forward with her account of sexual assault and rape on August 9, 2023. Her husband opposed her going to the police, fearing social ostracization. However, other members of the community persuaded her to come forward publicly for the sake of her entire community not only to secure justice for herself but as a living proof that rape also happened to women from the Meitei community.[26] This incident highlights how women's bodies and their sexuality are manipulated into becoming battlefields, with a disturbing trend of sexual violence being weaponized.

Below are some of the widely covered stories of sexual assault in the media, which came into focus after the viral video:

1. On May 3, 2023, at about 9 p.m., mobs stormed the Manipur University campus in Imphal. They brandished sticks and knives and went about systematically locating students, staff, and faculty from the Kuki-Zo communities. Female students were forced out of their hostels and berated and abused by the mob. A Kuki-Zo PhD research scholar hid in her hostel bathroom for several hours until the Assam Rifles rescued them at 3.15 a.m. All this time, she could hear the mob conducting room-to-room searches and shouting slogans such as: *'Sida Kuki Nupi Leibra?* (Is any Kuki Woman in here?) and *'Kuki Nupi Hatlo'* (Kill Kuki women).

2. On May 4, the B. Phainom village in the Kangpokpi district was burned down, and the villagers were forced to flee into the adjoining forests. The perpetrators pursued them, bludgeoning two men to death, and disrobing, parading naked, and sexually assaulting three women in broad daylight. According to the first information report (FIR) registered on June 21, 2023, a nineteen-year-old boy was murdered while he tried to protect his twenty-one-year-old sister from sexual assault. B. Phainom came under attack on the very first day of the violence in Manipur, but the FIR was registered two days after the viral video.

3. On May 4, twenty-two-year-old Hatneo (name changed) and her friend, students at the Nightingale Nursing Institute in Imphal, were harassed, assaulted, and left to die by a mob comprising the Meitei people. She remembered them shouting, 'Rape her! Torture her! Cut her to pieces!'

4. On the same day, less than three kilometres away, two young women in their twenties from H. Khopibung, a village in the Kangpokpi district, were gagged, dragged, and confined in a closed room for hours by a Meitei mob in the Konung Mamang area of Imphal. Their co-workers from other tribal communities could do nothing to help

them, but they could hear them screaming and pleading to be let go, clearly indicating the possibility of rape and torture. When the room was finally opened, it was filled with blood and hair, and the victims had died of injuries from the assault. Their bodies remained in a morgue in Imphal until December 14, 2023, when they were airlifted along with sixty others dead to the hill districts.

5. On May 6, a forty-five-year-old widow and mother of two was hacked to pieces, shot, and burned by a Meitei mob in Pheitaiching village of Kangpokpi.

6. On May 15, an eighteen-year-old girl was abducted and raped. She remembered her assaulters kicking her in the stomach, hitting her in the eyes with the butt of their guns, and threatening her with death if she resisted sexual assault. Her medical report, from a hospital in Kohima, confirmed assault and rape.

These survivor testimonies are not isolated incidents but emblematic of deeper systemic issues in Manipur. They underscore the pervasive gender-based violence rooted in political unrest and the reluctance of law enforcement to act decisively to protect vulnerable populations. Moreover, the shifting stance of influential community groups like the Meira Paibis illustrates the complex interplay of ethnic divisions stoked by politics. That is why, rather than focusing on understanding the psychological well-being of traumatized survivors, there have been numerous attempts to politicize and trivialize the violence they endured (which extends to all women in similar situations). The Coordinating Committee on Manipur Integrity, or COCOMI, the Meitei civil society-led outfit, swiftly dismissed the incident shown in the viral video, asserting that no rape occurred and that the mob 'just' stripped and groped ['touched'] the women. However, one of the forty-four-year-old survivors disclosed to *The Wire* (July 21, 2023), 'My private parts were touched; fingers were put into my vagina; some [people] put their tongue into my mouth.'

Following the Justice Verma Committee Report, 2013, the

definition of rape is no longer limited to a penetrative assault. The fact that an act was non-consensual and involved disrobing women still categorizes it as a sexual offence under the penal code. And yet the National Commission for Women Chairperson Rekha Sharma and the Assam Chief Minister Himanta Biswas Sarma pointed out that incidents of parading women naked had also occurred in Opposition-ruled states, such as West Bengal, Rajasthan, Chhattisgarh, and Kerala. Sarma even suggested that the release of the viral video on the day before the Parliament session might have been a political manoeuvre. Eminent legal scholar Upendra Baxi argues[27] that rape culture sees violence against women as a misfortune rather than an injustice. That is why it often reflects competitive party politics and governance practices where contrived and escalating levels of impunity shield severe collective sexual assaults on women. The Supreme Court, however, firmly responded to the attempts to diminish the issue, stating that the 'systematic' and 'unprecedented magnitude' of sexual violence against women in Manipur during ethnic clashes cannot be justified by pointing to women in other parts of the country.

Lastly, another crucial aspect to consider is women's sense of 'shame', both imposed on them and real. For the survivors, the psychological wounds of assault and sexual violence run very deep, as both women seen in the viral video have expressed. They felt traumatized and fearful and experienced a profound sense of loss—of dignity, pride, and the ability to lead a normal life. According to a BBC report[28] published on November 10, 2023, one of the women lamented, 'I was treated like an animal. It was hard enough to live with the trauma, but when the video of the attack went viral two months later, I almost lost all hope to continue living.' The other woman said, 'I find it hard to face other people, even of my own community. My [sense of] pride is gone. I will never be the same again.' Let us not forget that after the attack, both women had to flee their towns and live in hiding.

When Prime Minister Narendra Modi finally discussed the violence seventy-eight days later, he, too, highlighted the theme of shame, only taking it to a national scale now. He stated, 'What happened to the daughters of Manipur can never be forgiven... It is an insult to the whole country...This is an incident of national shame, inappropriate for any civilized society.' This statement attempts to connect the violation of women's bodies to an assault on the State and the country. It invokes paternalistic State protection by linking the public humiliation experienced by the victims to the broader concept of national pride and shame. This framing overlooks the numerous survivor accounts where they describe the police as either indifferent or complicit with the perpetrators (as acknowledged by the CBI charge sheet).

Indeed, the rape and sexual violence against women could not have happened without the implicit endorsement of the State. They are deeply entrenched within the fabric of the State's institutions. In a society being made to fragment afresh along ethnic lines, many perpetrators were not strangers to the victims but familiar faces. Thus, the perpetrators are not just those directly seen assaulting the women in the viral video but encompass a broader institutionalized 'ecosystem' that empowers them to commit these crimes of hate.

THE DEFIANT WOMAN

Teresa Rehman

Some of the most productive years of my career have been marred by unnerving incidents. I have done hardcore conflict reporting in strife-torn Northeast India, which inevitably meant flirting with danger, both from the State and non-state actors. My experiences range from being caught in a crossfire, to being summoned by the CBI, a 'special' investigative team, or another state authority, apart from exploring difficult and unknown terrains and people to get to stories. I can declare that being a journalist reporting from a conflict zone has a fear factor that is very real, and I have encountered it several times in my career. And yet, like most journalists from the Northeast, I went into the field without any precautions to protect me in case of a mishap or difficulty. My vast and varied experiences have taught me that we have still not developed the ability to reach out with empathy when a conflict emerges. We choose, instead, to point incriminatory fingers and hurl stones that are hewn from our own ignorance—an ignorance further cemented by a mostly thoughtless media that puts forth news and views selectively.

I have discovered, excavated and narrated the lives, trials and triumphs of women involved with social, cultural and political resistance across the region, learning that women's defiance to different forms of power and domination can be a formidable instrument of social change. Over the years, women everywhere have emerged as both symbols and catalysts of change and dissent in the face of repressive governments. It can be described as a kind of soft power that can shape the preferences of others through the use of culture, values, and ideas. This power can take different forms—reflection, shrill debates, marches, picketing, candlelight vigils, fasts unto death, sit-ins and extreme measures, like stripping oneself naked.

The searing image of a fiery nude protest by twelve irate elderly women on the hot summer morning of July 15, 2004, continues to resonate to this day, not just in Manipur, where it played out, but in the entire country and the world. The protest was held by a community women's organization called the Meira Paibis (torch-bearers) in front of the Kangla Fort, which was the headquarters of the Assam Rifles in Imphal, the capital of Manipur. The Assam Rifles is one of the Central Armed Police Forces responsible for border security, counterinsurgency, and maintaining law and order in Northeast India. Rumblings of discontent against it began as news poured in of the alleged rape and killing of a purported woman militant called Thangjam Manorama by the security forces. The Meira Paibis across Imphal city and neighbouring areas got together to do something to 'safeguard the dignity of their daughters', and twelve of them took the call to strip naked.

Contemporary India had not seen a protest like it before. Soldiers and officers watched aghast as a dozen women, all in their sixties or seventies, positioned themselves at the gates of Kangla Fort and then, one by one, stripped until they were naked. Because of the very nature of their protest, the disturbing sight continues to linger to this day, more than two decades after the incident.

On my trips to Manipur after this protest, I tried to meet and focus on the courage of these twelve older women who, when caught in a bizarre and sinister twist of fate, did what every responsible and forthright citizen is meant to do but rarely does. I tried to see the women behind these faces—give them an identity, understand their domesticity, their sociocultural milieu, and their larger worldview. In short, I tried to take a serious look at their lives and why what they did mattered to all.

* * *

The disquieting images of the Meira Paibis protest lodged themselves somewhere deep within my inner consciousness. This group of elderly women from a conservative society had defied social norms and commonly held notions of women's sexuality, especially the act of undressing and privacy. Their protest reminds me of the story of resistance of Nangeli and the 'breast tax' that was imposed by the king of the erstwhile State of Travancore, one of the 550 princely states in British-ruled India. It is said that women from the lowest caste were not allowed to cover their breasts, and taxed heavily if they wore an upper-body garment. It is also said that a woman called Nangeli defied this order, cutting off her breasts in protest, and died of excessive bleeding thereafter. Though there are claims and counter-narratives about the authenticity of her story, the fact remains that it is a powerful feminist tale of defiance against patriarchy, the lewd gaze and feudal and caste hierarchy.

As a journalist, I always try to explore conflicts from a gender lens. I had a compelling urge to 'unveil' the woman behind each of those twelve protesting faces in Imphal, and the public statement they were trying to make through their action. I felt that their oral narratives would be important to understand the import of their defiant act. The actual protest—disrobing while holding the challenging banner that said 'Indian Army Rape Us' in red—may have lasted for just a few minutes, but the imprint remains to this day.

The use of rape as an instrument of war is nothing new. British journalist Christina Lamb's book, *Our Bodies, Their Battlefield: What War Does to Women*[29] documents testimonies of abuse from wartime rape survivors around the world. She travels the world compiling survivors' testimonies, including of Yazidi women and girls captured by the Islamic State in Iraq and

Syria (ISIS), schoolgirls abducted by the Boko Haram in Nigeria, Rohingya women raped by Myanmar's military, and the last remaining 'comfort women' of Imperial Japanese soldiers, who are still seeking justice more than seventy-five years after their ordeal.

Through the stories of these twelve mothers and grandmothers, I tried to understand the resilience of the people of contemporary Manipur. Their protest occurred before the advent of social media; its images were captured by a few local photographers and television channels, and word spread all over India and the world. The voices of these women were amplified to a global audience in my book, *The Mothers of Manipur*.[30] Though these women apparently belong to the same sociocultural milieu, their life experiences are touching and unique. While one ran a shop at the famous Ima Market (also known as Nupi Keithel or the Khwairamband Keithel), run entirely by women in Imphal, one of them personally knew Manorama, while another's son writes protest songs and plays the villain in Manipuri films. These women have seen Manipur evolve into a bloody land, and they reminisce about the peaceful days of their youth. These are extraordinary women leading seemingly mundane lives.

Northeast India has witnessed years of internal conflict and discontent. The perception that the region is a dangerous militarized place has only pushed it further into remoteness. Violence and peace initiatives have for a very long time moved on parallel tracks in states like Manipur, which have witnessed several kinds of angry resistance against the draconian Armed Forces (Special Powers) Act, 1958, also known as AFSPA. This law gives extraordinary power and impunity to the armed forces in areas declared 'disturbed' in India. The AFSPA was passed on September 11, 1958, and was first applied in the Naga Hills (then a part of Assam). Gradually, it was enforced in the seven northeastern states. It was also in force in Punjab as the Armed Forces (Punjab and Chandigarh) Special Powers Act from 1983 to 1997. The most condemnatory in AFSPA are its Sections 4 and 6. The former enables the security forces to 'fire upon or otherwise use force, even to the causing of death' to maintain 'public order' or when 'any law' is being contravened. Section 6 says that no criminal prosecution will lie against any person who has taken action under this law. The AFSPA has been resisted for years by the civil society of Manipur, and many people have been arrested, tortured and harassed on the pretext of maintaining law and order. The state of the enforcement of AFSPA remains fluid. If the state wants to, it relaxes it a bit in some areas, and if it feels the need, it reimposes it. Activists term the AFSPA as a symbol of oppression and legal cover for the violation of human rights by the security forces. The Army, on the other hand, demands its continuation as it provides it with a protection cover against 'false prosecutions' by the state police at the behest of militants and corrupt politicians.

As a young woman, Irom Chanu Sharmila embarked on a hunger strike on November 4, 2000, demanding the repeal of AFSPA. The killing of ten civilians, allegedly by the security forces at a bus stop in Malom, a town in Manipur, triggered Sharmila to take this vow and continue fasting until the Act was repealed in the state. A few days after she started her fast, she was arrested by the police and charged with 'attempt to commit suicide', an unlawful act under Section 309 of the Indian Penal Code (IPC). She was later shifted to judicial custody. After a few days, the authorities decided to keep Sharmila alive through force-feeding by implanting nasogastric intubation—a tube inserted through her nose which fed her liquids.

The IPC states that the maximum sentence for the charge of 'attempting suicide' is one year in detention. Amidst a full media glare, Sharmila was released from detention after the completion of one year, then ceremoniously rearrested as she continued with her fast. In 2008, I met this frail woman at the Special Isolation Ward of Imphal's Jawaharlal Nehru Hospital. I was inspired by her unadulterated zest and vigour. She seemed unfazed and wrote poems in the time she spent alone in the high-security ward. She reminded me of Draupadi in the Mahabharata, who vowed not to comb or tie her hair until her wish for revenge against her aggressor was fulfilled.

* * *

The use of nudity as a political tool has been debated time and again. 'Nakedness can be a pleasurable experience, a mundane activity, or a humiliating event depending on the situation, on who is shedding the clothes, on whether there is a spectator, and in that case, on the spectator's relationship to the naked person,' writes Barbara Sutton.[31] Further, she writes, 'Because prevailing norms in most contemporary societies prescribe the use of clothing in public spaces, naked bodies can be used in quite sensational ways to call the public's attention to a social problem, particularly in the information age, when media resonance is a crucial political strategy.'

The tactic of shocking onlookers with public nudity has always been a part of the long history of activism. For instance, the Ukrainian feminist group, FEMEN, has been using naked bodies to protest against a whole range of issues like rapes, corruption, religious repression and political scandals. The animal rights organization People for Ethical Treatment of Animals (PETA) launched the nearly decade-long 'I'd Rather Go Naked Than Wear Fur' campaign in 1991. It had many celebrities pose with nothing on but their own skin to raise awareness of the brutal treatment of animals killed or trapped for fur.[32]

Any struggle is a pushback against prevailing circumstances. The use of women's bodies as a tool of protest is a potent device to challenge patriarchy in all its forms and amplify their political voice. Any such protest seems to have a ripple effect all over the world.

Women protesting over socio-political issues against all odds is not a new phenomenon. The women's suffrage movement was a long struggle over several decades that finally culminated in their right to vote in the United States of America. I remember visiting Seneca Falls in New York, where the first Women's Rights Convention was held on July 19 and 20, 1848. The convention had been advertized on July 11 in the Seneca County Courier. Despite the minimal publicity, there were an estimated 300 attendees at the inaugural meeting. It is not surprising that many of the convention attendees were locals, as a number of abolitionists also lived nearby. Many women and men working in the anti-slavery movement eventually became a part of the struggle to obtain equal rights for women.[33]

In retrospect, when we look at the Arab Spring, women were always at the forefront of the demonstrations. However, they were sidelined in the political arrangements when governments were formed. They remained observers, however, highlighting the shortcomings of the authorities. Though Arab women have done their best to support democratic transitions—their involvement reached its peak during the Arab Spring—they have since lost steam. Today, with the exception of Tunisia, women in the Arab Spring countries are paying the price for having stood up for change. Counter-revolutionaries have decided to punish women for their role in the uprisings, but such measures have failed to break them. In Yemen's capital, Sana'a, which is currently controlled by the ideological Houthi militia, only women hold protest demonstrations and take part in sit-ins, a clear indication that they have decided to continue the struggle for freedom. In Syria, women have remained steadfast in the face of both tyranny and extremism, while women in Egypt are still bold enough to criticize the lack of fundamental rights under the shadow of military rule. This shows that after the Arab Spring, women are different from what they were before.[34]

***

In a conflict zone, women are often the worst sufferers. Closer home, in Northeast India, women have always been at the forefront of the battle for peace and justice. A civil society organization formed in 1984 by the women of Nagaland, called the Naga Mother's Association, works for a peaceful society in a state that has witnessed several decades of violent conflict. They have also been advocating for reservations for women in the political space. The Kuki Women's Forum has also been consolidating the tribal voices demanding justice for the Kuki-Zomi people in the wake of the ethnic clashes in Manipur in 2023.

However, it has been alleged that most of these organizations are vocal only when they have to speak up for the women of their own community. In fact, during ethnic clashes, they even throw allegations of helping their men capture and rape women of the opponent community against each other. 'With all its heroic strengths, a community-focused organization like the Meira Paibis has inevitably had to wrestle with real dilemmas that have exposed the women's own inadequacies of judgement and response. Because their activism against rape arose largely out of their sense of solidarity with their own community, and not from a feminist understanding of the gendered nature of the crime,' writes Pamela Philipose.[35]

In a highly militarized zone like Northeast India (or in places with a similar history or situation), there are too many stakeholders and too many versions and narratives. Indeed, violence and peace initiatives have long moved on parallel tracks, including in Manipur. In the murky maze of conflict zones, seemingly 'frail' and 'bewildered' women have responded in various ways, often coming together in solidarity as mothers, crusaders, protesters, volunteers and citizens. It is intriguing to see women metamorphose into energetic, loveable and inspirational figures who bear this unkind history with extraordinary fortitude. They take on the big questions of our time bare-knuckled, and their stories hold the seeds of future resolutions. One can always look back to them when in crisis for answers and solace.

HIDDEN VULNERABILITIES

Ngurang Reena

Living through India's race and gender wars has been stifling. After experiencing two racialized attacks in 2022, including a sexual assault in September, I wrote an editorial for *The New Indian Express*.[36] I wrote about the racialized crimes that continue to be committed in India against the people of the Northeastern Region. Recollecting my own and several others' haunting experiences with racially targeted assaults in cities, I called for a collective political and moral reckoning from Indian society, including demanding retributive justice through reforming the existing legal apparatus.

Ever since I moved to New Delhi in 2009 for higher studies, my Mongoloid phenotypes have remained marginalized in the 'Indian face'. This situation continues to subject me to absurd, harrowing experiences and sometimes, tragically, even life-threatening ordeals. A disquieted, angry girl initially, I blamed myself for all those experiences and almost left the city. I am no longer hurting, thanks to my father, who encouraged me during his lifetime to put up a resistance and fight for my place in this city and country. Now, after a decade of ethnographic work on racism, gender and migration in India, I examine key debates on racialized gender violence and illustrate the vulnerabilities of ethnic minorities in India's cities as a researcher and writer.

Drawing upon a long history of decolonial efforts and the anti-racism and feminist movements in South Asia, my scholarly and public engagements have called out coloniality and racialized policing as responsible for the continued social and private disciplining of Northeast Indian women's bodies. The historical and contemporary political and social relations must be accounted for within and outside the Northeastern Region if we want to grasp the complete nature of this ongoing injustice.

Ethnicity and identity studies draw a lot of academic curiosity about Northeast India. Intersectionality can serve as a powerful analytic tool to redefine racial and gender justice and perhaps redress the multiple injustices that may seem impenetrable in the Indian experience. Race relations, I am convinced, underline how the rest of Indian society justifies and regulates the everyday racialized attitudes and mindsets towards people from the Northeast. These racialized experiences violate, infiltrate and penetrate our lives, bodies, psyches, and minds. Racially-targeted crimes have entrapped and penetrated the intimate spaces of my family, friendships, and beyond. They have penetrated the basic aspects of my life, such as health, education, housing, neighbourhood, the public, and other impenetrable spaces.

In July 2022, two men verbally assaulted me at a café in South Delhi, ending with a note on nationalism and 'Indianness'. One morning, two weeks later, a young man followed me into a public park, also in South Delhi. He tried to force himself on me; he said he wanted to have sex and practice yoga with me. I had to push him and run, scared for my life. After these events, naturally, I stopped visiting that café. I also did not go to the park for a very long time.

Even today, the prospect of finding a decent house in an affordable neighbourhood is a daunting experience. Nobody— from the landlords to the brokers and sometimes the neighbours— shies away from revealing their racial biases. Cultural and moral policing with regard to diet, attire, mode and means of income, relationships and recreation have made house-hunting a truly exhausting endeavour. This explains how racialized violence penetrates every space and aspect of our lives.

Belonging: The In-between

In pursuit of dreams, hopes and aspirations, and sometimes even for survival, many of us 'leave the land'. Researchers interested in this field of enquiry engage in ethnographic understandings of alternative spaces beyond the idea of 'home', which foregrounds the narratives of individuals and communities from Northeast India with what we popularly call the 'mainland' India.

Between 1981 and 2001, the total number of 'migrants' from the Northeast to other parts of India increased from 0.4 million to 1.1 million [4 lakh to 11 lakh]. Additionally, between 2005 and 2010, half a million [5 lakh] more moved, with Delhi as the most preferred destination with 2 lakh people.[37]

Anthropologists Dolly Kikon and Karlsson BG, in *Leaving the Land*,[38] emphatically underscores the political, social and economic transformation that has transpired in the Northeastern Region due to the increasing migration of indigenous youth to Indian metropolises. Through telling stories and narratives, the authors enable us to understand and expose the intersections at which racial violence develops, intensifies and is normalized, notably for migrants of affective labour (in the service industry) in big cities such as New Delhi, Bengaluru, and others. Similarly, Duncan McDuie-Ra's 2012 essay, 'Leaving the Northeast' in the book *Northeast Migrants in Delhi*,[39] documents the migration in what he describes as the migrants creating their own 'map' within one of the most unfriendly metropolises—Delhi—through community linkages.[40]

Whilst millions of us continue to cross the borders of state and region for several reasons, we also embark on transcending the multitudes of mental maps that push us to negotiate the idea of belonging. Amidst the economic, political, social and environmental transformation, 'crossing borders' isn't a new phenomenon for the people of the Northeastern Region. As migrants, we undertake this exercise on many levels.

According to the vast literature on national identity and State-building, borders and boundaries of place, nation, and culture are not necessarily isomorphic. In fact, national identity, like nation-building, is defined relationally and emerges from a dynamic process of interaction, engagement and negotiation between local and national forces.[41] New perspectives on borders have also come to offer a fresher understanding of the phenomenon as 'sites for interaction between individuals from many backgrounds, hybridization, creolization, and negotiation'.[42] Subsequently, borders represent a sense of inherent duality, often fostering a 'process of mirror imaging'[43] where the construction of 'otherness' constantly takes place on both sides of the border (also).[44]

Migration due to conflicts such as the one currently ongoing in Manipur has made thousands into the displaced with no hope of return. Such an event is yet another testimony to the historical, political, social and spatial marginalization, mainly of young indigenous people from the Northeastern Region. Those fleeing the ongoing persecution in Manipur have found refuge to some extent in India's metropolises, such as New Delhi and other cities. Although marred by racialization towards the people of the region in various forms, these cities also happen to provide alternative spaces for belonging and, to some extent, an intergenerational experience of belongingness.

I write about the *in-between sense of belonging* to inform the readers how a new location outside the Northeastern Region, such as New Delhi, is crucial for us, alongside the existence of collective and associational spaces such as the cultural, political and religious, forged to some extent to represent our new 'home'. Neighbourhoods such as Humayunpur, Lajpat Nagar, and others, filled with migrants from the northeast, display distinct ways of simultaneously articulating difference and belongingness. Such new places offer alternative ways of building relationships, networks and linkages within food enclaves and other representational spaces in different cosmopolitan-urban settings, affording us the privilege of experiencing unique meaning-making endeavours.

These meaning-making endeavours enable us to convey the peculiarities of the frontiers at the Centre, revealing the complexities of the diverse sociocultural region and, sometimes, helping us assert our 'empowerment' to contest and navigate the borders and increasing political actions through forums and associations such as cultural and political gatherings in India's capital also, more or less, leverages political faculty.

Interestingly, the historian Joy Pachuau, in her 2014 book *Being Mizo: Identity and Belonging in Northeast India*,[45] underscores the distinctive struggle between the different stages of belonging. She argues that the phenomenon of categorization of the 'significant other' experienced by a Mizo[46] enables the agency in 'identity creation, and allows for itself its own mode of functioning and social practices'. In this regard, the effort of becoming and belonging, as noted by the historian, finds itself in a state of intermittent contestation. However, when examining Northeast India's relationship with the 'mainland', these perplexities should not be viewed or perceived as anything directed against, or less than, being 'Indian'. This is a crucial observation, strikingly expressed and shared by the historian of South Asia, Prof Bérénice Guyot-Réchard.[47]

To me, it simply means this: whilst my identity as a Nyishi woman finds its meaning in history and geospatial location primarily in my home state, Arunachal Pradesh, my in-between identity when moving to Delhi and other metropolises may experience spatial anxieties to a great extent. Therefore, to sustain my distinctive 'tribal' identity, I must 're-enact and keep it alive' by engaging with and participating in the new locality's activities, as observed in *Being Mizo*.

How Racialized Gendered Violence is Produced and Reproduced in Urban Spaces

It is against this backdrop of experiencing 'othering' that understanding the race, gender and violence questions requires a nuanced knowledge of the Northeast Indian's 'migrant' stories. Concomitantly, to understand how responses to such violence are shaped in the light of historical, spatial, and social conditions, one must investigate our (the migrant's) relationship with the Indian state, cities, urban landscape and the many configurations in between. Additionally, it requires rigorous application and interdisciplinary deliberation between history, political science, anthropology, sociology, law, and other related fields.

Several narratives and stories of those who experience this violence, notably gender-based violence, will enable us to understand and unveil the intersections at which racial violence originates, develops, intensifies, and becomes embedded in the individual's life as well as in the wider community.

Women's safety in Indian cities has been a major concern. Apart from the 2010 Draft Strategic Framework for Women's Safety in Delhi, the National Crime Records Bureau has repeatedly listed cities such as Delhi as the most unsafe for women. According to feminist geographers, urban landscapes, to a great extent, do not recognize the gendered aspect of city infrastructures and fail to accommodate the interests of women and other marginalized sections of the society. This gendered aspect of urban planning gained traction during the 1970s and 1980s and has become a critical aspect of urban and city planning.

Whilst the 'crisis of masculinity' and other dependent variables as explanations of gendered violence continue to provide a fair share of the argument, they fail to offer conclusive narratives that reveal the peculiarities of racially targeted gendered violence. Thus, we must call attention to the plurality of women and women's experiences.

In July 2007, Delhi Police published a booklet aimed at providing 'safety tips' to students and visitors from Northeast India. To most of us, the booklet embodied absolute colonial misgivings and cultural policing and, most profoundly, a reiteration of patriarchal undertones on women's bodies and sexuality.

> *On Attire: Be Roman in 'rooms'—revealing dresses should be avoided.*
> *Travel: Avoid lonely roads/by-lanes when dressed scantily.*
> *Help: Dial 100 and always carry pepper spray.*
> *Dating: Go to decent places.*[48]
>
> —An excerpt from the Delhi Police booklet titled
> *Do's and Don'ts for Northeast Students in Delhi.*

With evolving global feminist movements, the role of race found a place in feminist theories. Intersectionality, a theory coined through Black women's experiences by African-American academic and writer Kimberlé Crenshaw in 1989, first exposed the many facets of racialized gender vulnerabilities in the United States system. Crenshaw discussed the need for an intersectional framework to describe how race, class, gender, and other individual characteristics intersect.

In the Indian case, the 'burden' of sexual promiscuity attached to women from the Northeastern Region has resulted in unwarranted attention and desire in the form of sexual pursuit and assault. Based on my lived experiences, I can testify that my ethnicity exposes a type of unique vulnerability wherein most acts of violence are perceived as 'justified'.

A January 2013 study[49] jointly sponsored by Jamia Millia Islamia's Centre for North East Studies and Policy Research and the National Commission for Women reported that not less than 60 per cent of women who have migrated from the Northeast to the four metros—New Delhi, Mumbai, Kolkata and Bengaluru— have faced harassment and discrimination. Based on a sample survey, the report concluded that Delhi ranked at the top with 81 per cent of respondents reporting harassment in the city, followed by Bengaluru at 60 per cent, while Mumbai emerged as the safest city, although there were reports of extortive behaviour by auto and taxi drivers.

In 2010, a Mizo woman was raped in Delhi in a case that is popularly known as the Dhaula Kuan rape case. It signalled a compelling foreboding of the intersection of race and gender, wherein the assault on the Mizo woman was almost 'justified' because of the sexuality attached to her ethnicity.

The MP Bezbaruah Committee,[50] amongst others, have concluded that the number of attacks on people from the northeastern states in Delhi has been proportionately very high considering the small number of people from the region living in the city and that the numbers of incidents that are racial in nature, apart from molestation and prejudices, were growing.

In 2017, while visiting my friends at a hotel in South Delhi, I was assaulted in a lift by two hotel guests. The men enquired about my 'rate' and offered sex for the night. Naturally, the unpleasant and traumatic encounter paralyzed my mental faculties. After a week, when I had found my bearings, I consulted with my friends and family and sought accountability from the hotel management. However, it was only after intervention from the city's SPUNER—Special Police Unit for North Eastern Region and North East Helpline—and the media[51] that the hotel management heeded my plea. It is pertinent to highlight the racist attitudes the hotel management also displayed towards me. The management sided with the unruly, inebriated guests and demanded my 'dishonourable' exit from the hotel.

Analyzing the cosmopolitan experience with regard to the accounts of online dating of women from the region can additionally provide a good ethnographic inquiry into the dynamic processes of interaction between people, places and cultures involving opposite forces and processes—in other words, between the frontiers and the rest of India. Whilst acknowledging the vulnerabilities of all women in online spaces, I am convinced that women from the Northeastern Region, unique in their socio-cultural distinctiveness, are likely to have similar experiences in online dating spaces, be it Tinder, Hinge, or elsewhere.

Esther, a development strategist from Arunachal Pradesh (name and profession changed), revealed to me the complex intersection of race, gender and the politics of desire while narrating her online dating experiences. She confided that sexual exploration outside her home state afforded her a new sense of freedom and personality. She affirmed that, initially, it was impossible for her to trust meeting men online due to her traumatic experiences in the city. Despite having lived in Delhi for over a decade, she allowed herself to embrace a rekindled relationship with the city and its people only years later, and then with caution, once she had regained her lost confidence, she told me.

Additionally, her dating experiences revealed the duality of gendered vulnerability as a 'tribal' woman on either side of the 'border'—restrained by cultural and moral oversight on both ends of the road. On the one hand, several indigenous institutions regulate women's bodies and sexual desires through regressive customary beliefs, values and practices. On the other hand, when subjected to the racial attitude towards women from the region of most Indian men in urban landscapes, sexually confident women like Esther often get viewed as promiscuous. She said that the 'pressure' to have sex on the first date was always imminent, and some men asked her to introduce 'nice Northeast women' to their friends. When she chose to take things slow, most of her dates either 'unmatched' her on dating apps or blocked her, and some didn't even show up for dates! Other women from the region have also informed me about having received threats when they exercised their choice, including blackmailing based on previously exchanged texts and photos.

As observed in the beginning, to understand how the responses to such violence are shaped and formed by varied settings, one must investigate the many configurations migrant relationships can take. In the light of historical, spatial, and social conditions, perhaps, these narratives present us—the academics, researchers, writers and practitioners—with the opportunity to interrogate and analyze women's sexual desire experiences, notably with regard to understanding and supporting diverse women's sexual empowerment.

Embodied Coloniality in Indian Society

Modern nation states often use a desultory discourse of justification to continue racial oppression, while, as a collective of Mongoloid descent, prompting cultural disposition, we are often reminded of our 'savagery'. Expectations of assimilation for the people migrating from the Northeastern Region is another political ploy in the context of discrediting sub-national and regional cultures. Calling out women from the northeast when they come under attack from various sections of society uncovers how women are perpetually made to bear the burden of such cultural tropes, particularly related to 'provocation' and shame with regard to our bodies. The Mizo woman's case verifies this claim.

Tehelka magazine's 2012 sting operation conducted on thirty police departments in the National Capital Region (NCR), which included police officials in Delhi and its neighbouring cities, Gurgaon, Faridabad, NOIDA, etc, exposed the deeply-rooted male-chauvinist beliefs and attitudes among police officers towards women in general. The institutional predisposition to misogyny with regard to women's bodies, sexuality and character emerged the biggest concern from the airing of the sting. The investigation revealed, for example, that the majority of police officers agreed that a woman's clothing was directly linked to assaults such as rape against them.

The apparent problem of racism and racial discrimination within law enforcement agencies, primarily police brutality, is another form of racism that people of the northeast endure. Notably, police violence in the form of little or no action against a complaint made by women from the region is a serious crime.

Delhi Police's 'safety tips' booklet from 2007 is another great case study to understand attitudes of the police force towards women from the region. My 2017 assault at the South Delhi hotel is another example. In the aftermath of that unwanted rendezvous, the police, to a great extent, profiled me based on my ethnicity and wouldn't heed my complaints until I called the SPUNER helpline and visited the local police station with a male friend.

In another case, according to reports, an officer assumed that the two complainants who had approached him with a sexual assault complaint were from the northeast and delayed the registration of their case. The complainants were actually women of Chinese descent from Singapore, on vacation in Goa.

It is not an exaggeration when we say that most of us distrust the Delhi Police in handling race-related crimes. There are no provisions to check any form of systemic police discrimination. According to research conducted by R Bhattacharyya and Venkat Pulla in 2020[52] 80 per cent of respondents did not approach the police even if they suffered discrimination and harassment. Some respondents said that it was futile to approach the 'corrupt and insensitive' police. And those who did complained of 'dissatisfaction'.

Owing to the growing number of cases of violence against people from the northeast, in August 2020, the National Campaign Against Torture (NCAT), a platform for action of NGOs committed to stamp out torture in India, submitted a report to the Committee for Reforms in Criminal Laws set up by the Union Ministry of Home Affairs. Its 168-page report, 'Racism in India: The Need for Criminalization of Racism and Racial Crimes', underscored the need for a constitutional and legal framework based on racial discrimination.

The report also underlined the inadequacy of existing provisions to criminalize and penalize racial offences. Through detailed documentation, it highlighted the continued racial violence against Tibeto-Mongoloids from the Northeastern Region. The report, through careful categorization, revealed a series of racial attacks prior to the COVID-19 pandemic and spurts of racist attacks during the pandemic as well. The NCAT report, whilst delineating the wide-scale racialized violence in Indian society, also revealed its distinctive gender-based vulnerabilities. The same report dedicated a chapter to racial violence against African citizens who reside in India.

Charting the Way to Mitigate Racialized Violence

Acknowledging the multitudes of maps along the borders of Northeast India and the 'mainland' is an apparent necessity—these borders are beyond geo-spatial; they are politicized. And the distances between these borders are wide because of the continued complicity, in colonial and post-colonial India, in fostering reductive discourses on tribe(s). There is an urgency to identify and bridge the distance from these border worlds, starting with legislative reform based on a reinvigorated discourse on tribes and 'tribals'.

Rooted in the exercise of theorizing nationalism, physical maps and figures first imagined and conceptualized the nation-space as a methodically demarcated/organized territory. In this sense, the imagination of phenotypes that remain outside the contours of the 'Indian face' is mine and of other people from the Northeastern Region. However, a 160-page supplementary publication of the National Council of Educational Research and Training in 2017, 'Northeast India: People, History and Culture'[53] is an encouraging step in attempting to delineate aspects of Northeastern India's land, people, history and culture.

Making sense of the racially motivated behaviour faced by people from Northeast India in Delhi, Duncan McDuie-Ra describes in his book, *Northeast Migrants in Delhi: Race, Refuge and Retail*,[54] one category of racial violence as 'harassment'. He describes these experiences as everyday encounters that involve verbal taunts and unwelcome attitudes and gestures in public places. And violence is an extreme form of harassment that is intolerable. It signifies murder, rape, molestation, and other such crimes.

The absence of a solid definition of racism and race-related crimes, including stringent anti-racism laws, may have resulted in the pervasiveness of overt acts of racism. However, even for covert racially motivated criminal acts, there's a substantial amount of work to be done. Drawing on Corlett[55] and the United Nation's definition of racism rooted in atrocity and ethnic persecution, race-related crimes in the Indian context require urgent intervention. Legal and legislative reforms with regard to protecting the people of the northeast from race-related violence will also facilitate provisions to protect people from African nations living in India.

It is uncanny that Northeastern Indian migrants' high demand in the neo-liberal labour market, with our 'special skills' imbued with a touch of 'internationalism', hasn't helped the community overcome the race discrimination it encounters in urban India. Indignity in various forms of racialized experiences only confirms that both cultural and economic capital are located within notions of power as both play vital roles in social reproduction.[56]

There are multitudes of 'positive stories' about migrants from the Northeastern Region living and flourishing in urban spaces beyond the northeast. To my mind, investigating such stories also requires an understanding of the journey—the in-between stages of belonging and the contestation of identities I mentioned earlier. It is also interesting to note that most migrants (women) do not want to go back home; the illimitable expanse of urban life is indisputable; however, ensuring women's safety and well-being ought to be paramount for urban leaders and planners. Thus, a comprehensive understanding of social justice must include—though, crucially, must not be limited to—the ability to live in a dignified, safe and nurturing environment.

A FACE THAT MAKES DEATH SHIVER

Ratnottama Sengupta

At first, I thought it was just cold water, thrown as a silly game. Then the ice-cold liquid became unbearably hot. It felt like someone had stripped off my skin and sprinkled chilli powder inside...

—Saira, a survivor

Acid. When, in our school labs, we held in our hands a bottle of acid—nitric, sulphuric, hydrochloric—we were careful not to spill it because we were warned it can dissolve or raze substances it came in contact with. Later, in the course of authoring *Krishna's Cosmos: The Creativity of an Artist, Sculptor & Teacher,*[57] on the life of the pioneer printmaker Krishna Reddy, I learnt of the liquid's use in the art of creating etching plates. Occasionally, when the bathroom got clogged, I did pour a bottle down the drain to clear the muck and let the water flow free again. Little did I know how dangerous the chemical can be when it is poured on a human body. How much damage it can cause to live tissue, destroying the skin, the flesh, the nerves, the identity, the very soul of a person who is subjected to its attack.

I came alive to the vicious use of acids when I watched *Chirodini Tumi Je Amar/2* (You are Mine Forever/2) a 2014 Bengali adaptation of the Tamil-mainstream hit *Vazhakku Enn 18/9* (Case Number 18/9, 2012). The crime thriller directed by

Soumik Chatterjee unspooled on the pivot of such attacks to drive home the message of juvenile delinquency, misuse of technology and abuse of administrative power. Jyoti, Shreya's house help, is admitted to hospital following an acid attack that has burnt her face. The police zero in on Bhanu Sardar, as he used to 'follow' the girl around. But Shreya suspects that Raj, the spoilt kid of a wealthy single mother with political connections, threw the acid, mistaking Jyoti for Shreya. Rightly, as it turns out. But Raj's mother gets him off the list of suspects, and Bhanu is made the scapegoat. Jyoti, now out of the hospital, avenges this by paying the corrupt policeman back in the same coin.

Soon after, I watched *The Woman and the Man* (2016). A milk-delivery man is infatuated by a free-spirited single woman and fantasizes about her every night—until she is scarred by a vicious acid attack. Sharmila Maity and Rajdeep Pal—recently awarded the Silver Lotus for *Kalkokkho* (House of Time, 2021), their philosophic take on the COVID-19 crisis—had built the nuanced eighteen-minute short on the wantonness of the male gaze and objectification of the female body; on sympathy turning into empathy and lust giving way to love.

In *One Last Time*, Mohinder Pratap Singh's 2024 movie, the rejected lover pleads, 'Come and meet me.' But in a patriarchal society, men cannot take 'no' from a girl. So, when Mukti, young, attractive and soon-to-be-married, refuses the lusty advances of Janardan, the 'boyfriend' plots to deface her. But fortunately, it takes all kinds to make the world: a turbaned taxi driver overhears him plotting the savagery with his friends, and swings into action. The denouement? The tables are turned on the attacker…

A perceived slight to the dignity of a rejected lover is common to acid attack and rape. Subscribing to a patriarchal mindset that expects a woman to dress conservatively, smile demurely, be gratified by male attention and acquiesce to a marriage proposal or succumb to lusty advances, men get enraged when a woman says NO. 'She's being coy,' they'd like to believe, for 'women like to be possessed, don't they?' Brute force, that's what they're asking for! Agency? Autonomy? Consent? Whoever thought up these terms!

It was only with *Chhapaak* (Splash! 2020) that the establishment sat up and took note of the horrific 'crime of passion' that raised its head in Bangladesh (reportedly in 1967), took root on other South Asian maps—India and Pakistan—and spread further East, notably to Malaysia and Cambodia. India's National Crime Records Bureau recorded 1,483 cases between 2014 and 2018, and studies have indicated a rapid rise in such incidents.

Why?

In most movies—and many have been made in recent years—the reason for the brutal attack is rejection by the woman. Refusal to marry. Turning down sexual advances. In reality, are there other so-called reasons? Yes, the inability to give birth to a son! Of course, there could be an extramarital affair going on—or suspicion thereof. Perhaps, she refuses to give him a divorce when he fancies another woman. Sometimes, there's a land dispute, or a business deal gone sour. In a patriarchal society, any of these reasons is good enough cause to fault a woman. Caste, class or creed no bar: from family feuds to communal clashes, a woman's body bears the brunt of violence. Strange, isn't it, that sometimes men have women as accomplices—as we saw in the socially-committed biographical Hindi drama film *Chhapaak*, in which it was Babbu's sister's character who actually splashed the acid on Malti.

'In the past, sometimes, I have wondered how it would be to empty a full bottle of acid on you [the man who attacked her],' wrote Dolly, a real-life fourteen-year-old acid attack survivor, in a 2015 open letter addressed to the attacker. She wrote, 'My hands would tremble...But you burnt my face, not my will to live. You can't throw acid on that.'

Malti, the protagonist of *Chhapaak*, is infused with this very human spirit. And she is the barely masked alter ego of Laxmi Agarwal, another battle-scarred crusader against acid.

Splash!

> *'When acid is thrown on a person's face, the eyelids and lips may burn off completely. The nose may melt, closing the nostrils, and the ears shrivel up. Skin and bone on the skull, forehead, cheeks and chin may dissolve. When the acid splashes or drips over the neck, chest, back, arms or legs, it burns every inch of the skin it touches.'*

—Dr Ashok Gupta, plastic surgeon who has operated on more than 150 victims, talking to Harsimran Gill and Karen Dias for an article published in *Al Jazeera* on March 10, 2016.

Chhapaak was directed by Meghna Gulzar, who has carved a niche for herself with woman-oriented films like *Filhaal* (Momentary, 2002), *Talwar* (Sword, 2015) and *Raazi* (Agreed, 2020). And, interestingly, it was co-produced by Deepika Padukone. It was right after her triumphant portrayal of Padmini (*Padmavat,* 2018), the queen of Mewar whose fabled beauty drew the Sultan of Delhi, Allauddin Khalji to Chittorgarh. To portray Malti, Deepika had to trade enticing looks for the repellent face of a survivor, defaced for life and yet willing to knock on the doors of court after court for justice.

Shot in locations near Delhi and Mumbai, *Chhapaak* was accorded tax-free status in Chhattisgarh, Madhya Pradesh and Rajasthan. Still, it grossed only Rs 55 crore (US$6.9 million)—a failure in commercial terms. However, the story of a woman standing up to injustice and making societal and legal changes in how the world looked at the disfigured faces of victims, inspired a leading actress like Deepika to put her money where her face is. Literally.

The superstar's incandescent beauty was concealed under layers of silicon and glue. The agony of Malti, the fictionalized Laxmi, plays out on her face. After the attack, first, Laxmi's face was covered by red blotches, then the upper layer of her skin peeled away, taking many of her facial features out. What was left was the ghost of a face that required a series of painful–and pricey–surgeries to be rearranged into a semblance of what it used to be. But what lay at the end of the ordeal? On seeing her, a child shrieked out and shivered in fear.

To be realistic, the film had to show the full horror of Malti's plight. At the same time, it had to compel viewers to keep watching so that they absorb the full import of the violence done to her. For the prosthetic and make-up artist Clover Wootton, who has a skilled understanding of silicone, resin, polyurethane and metals, it was a challenge to strike a balance between the visceral horror of what acid attacks mean, without sensationalizing or turning the viewer away.

The other challenge lay in the technical process of prosthetic make-up. In real life, acids turn the skin black and it starts to peel off. By contrast, with prosthetics, one adds something to the player's face. While acid attack victims lose mass on their face, which then goes from dark to light over time, leaving white blotches and constricted skin, make-up artistes have to *add* layer after layer to the subject's face. So, Deepika had to ensure that the prosthetics didn't swell up her face. Prosthetics, in this case, had to battle with aesthetics and let it win.

With glue all over her face, Deepika must have found it hard to breathe. This also made her empathize with the victims, whose nose melt makes it difficult to breathe through their nostrils. Having come out of a numbing bout of depression, Deepika could relate to women who have gone through experiences that imprisoned them, made them withdraw into themselves, away from the world, society, families, even themselves. Yet, she stood up and moved forward, and could soon identify with the plight of Laxmi Agarwal, Pinky Rathore, Preeti Rathi, Aarti Thakur and other victims of the monstrosity.

'The common thread,' she said in an interview, 'is what we chose to make out of the incident. The fact is that after going through such [immobilizing] experiences, we chose to speak up. We learnt from the experience and are on a path to help other people. To impact their life positively. I was attracted by this human spirit and wanted to make this film.'

Before Padmini, Deepika had essayed the fabled beauty

Mastani—again, a strong-willed warrior who made her life with the seventh peshwa of the Maratha Empire, Bajirao I. Defying expectations and conventions, Deepika fearlessly took on the unconventional role of the disfigured Malti and left the comfort zone of fitting into stereotypes. Such was her dedication to the cause that she joined a team that acted as plumbers, students, businessmen, housewives, even a drunkard—to find out how easy it was to procure a bottle of acid. The aim? To ascertain if the amended laws were being implemented.

Laws and Changes

'Whether I throw water on you or acid, I will suffer the same penalty.'

Through this one dialogue, director Meghna Gulzar could easily drive home to her viewers the laxity in Section 326 of the IPC—voluntarily casing grievous injury by a dangerous weapon—and sections 326A and B. To clarify this further, until 2013, acid attacks were not considered a distinct offence—they were covered under general laws such as for causing grievous hurt (Section 322, which defines the criminal act), or murder and attempt to murder (sections 302 and 307).

But following the rise in incidents, the determined efforts of many victims, and the founding of outfits for the rehabilitation of survivors, the courts saw the need to amend the laws in 2013. To help tackle the sense of impunity, acid attacks—both successful and attempted—were made cognizable and non-bailable offences through the Criminal Law (Amendment) Act of 2013. Under Section 326A of the amended law, if a person uses acid to cause any injury—whether permanent or reversible—with the knowledge that the substance burns, disfigures or maims an individual, they are liable to be sentenced to imprisonment for not less than ten years. It can be extended to life imprisonment with a fine.

And under 326B, even if no injury is caused, the offender will be held liable for throwing—or attempting to throw—acid on the victim. They will be awarded an imprisonment of not less than five years, which can be extended to up to seven years, and a fine. Further, if an acid attack leads to the victim's death, then—under Section 302 meant for murder—the accused can be sentenced to death; if not, then life imprisonment and a fine.

Additionally, the 2013 amendments laid down the punishment for failure to register crimes against women by adding sections 166A and 166B to the existing Section 166. Public servants in particular would be pulled up for disobeying the law if they acted or behaved in any manner prejudicial to a victim. Or, if they do not record information in relation to a cognizable offence.

The Act of 2013 imposed fines on offenders which should directly go to the victim. It also laid down that governments should provide the victims with compensation that is appropriate to cover the medical expenses. Based on Supreme Court of India directions, the Union Ministry of Home Affairs directed: i) The states to ensure that victims receive Rs 1 lakh and the balance of Rs 2 lakh within the next two months. ii) To provide free treatment to acid victims in any hospital, government or private. iii) To set aside one or two beds for vulnerable victims who might get discriminated against because of their background. iv) To initiate social integration programmes for victims and provide funds (and opportunities) for their rehabilitation. A number of legal aid services and organizations were also set up under this initiative.

Laxmi vs Union of India

'When the wounds from an acid burn heal, they form thick scars that pull the skin tight and cause disfigurement. In 90 per cent of cases, the eyesight of the victim is adversely affected, causing blindness. And then there is the psychological trauma. With a high survival rate among victims, acid attacks are rarely carried out with murder in mind. They are intended to disfigure and mutilate—to condemn the victim to a lifetime of suffering.'

—Dr Ashok Gupta, cited in *Al Jazeera*, March 10, 2016

The fight to change this story started in earnest in 2005 when sixteen-year-old Laxmi Agarwal was doused with acid on her way back from the market near Tughlak Road in Delhi. Because? Ten months earlier, the Class 11 student had refused to accept a marriage proposal from thirty-two-year-old Naeem Khan who lived in the same neighbourhood. Laxmi lost consciousness for a while but survived the attack, albeit with disfigured face, neck and other body parts, and mustered courage to file a Public Interest Litigation (PIL) in the Supreme Court in 2006. The fallout? She succeeded in getting not only compensation; she got acid attacks recognized as a separate, serious category of crime. And the footnote? Naeem Khan, initially let off on bail, was sentenced to life imprisonment.

The apex court had directed the Centre and state governments to amend existing laws and draft new legislations. As a result, The Prevention of Acid Attacks and Rehabilitation of Acid Attack Victims Bill, 2017 came into being. It raised the penalty for the crime from seven to ten years and regulated over-the-counter sales of acid. Dealers could not sell unless they kept a record of the buyer's address, the quantity purchased, and the reason for the purchase. That is, people could buy only after showing a government-issued photo ID. The other major steps included the financial support towards the repeated surgeries required to reconstruct the face or body, and the rehabilitation of women who account for more than 80 per cent of the victims.

Laxmi, daughter of an alcoholic father, a domestic help mother, and sister of a brother suffering from intestinal tuberculosis, rose from being only an 'acid attack survivor' to a television anchor. Through her ordeal, she became a symbol of courage, hope, positive action. She was NDTV's Woman of the Year. In 2014, she received the International Women of Courage award presented by Michelle Obama. In 2019, India's Ministry of Women and Child Development honoured her with the International Women Empowerment award. UNICEF bestowed her with a recognition for her 'Stop Acid Sale' campaign. She also became the mother of a daughter named Pihu. All because she did not give up on life.

The Attack

> *'So much beauty, Parvati! It only fans vanity. You know how beautiful the moon is—that is why her face is scarred. Come, let me scar your face...Don't be scared Paro, your wound will heal soon enough! Only the scar will remain in memory of our parting. So, whenever you will see your moonlike face in the mirror, you will think of me.'*

> —Dilip Kumar as Devdas in the eponymous 1955 film.

Acid attacks are, likewise, intended to disfigure in order to mark a person for life. To teach a lesson, not kill. With a high survival rate, the victim is expected to suffer a fate worse than death, which is momentary. All because the girl had a mind of her own: she said a firm 'no'. How dare she! Proud of her looks, is she? Of herself? Destroy her. No, acid is not a murder weapon, it is meant to mutilate. She won't suffer once she's dead, right? So, let her remember for as long as she breathes, heavily, with difficulty, Whom She Dared Reject.

Sufiya Bano from Budaun in Uttar Pradesh had refused her cousin brother who lived in the same house and wanted to marry her, then twenty-four. So, one day in 2004, he stood in front of her and said, 'You are too proud of your face. Now enjoy!' And he poured acid over her face even as she screamed and cried for water. After a lot of water had flown down the Ganga, the culprit was sentenced to ten years imprisonment but released on the 75th anniversary of India's independence. This was reported by the Kashmir-based South Asian journalist Safina Nabi in *NewThinking.com* on April 6, 2023.

It is hardly surprising that most acid attacks target the face—which may not be critical to survival but is the most critical part of an individual's identity. That is perhaps why a face is equated with vanity. It helps the attacker that in most contemporary, modern societies a woman's face is not covered.

The Aftermath

Acid attack requires immediate attention. But how many of us know what first aid ought to be administered to the victim? Onlookers are too stunned to immediately wash the acid off with plain water. Only after stabilization, the victim ought to be shifted to a clinic or hospital. But even ambulances and emergency rooms lack the special neutralizing agents that can limit the damage. Often, private hospitals refuse treatment citing lack of specialized facilities. In doing so, they contravene the provisions of Section 357C of the Code of Criminal Procedure, 1973. But there is no law to take action against these hospitals or clinics.

Inadequate compensation under the survivor compensation schemes. Lack of legal guarantee to free medical care, rehabilitative services...And the psychological trauma? Let's not even talk about it! Depression, loneliness, lack of concentration and memory, insomnia, nightmares, lack of confidence in themselves, lack of faith in education, skill, or professionalism, fear of ridicule—you name it, they suffer it. Which is why psychological counselling for trauma and depression is now strongly suggested by NGOs that have sprung up in robust numbers in recent years.

Economic disaster is spelt by acid not only by the surgeries and medical care that has to go on for life. It is also caused because often, an attack closes avenues for gainful employment. This becomes the most critical requirement, since being unemployed makes it tough to keep the kitchen fire going for the family (most of the victims have been found to have been the breadwinners in their family).

And it also takes a toll on self-confidence. Employers get impatient as court appearances translate regularly into a day's absence from work. And when they commute by train, often, co-passengers cringe, if not refuse to sit next to the survivors. And still a complete ban cannot be imposed on the sale of hydrochloric, sulphuric or nitric acids, since they are widely used in the automotive industries, polish manufacturing and in the medical industry, too: say, as agents in rust cleaning.

Statistics

The first acid attack in India was recorded in 1982, Safina Nabi writes in *NewThinking.com.* Since then, this cruel form of gender violence intended to silence women who refuse to be controlled or dictated has risen across the developing nations of South Asia. The tragedy is that for varied reasons, the true number of this repulsive crime doesn't come to light. Still, the journalist writes with certainty that '80 per cent of attacks are against women and 60 per cent of them go unreported'. She adds that 'globally, there are approximately 1,500 attacks a year perpetrated by men who suffer loss of face, or loss of honour'.

Data from the NCRB (National Crime Records Bureau) on December 19, 2022 lays down that in India, 150 cases were recorded in 2019, 105 in 2020 and 102 in 2021. Since the number of cases of acid attack against women are being said to rise in South Asia, but the number of cases in India are shown declining according to these cited NCRB figures, it is important to note that when it comes to justice for the victims, it is not just the apparent fall in recorded cases that matters but putting a leash on the impunity that comes with perpetrating such an attack. Year after year, Uttar Pradesh and West Bengal have accounted for nearly 50 per cent of the cases. The charge sheeting rate stood at 83 per cent and conviction rate at 54 per cent in 2019. These figures improved in 2020 and stood at 86 per cent and 72 per cent, respectively, but in 2021, they stood at 89 per cent and a mere 20 per cent.

Dignity: A Journal of Analysis of Exploitation and Violence, Vol 6, Issue 1 (2021), Art. 5 details in its findings and conclusions that 'the primary causes of the growing incidence rates of acid attacks are India's patriarchal culture and its inadequate legal system'. Due to this, many victims don't receive compensation on time. 'In 2020, only 799 of 1,273 victims received compensation,' it notes.

Before we Sleep...

The amazing stories of Laxmi Agarwal and other strong-willed women who had the courage to face every adversity tell us never to give up hope. Their admirable actions have sparked a fire in people, in society, to speak out against the horror of hate crimes that still dog women in society—be it ours, theirs, or others.

And still, there are miles to go before we sleep. For instance, the NCRB could prepare annual reports in conjunction with NGOs to get a true picture of how diligently states and authorized organizations and offices are following the rulings of the Supreme Court. The police could be encouraged to treat victims with a greater understanding of the gravity of the attack, and the urgency to complete the investigations and book culprits. Clinics, nursing homes and hospitals could be sensitized to attend to survivors with greater haste and sensitivity. And common men and women could, perhaps, be made aware to respond with alacrity, and plain water.

But violence against women—or children, for that matter—cannot be resolved in a court of law alone. So, perhaps the ideal situation could be obtained only when the government and mass media join hands to educate young minds about the equality of men and women. About the ills of patriarchy and the gains of non-violence. Most of all, about the need to look upon disfigured and maimed faces as humans like us, not aliens.

Note: *Opinions are based on numerous conversations with directors and activists and travels around the world as a film critic and journalist. Not all of it can be sourced to books and papers.*

NEPAL'S BATTLE AGAINST TRAFFICKING: STORIES, STATISTICS, STRUGGLES

Babita Basnet

Sanu Rai's journey began in the harsh realities of a poor peasant family in the Khotang district of Nepal, where life was a constant struggle. 'I was born in 1978, the youngest among two older brothers and five sisters,' she recounted to me in 2005, when I was chronicling the lives of ten women, including Sanu, who were rescued in 1998 from red-light districts in India. 'My father passed away when I was just nine, leaving my sick mother to bear the weight of raising us all,' Sanu told me. By the time she turned thirteen, she found herself shouldering the responsibility of caring for her ailing mother and younger siblings. It was during this challenging period that a glimmer of hope emerged when a village sister, who worked in a Kathmandu carpet factory, returned home.

'She told me, "Life in the village is hard; no matter how much we work, it's difficult to make ends meet. Let us both go into carpet weaving,"' Sanu recalled. Eager to ease her family's burden, she embraced the opportunity and followed the woman to Kathmandu, Nepal's capital. However, what awaited her there was far from the promised escape. 'I endured immense hardships in the carpet factory for a year, only to find myself unpaid and unable to send any money back home,' she lamented.

Amidst this struggle, a man named Badri Pariyar, along with his wife, who also worked at the factory, offered Sanu a chance for what they described as a better job in Pokhara town in Nepal. 'I trusted them like older siblings,' Sanu remembered. However, the journey they embarked on led Sanu far away from Pokhara and into the heart of Mumbai's dark underbelly. 'I never saw Badri again,' Sanu recounted sorrowfully. 'In those brothels, filled mostly with Arab patrons, marine crews, and foreign visitors, I spent three harrowing months that stripped me of everything. It was there that I learned I was HIV-positive.'

Returning to Nepal marked a turning point for Sanu. Determined to turn her pain into purpose, she dedicated herself to counselling HIV/AIDS patients and tirelessly advocated against women trafficking. Initially known as Sanu Rai for her safety, today she proudly stands as Natishara Rai, a beacon of resilience and courage. In 2022, her relentless efforts were honoured with the Kamala Bhasin South Asian Award for her outstanding contributions to gender equality. I documented her story—along with those of nine other women rescued in similar circumstances—in *In Search of Self Reliance*, a book published by UNIFEM in 2004 in collaboration with Shakti Samuha, a prominent NGO.

Another inspiring figure, Charimaya Tamang, honoured in 2011 as a 'TIP Report Hero Acting to End Modern Slavery', was trafficked to India at sixteen, and spent twenty-two months in a brothel before her rescue. Upon returning to Nepal, she faced community stigma but bravely reported her traffickers, leading to their conviction in 1997. The organization she co-founded in 2000, Shakti Samuha, received the Ramon Magsaysay Award in 2013 for its anti-trafficking efforts. Today, Charimaya advocates for survivor inclusion in anti-trafficking initiatives across Nepal.

These stories tell us about the indelible mark of human trafficking that continues to shape Nepal's present. Both within the country and across its borders, it manifests in various forms, reflecting its complex nature, emphasizing the persistent challenge it poses, and the slow judicial process in resolving cases.

Natishara's story is unique and inspiring, but her travails were hardly as rare for women in Nepal as they ought to be. According to the Nepal Police Human Trafficking Investigation

Bureau, in 2021-22, there were 14,511 cases related to human trafficking, with females accounting for 94.7 per cent of the victims. Similarly, the Office of the Attorney General documented 867 trafficking cases in its 2022 report. These statistics illustrate how the majority of trafficking victims registered with Nepal's authorities are female. All of them are witnesses to the illegal trade in persons, which has transitioned from exploitative labour practices to the rampant trafficking of women for sexual purposes.

Historically, Nepalese women were primarily trafficked to India, but now they face risks in various countries, where they are often taken under the guise of foreign employment. It was in 1996, after the rescue of eighty-eight Nepali women and children from brothels in India, that the world first saw the harrowing conditions of the victims of this illegal practice in unpitying detail. This rescue also highlighted the diverse backgrounds of the victims, shockingly revealing that most of the rescued women were from Nuwakot, Sindhupalchowk, Chitwan, and Makwanpur, districts near the capital, Kathmandu, rather than the remote parts of the country.

A staggering sixty-five of these women were illiterate, highlighting their vulnerability, while twenty-three were literate but could still be tricked into trafficking. Traffickers used various methods, including exploitation by relatives, villagers, colleagues, and brokers who promised marriage, but delivered them into brothels instead. Many rescued women were unaware of the sums for which they were sold. Among them, fifty-three were lured under false promises of better job opportunities, while seventeen rescued from carpet factories had hoped to eventually work in Mumbai.

Historically, traffickers would traverse villages under the guise of marriage propositions to lure young women and girls to cities in India. But something even more sinister transpired in 2019 and 2020, when Nepal saw a surge in newspaper advertisements targeting women interested in marrying Korean men. Locally known as 'Biwahwari', these ads typically sought women aged between twenty and thirty-two, including divorcees. Agencies like

Blue Bed International Marriage Bureau, International Marriage Bureau, Nepal Korea International Marriage Bureau, and others frequently published these ads under titles such as 'Are you looking for a Korean husband?' and 'Korean Husband Wanted'.

While arranged marriages through relatives traditionally dominate Nepali culture, the rise in independent partner selection opened avenues for such advertisements. However, soon, concerns about the exploitation of Nepali women under the guise of marriages in Korea surfaced. This issue gained attention on social media, prompting a public outcry and police intervention, leading to a cessation of such advertisements. Despite this action, the current circumstances and well-being of Nepali women who married and moved to Korea remain largely unknown due to the absence of comprehensive investigations into their situations.

In 2023, Nepal's Human Trafficking and Investigation Bureau intercepted 6,466 individuals at Tribhuvan International Airport, suspecting them of being at risk of trafficking or smuggling. Over the past five years, the Lumbini province alone has reported 115 trafficking cases involving individuals seeking foreign employment. Earlier in 2013, during a visit to Khasa, a bustling market on the China-Nepal border, I witnessed Nepali girls coerced into prostitution in so-called dance bars that operate in the evenings. Nepali men, including truck drivers and businessmen, frequented these bars, contributing to a cycle of exploitation where the profits often benefited Chinese businessmen. The 2015 earthquake temporarily halted this exploitation, but with the border reopening, concerns arise afresh about the resurgence of such practices.

We must remember that migration for foreign employment and trafficking are distinct, though they are often interconnected. Foreign employment entails legal work abroad, while trafficking involves coercion or deception into labour or sexual exploitation. Trafficked individuals, unlike migrant workers, are typically unaware or misled about their work conditions and rights. While migration overseas is a valid route for women in pursuit of economic independence, the problem is that many women fall prey to traffickers in their search for work to end their economic vulnerability.

Recent data from the Nepal Police Human Trafficking Investigation Bureau also highlights a concerning rise in internal trafficking within Nepal. A recent case on May 16, 2024, saw the rescue of six teenage girls from a massage centre in Pokhara, underscoring the growing prevalence of such incidents across major cities, including Kathmandu. Particularly prevalent in urban entertainment and hospitality sectors such as dohori sanghs ('duet venues'), dance bars, massage centres, khaja ghars (snack restaurants), and parlours, these incidents often involve labour exploitation, sexual abuse, and severe psychological distress, predominantly affecting women and girls. Many young girls from rural areas are lured with false promises of legitimate work, only to find themselves coerced into exploitative environments in urban centres within the country. This trend dates back to Nepal's Maoist conflict in 1996 and has escalated since the 2015 earthquake.

Making things worse, traffickers have now started exploiting social media platforms to identify vulnerable women, particularly those without spouses or in distress. (Facebook, for example, is a prominent social media platform in Nepal, with 43.9 per cent of Nepali women actively using the platform according to NapoleonCat.com.) According to the Nepal Police Cyber Bureau, there were 9,013 cases of online violence reported in fiscal year 2078 (July 16, 2022 to January 15, 2023), with women accounting for 54 per cent of these cases. Disturbingly, some of these cases have involved traffickers using social networks to deceive women under the pretext of foreign employment, perpetuating the cycle of exploitation. In the preceding year, the Cyber Bureau received 4,686 complaints, of which 80 per cent related to sexual violence, highlighting the grave risks posed by online platforms. While precise figures on the extent of trafficking facilitated by social media remain elusive, it is evident that these platforms have significantly streamlined traffickers' ability to prey on vulnerable women across Nepal, from remote villages to bustling cities.

There are robust legal protections against exploitation (including labour trafficking, sex trafficking, as well as organ trafficking) guaranteed by the Constitution of Nepal (passed in 2015). Article 29 expressly prohibits human trafficking, forced labour, and slave trade, recognizing them as severe violations of human rights. However, the bottleneck seems to be in terms of how speedily and effectively cases are executed by the Attorney General's office and the courts. The annual report of the Office of the Attorney General recorded 867 trafficking cases in 2022. Of these, 349 cases were resolved, while 518 cases remained pending from 2020-21. A similar report for 2022 of the Supreme Court of Nepal recorded 1,106 cases involving trafficking survivors in 2020-21, of which 429 were resolved, and 677 cases remained pending. These indicate a slow implementation process within legal institutions.

The government has announced forthcoming amendments to the Human Trafficking Control Act, currently under review by the Ministry of Finance. Nepal has adopted legislative measures such as the Act Relating to Children (2018), Labour Act (2017), Bonded Labour (Prohibition) Act (2002), Foreign Employment Act (2007), and Local Government Operation Act (2017). The National Criminal Code (2017) also criminalizes forced labour and trafficking-related offences, and perpetrators face imprisonment and substantial fines. Offences such as selling or enslaving individuals, forcing them into prostitution, or subjecting them to coercive labour carry penalties of seven to ten years' imprisonment and fines from 70,000 to 100,000 rupees.

However, despite the advance of legal protections, many Nepalese women end up trafficked under a variety of pretexts, including foreign employment in India, the Gulf states, and various African nations. In the Gulf, repeated trafficking leaves women highly vulnerable, with some returning pregnant or with children, requiring shelter upon their return to Nepal.

The Human Trafficking and Transportation Control Act (HTTCA) (2007) stands as a cornerstone in Nepal's legal framework against human trafficking. It provides comprehensive provisions for prevention, rescue, rehabilitation of victims, and stringent penalties for traffickers. Convictions under this law can lead to up to twenty years' imprisonment and fines up to 200,00 rupees, though challenges remain in addressing organ trafficking adequately.

However, a study of the complaints registered at the Nepal Police Human Trafficking Investigation Bureau shows that the situation of internal trafficking within Nepal is increasing. Furthermore, there is a trend of people going abroad illegally (without suitable documentation) through irregular routes in the name of foreign employment, which often leads to trafficking.

Nepal's policies against trafficking underscore the country's commitment to combat trafficking across various sectors and demographics. Its legal efforts encompass prevention, victim protection, legal remedies, and institutional capacity building, emphasizing inter-agency collaboration and cooperation. But while progress has been made nationally, challenges persist in localizing policies and mechanisms across provinces and municipalities.

There is a draft of a legal document prepared by the Ministry of Social Development in the Bagmati province that awaits parliamentary validation, which may address some of these concerns. However, not all provinces and municipalities have formulated such policies, highlighting the ongoing need for nationwide, comprehensive, and coordinated approaches against trafficking. In the final analysis, far more effort is required to develop and implement strategies tailored to address the problem, for exploitation coexists with the root causes that contribute to vulnerability of women, such as poverty, lack of education, and social norms.

WHEN KIN SAYS KILL!

Ratnottama Sengupta

They shot her in the head, they stuffed her in a sack, they threw her in the river to drown...Yet Saba Qaiser lived to tell her tale because, at the very last moment, she had tilted her head just that bit. The bullet grazed her temple and as blood spilled out, her father and her uncle—yes, her father and her uncle—hurried to finish the 'job' and threw her into the waters. But why? Simple: the eighteen-year-old had eloped to marry a youth she loved, defying her uncle who wanted to marry her off to his brother-in-law.

Sharmeen Obaid Chinoy of Pakistan was looking for a subject to film after she won an Oscar for *Saving Face* (2012), her documentary on acid attacks. She chanced upon a news item about a girl rescued from the river, followed it up, and ended with the documentary, *A Girl in the River* that won her a second Oscar in 2016. A rare feat since most victims of such violence do not live to tell their tale. The Oscar wasn't the only achievement worth celebrating. The then Prime Minister of Pakistan, Nawaz Sharif, said he would pass a law to end honour killing. In October that very year, Parliament passed a Bill that took away the right of forgiveness.[58] That was crucial because after all the pain Saba put up with, she ended up 'forgiving' her father who—ironically—gained in status in the male-dominated society for 'deservedly punishing' a disobedient daughter!

* * *

It is evident even as we utter the term that 'honour killing' is a violation of the Right to Life of any individual—the foremost fundamental right that is enshrined in all human rights instruments starting with the Universal Declaration of Human Rights (UDHR), 1948. So, any instance of honour killing is actually a murder.

Still, for decades, such killings have been defined—even by dictionaries—as 'an act of violence committed by one or more male members of the family against female family members' who are considered to have brought dishonour on the family by refusing to enter into an arranged marriage; being the victim of sexual assault/rape; committing adultery and/or seeking divorce.

But don't rush to conclusions: fathers, brothers and uncles aren't the only ones to 'restore honour' by killing a girl who marries a man of another caste, creed, class or of the same gotra or lineage; mothers have been equally guilty.

Again, while more often than not, it is the girl who is targeted, in Delhi, Kolkata, Bulandshahr and Thiruvananthapuram, instances abound where the man the girl chose to garland has been annihilated and the girl taken back into the family fold. And, though practiced with frightening ferocity and revolting regularity in African and West Asian countries like Turkey, Iran, Egypt or Iraq, Afghanistan, Pakistan and India are equally guilty of the crime that has sullied the honour of the United Kingdom, the United States of America, and Mexico, too.

Indeed, these false notions of honour and shame that lead to horrifying murders by kin is not unique to any culture or religion. A couple of centuries ago, duels were an 'honourable practice' in the advanced countries of the West, while Anne Boleyn, the second wife of the English King Henry VIII and mother of Queen Elizabeth I, was beheaded on allegations of adultery.[59] Shakespeare gives us *Othello*, the Moor of Venice who strangled Desdemona, suspecting her of infidelity.[60]

In Brazil and other parts of Latin America, machismo is a code of 'honour'. We cannot forget Helen of Sparta who eloped with Prince Paris of Troy. This prompted her father Tyndarus to demand that all her suitors defend his choice of husband for Helen, setting all of Greece against Troy.

* * *

At the outset, let me clearly state: no part of this essay is fiction. If any incident or observation is not ascribed to a source, it is because my entire understanding of the subject comes from having watched numerous films, conversations with filmmakers from Turkey, Egypt, Iraq, America, Kazakhstan, Pakistan and India, and reading and reporting on the issue over a lifetime.

The origin of the code of honour can probably be traced to tribal history. Long before the Ottoman Empire brought much of southeastern Europe, western Asia and northern Africa under a khalif, relations between the settled people of Central Asia and the nomadic tribes of the Steppe—be they the Huns, Turks, Persians, or the Indo-European Sakas, and the horse people, the Mongols, Uzbeks, Kyrghyz, or Kazakhs—were marked by conflicts. The major centers of population and high culture in Eurasia were China, India, West Asia, and Europe. These regions were connected by the Steppe route, which was an active predecessor of the Silk Road that ran from China to Rome. The aridity made agriculture difficult in the Steppes, while distance from the sea made trade equally difficult. So, when they spotted a caravan, they would rob it, tax it, or hire themselves as its guard.

Naturally, the nomads had to be aggressive and frequently resort to warfare. Raids between the tribes have been common throughout the region and through history. With ease, they would raid a village and drive away the tribe's flock; especially as they had more mobility on their horses, the horsemen could ride away before an infantry-based army could be assembled. Soon, they developed devastating military technique, and before long, the Steppe horse-archers became some of the most militarily potent people in the world.

In that world order of tribal confederation, the tribe's leader was supreme—and the tribe that had a bigger number was more powerful. In fact, the lesser tribes often sought the protection of the more powerful tribes. Periodically, a number of such tribes would organize themselves as a single military force to launch campaigns of conquest against the more settled and civilized regions. For example, the Hun invasion of Europe, the Turkic migrations, the Mongol attacks on India...

Now, as mentioned a while ago, the strength of a tribe lay pretty much in its numbers, and its numbers could increase only through procreation. So, honour killing was but the result of men of a family, clan or tribe in a patrilineal society seeking to control the reproductive power. Women for these tribes were but a machine—better still, a factory for making babies. So, the daughters had to be married to the men within the tribe, often to first cousins. If a daughter married outside the clan or tribe, the enemy would go up in number, and the offspring of the daughters would be absorbed by the enemy's civilization. Both these possibilities had to be curbed at any cost. Therefore, a man who killed his daughter or niece 'set an example' for the tribe. He won their approbation and respect rather than condemnation for taking a life.

Before long, honour killing became a standard manifestation of a woman's commodification in patriarchal societies. In later societies, it was followed by other violent manifestations, such as female genital mutilation, female foeticide, and acid attacks. In more recent times it strikes at a woman's agency—and we will come to that later.

* * *

Sex outside the bonds of marriage renders the partners in crime karo—blackened man—and kari, blackened woman. The term karo-kari, commencing from Sindh, is synonymous with honour killing across Pakistan but in most cases, the woman is attacked by the men in the community. Particularly in the rural areas, the male-dominated jirga or tribal council decides affairs, and its decisions are given primacy over state legislation. A jirga arbitrates according to the tribal values and concerns. The tribal notion of justice has been defined by violence on the client's behalf. As a result, even a teenage couple, eighteen-year-old Ghani Reham and fifteen-year-old Bakhtaja were condemned to be electrocuted in December 2017 by a jirga in Karachi—and the respective fathers and uncles carried out the sanctioned killing.[61]

* * *

In most societies where honour killing is tolerated, the act falls under laws dealing with murder, but at the same time, the rules of defence relating to provocation and extenuating circumstances are found in their penal code. Such provisions usually originate from old colonial penal codes—Spanish, French, Ottoman—where honour killings were treated as 'crimes of passion'. In other words, the sentencing was not based on the act itself but on the feelings of the perpetrator. If 'defence of family honour' is regarded as an extenuating circumstance, killing in the name of honour could incur a sentence of only a few months.

In Pakistan, the roots of leniency towards tribal customs lie in a British colonial law of 1860 which was grafted onto the country's penal code. Britain granted a lenient sentence to the man who murdered his wife for 'grave and sudden provocation'. However, Pakistan's Federal Shariat Court reformed this law in 1990 to bring it closer to Sharia. It declared that 'according to the teachings of Islam, provocation, no matter how grave and sudden, does not lessen the intensity of the crime of murder'.

The karo-kari phenomenon of Sindh is mirrored in the Khap ordained killings of the Haryana-Rajasthan-Punjab-Delhi regions.[62] By being labelled as 'tradition' or 'culture of the ancients', these murders and homicides are venerated, not punished. This whole 'culture' is facilitated by the jirga, the traditional assembly of leaders in Pakistan; the tribal council of Afghanistan that has a legislative function; and the Khap panchayats of India's northwestern belt.

Khap, like jirga, is also a kangaroo court. But there is a

striking difference in the killings sanctioned by these two. While one favours enforced marriage between close relatives, the other finds marriage between cousins—even twice or thrice removed—totally unacceptable if they happen to be of the same gotra.[63]

In Rigvedic times, gotra was the tribal clan that traced patrilineal descent from a certain rishi—he could have been a sage, a warrior, or an administrator. To prevent inbreeding depression, three generations in the line of ascent through mothers, and five in the case of fathers, were to be considered as brothers and sisters. Hence, even the thought of such a marriage would be impure, vile, an unforgiveable offence—not just against the family but against society. During Rigvedic times, the heads of the community would pronounce the family outcast—and to prevent that, such marriages would be snuffed out. By the same logic, the Hindu Marriage Act of 1954, too, barred such marriages.

However, the Bombay High Court, after consulting the texts of Manu and Yagnavalkya, had declared that the requirements on gotra 'were recommendatory, not mandatory'. In the Manoj-Babli case, the Punjab and Haryana High Court dealt a body blow to the practice, ruling on March 29, 2010, that five of Babli's family members (brother Suresh, uncles Rajender and Baru Ram, cousins Satish and Gurdev) were to hang until death for killing the couple on June 15, 2007.[64] Additionally, the driver of the Scorpio car used in the crime was sentenced to seven years' imprisonment for kidnapping, and the leader of the Khap court was awarded life sentence for 'hatching conspiracy'.

Problems in tackling Khap killings lie in the fact that usually, a mob would set upon the 'offenders' and so, no definite accused could be found. Also, most parents would not go to the police against such mob violence. And the mobs would be alerted by the thirty-day notice clause in the Special Marriage Act, 1954, applicable to most inter-caste and inter-faith marriages contracted in courts of India.[65] As per Indian tradition, parents have the custody of unmarried daughters until they are 'properly married'—and they have a right to control their daughters' marriage because of the caste system. In fact, in strongly patriarchal societies, women often remained legally minor throughout their lives. They merely change from being the property of their father's family to that of their husband's family, without acquiring any political or economic voice and little possibility of independent action as an individual. Thus, honour killings were, essentially, against women's agency.

The cultural perspective is that family honour is all-important for both women and men. But, while women must protect it by modesty, men must uphold it by masculinity and restore the honour lost by her immodesty by killing her. Place it in the context of ancient times and you will understand the why of it: if an individual transgressed, and the family was outcast, where would they go? The tribes were a self-contained community, society, nation, government—in brief, their entire world.

This reality has changed in a world that is now a global village. Still, the criminality of these murders is not recognized; instead, it is justified as 'upholding justice and order'. In fact, one Pakistani politician is on record defending the killings by saying, 'These are centuries-old traditions and I will continue to defend them.' And if not outright condoned, they are treated with a certain leniency, if not deference, and masked as 'suicide' or 'accident.' The reality is horrific miles away.

* * *

To set an example that would deter other daughters, fathers and brothers have come up with the most brutal methods of snuffing out life. In 2012, Mehtab Alam, a garment trader in Kolkata's Ayub Nagar, decapitated his younger sister with a sword and carried the severed head to the police station where he asked for a glass of water, and then surrendered.[66] He had found twenty-four-year-old Nilofer, a mother of two who had eloped with a rickshaw puller, dragged her out and unilaterally beheaded her. He did it 'to punish her for the black act (extra-marital affair).'

In 2016, Shankar was hacked to death at a public crossroad.[67] The Dalit boy had dared marry an upper caste Thevar girl,

Kausalya. In February 2002, close to the capital city Delhi, educated and well-established Nitish Katara was battered to death with a hammer, had diesel poured on him, then set aflame and dumped, to be retrieved from a drain beside the highway in Ghaziabad. His crime? He had had an affair with his classmate, Bharti Yadav, ignoring the threats of her father, DP Yadav, an influential political figure with dubious links.[68]

In 2018, Delhiite Ankit Saxena, twenty-three, was killed on a public street by his nineteen-year-old Muslim girlfriend Shehzadi's father.[69] An obscure political 'sena' boasts of surveilling local courts to track impending marriages of Hindu women to Muslim men, then beats the women with wooden planks, or forcefully drugs them to physically separate the couple, then foists rape cases against the fiancé. A widely reported killing in recent times was the Rizwanur Rehman 'suicide' on railway tracks—after he married Priyanka Todi, daughter of a Hindu businessman from Kolkata.[70]

It is no better in Mumbai, the financial capital of India. In December 2019, Arvind Tiwari, forty-seven, killed Princy, the eldest of his three daughters, decapitated her, stuffed her body parts in two suitcases, threw one in a garbage pile at Titwala, another near the Kalyan railway station, and buried the knife near his house in Indira Nagar.[71] The reason for killing? 'Other daughters (living in Uttar Pradesh) will not find a groom,' since Princy, who worked at a call centre, was having an affair with a man from 'another community'.

Renowned actor Aamir Khan's much-accoladed television programme *Satyamev Jayate* featured in 2012 a young couple— Abdul Hakim, twenty-nine and Mehwish, twenty-three—who were hiding in Mumbai as they were threatened by the Khap panchayat after their love marriage.[72] But once they returned to Bulandshahr, Hakim was shot through his head when he was buying medicines. 'The panchayat had declared over loudspeakers that they will also kill me and my year-old daughter,' Mehwish told newspersons in Bulandshahr, providing them with a clipping of her conversation with her mother.

Bulandshahr or Bhojpur, Kanpur or Jodhpur, Hisar or Hyderabad—the ubiquity of the crime is mind-boggling, as is the brutality that goes with it.

* * *

Hyderabad, March 2020: Telangana real estate businessman Maruthi Rao, fifty-three, consumed insecticide and rang down the curtain on the gruesome killing of Pranay who had married his daughter Amrutha. In 2018, Rao had hired a killer for Rs 1 crore. CCTV footage showed the young man walking out of a hospital with his pregnant wife when assailants fell upon him from behind with a machete.[73]

Jodhpur, March 2020: Rinku from Pali was strangulated, burnt, and buried in the Rajasthan village.[74] After her charred body was exhumed and sent for postmortem, her mother, Sita Devi, and paternal uncle, Sewaram, were arrested. Rinku, just sixteen, was in a relationship with a boy in Pune and had eloped two months prior to the crime. The family lodged a complaint of kidnapping. The couple was arrested in Dadar, Mumbai and since she was underage, Rinku was handed over to her family. But she insisted on marrying the boy when he was released a month later. Her father, Sesharam, took her back to Jodhpur on the pretext of visiting a local deity. That's where she was killed.

Rajkot, May 2020: Sanjay Ram, twenty-four, and his bride Dhara, twenty-two, were axed to death on a national highway in Gujarat by an assailant who spared Sanjay's sister.[75] Junagadh Police held Dhara's brother responsible for the killings. Motive: same old caste difference. When they married, the bride's father had committed suicide—so the brother had meted out 'justice' to the 'root of trouble'.

In **Meerut**, Tina Chaudhary, who was studying in Class 12, was shot in her private parts and killed by her cousin a day after Valentine's Day.[76] How dare she, a nineteen-year-old, have an affair? In Amroha near Moradabad in Uttar Pradesh, a fifteen-year-old was missing for eleven months.[77] Her father and brother had shot her and thrown her in the Ganga. And near Mandu, a seventeen-year-old was forced to drink pesticide by her father, then at his instance, her throat was slit by her cousin.[78] She had the gall to refuse to end her relationship with a man from another…

You, reader, can fill in the blanks with any of the following words: caste, creed, class, or gotra. Does it really matter which word? The crux of it is that she showed spunk. A mind of her own. Agency. How can a chit of a girl be allowed that?

* * *

Pakistan probably has the highest number of documented honour killings per capita of any country.[79] In other words, about a fifth of the world's honour crimes are performed in the Indus Valley. The Human Rights Commission of Pakistan (HRCP) found that some 700 women were killed in 2017, and about 1,100 women in 2015. According to the Aurat Foundation of Lahore, 432 were killed in 2012; 705 in 2011; 557 in 2010, 610 in 2009, and 475 in 2008. And these are figures for women alone—men, too, are killed to 'restore' honour, the foundation underscores in its report.

Suspicions and accusations are enough to lead to the murder of innocents. And often, the reasons go beyond the 'immoral behaviour' (of alleged marital infidelity, refusal to enter an arranged alliance, demanding a divorce, or even rape and pregnancy). For, in contemporary patriarchal cultures, these pretexts hide inheritance issues—if not to clear the path to a second or third marriage. Scratch the surface and you will find that the victim—a girl/woman who wants to marry of her own free will—holds properties that the male members of the family do not want to lose. Tasleem Khatoon Solangi, only seventeen, was tortured and killed by members of her village in the Khairpur district of Pakistan, in the eighth month of her pregnancy.[80] Her father claimed they were told by her father-in-law that she had conceived out of wedlock 'because he wanted to take over our family farm'.

One may point out here that the long-outlawed act of Sati—bride-burning on the pyre of her husband—and the widows of Vrindavan resulted from the same root.

Sample some of the shameful deaths in Pakistan that shook the world:

1. Samia Sarwar was murdered in April 1999 by her elite, politically-connected family in the Lahore office of the celebrated human rights activists Asma Jahangir and Hina Jilani.[81] Logic? Samia sought their assistance to divorce her husband—a first cousin. In March 2000, the BBC documentary *Licence to Kill* traced this highly publicized killing, yet no arrests were made.

2. Ten years after Samia Sarwar's killing, in April 2009, Pashtun singer Ayman Udas from Peshawar was shot to death by her two brothers who found her divorce, remarriage and—worse—artistic career 'damaging to the family honour'.[82] No one was prosecuted.

3. Five years after that, in July 2016, Qandeel Baloch was strangled by her brother in Multan, Punjab, for 'posting controversial pictures of herself on the social media,' including one with a cleric.[83] The brother had gone on the record to say, 'She was bringing disrepute to our family's honour. I could not tolerate that.' But this outrage speeded up the passing of the law against honour killing.

4. A video of dancing and clapping at a private celebration—a wedding in Sartai, a remote village in Kohistan[84] in the spring of 2012—cost four girls who featured in it their life and, eventually, also four brothers: the two boys who recorded the video and the brothers who went to court against the clerics who had ordered the killing of the girls. A jirga consisting of 40-50 members claimed the girls were all alive. When the Supreme Court sent

rights activists to meet the girls, they produced four different ones, not the ones in the video. The case, dubbed the 'Kohistan killings', went on for eight years and in December 2018, Afzal Kohistani, the 'whistle-blower' brother who had revealed that the girls had been tortured to death, was also shot multiple times and died on the spot in Abbottabad.

5. The BBC tracked another honour murder in the 2018 documentary, *Murdered for Love? Samia Shahid.*[85] A British passport holder, Samia had flown in to visit her father in Punjab, where her ex-husband Mohd Shakeel also lived. Six days after her arrival, she was found dead in his house—raped and strangled. Earlier, Samia was forced to marry Shakeel, her first cousin, but in 2014, she left him to marry Syed Mukhtar Kazam and start a new life in Dubai. The horrific part of it? When Samia was fleeing her ex-husband's rape bid, her father urged Shakeel to mete out justice.

6. In May 2014, a pregnant Farzana Iqbal was stoned to death in front of a Pakistan high court for eloping with the man she loved, Mohd Iqbal.[86] Her father told the police, 'I killed my daughter as she had insulted all our family by marrying a man without our consent and I have no regret.' It was later revealed that the father was enraged because the groom—to whom Farzana was betrothed years ago—had refused to give the enhanced bride price demanded by the father.

This archaic custom of bride price prevailing in some societies where women are demographically fewer, worsens their plight. For one, it leads to 'marrying off'—effectively, selling—girls at the onset of puberty, often to men in their forties and fifties. For another, once sold to a man, she remains his property—she cannot seek a divorce even if she is abused, nor can she return to her parents. If she protests too much she is killed, sometimes in the name of karo-kari.

***

The nightmarish part of Farzana's tale is that Iqbal, who had strangled his first wife to marry her, was arrested for the murder and then released as he was 'forgiven' by his first wife's family.[87] Do you see a likeness with Saba Qaiser's situation? Yes, and no: Saba survived her father's murder bid, and 'forgave' him after marrying the man she was betrothed to—Qaiser. The culprit here was the society that pressured the girl to 'forgive' her father. The 'forgiveness law' was in place then, allowing perpetrators of murder to be freed if the victim's family forgave them.

How did 'forgiveness' become so important in law? Why was it legally binding? It is believed that in the wake of civil crisis, people turn to alternative models—traditions of the tribes, or customs. In a panel discussion following the screening of *A Girl in the River* in Lahore, gender studies expert Sualeha Qureshi explained (as reported in *The Dawn* newspaper on April 2016): 'The Qisas and Diyat law which follows Islamic traditions (not Islamic jurisprudence) allows for forgiving a murder. This is a convenient loophole for those involved in premeditated murders such as honour killings.' Qisas and Diyat allowed for forgiveness, so the murder was not a crime against the State, only against the victim's family. The enormity of the injustice is driven home by the quantum of punishment: if a murderer involved in honour killing was convicted, he would be imprisoned for only five years; but for a murder, the punishment in Pakistan is the death sentence.

To explain this further, Qureshi had said, 'A murder is a murder but in Sharia law your religion is public and not personal. Forgiveness by kin is accepted. Patriarchy enables the law to be misused and a culture of violence is enabled...' No one, then, asked Saba Qaiser if she wanted to forgive her father and uncle: her husband's elder brother decided, and she acquiesced to 'forgive'.

As noted earlier, this law was amended after *A Girl in the River* won the Oscar in February 2016. In fact, the indignation over Qandeel's death in July that same year had hastened the passing of the Anti-Honour Killing Law (Criminal Amendment

Bill), 2015 and the Anti-Rape Laws (Criminal Amendment Bill), 2015.[88] The legislation passed in October 2016 imposes life sentence on the perpetrator even if the family 'forgives' him or her. The forgiveness only saves them from the death sentence, which is the maximum penalty for murder.

* * *

Individual versus society: that is what constitutes drama from the times of Aeschylus, Sophocles, Euripides. Movies across the globe have, naturally, fed on the theme—sometimes in the form of feature films, sometimes as documentaries, and often as television series. Since this mass medium can appeal to the conscience of the common man, let's cast a glance at the attempts to raise awareness against the crime—in India and elsewhere.

Teenager Ayse is slow poisoned by her father Osman over a car journey in the movie *Where the Fire Burns* (Turkey, 2012, dir. Ismail Gunes). The reason: she got pregnant by a migrant worker and brought shame upon her kin. But once the caring child who dotes on her father is dead, the finality of the act dawns on him, to torture him until the end. The film picked up a top prize in Montreal and entered the 2013 race for the Oscars.

No one is surprised when Santiago Nasar is killed in a small town of Latin America. The Vicario brothers were openly declaring that they would kill him to regain the lost honour of their young sister Angela. It's the way of the country—nothing and nobody could prevent it, wrote Gabriel Garcia Marquez. It was the *Chronicle of a Death Foretold* (Italy, 1987, dir. Francesco Rosi).

Ahlam, in *Bride of Fire* (Iran, 2000, dir. Khosrow Sinai) studies medicine. She loves Dr Parviz and wants to marry him. But according to her tribe's laws, she must marry her cousin Farhan. Ahlam decides to face her family and seek a solution.

She's *A Regular Woman* (Germany, 2019, dir. Sherry Hormann). Her brothers insult her, hate her, threaten her for her lifestyle. But Aynur, a German of Turkish origin, struggles for a free, self-determined life opposed by her family. So, she reports her eldest brother to the police, takes her child and moves in with a woman friend. Now the brothers discipline a young Turkish woman to become a strict Muslim with a sinister aim: she is to become the child's mother when they kill their sister.

The documentary, *Price of Honor* (USA, 2014, dir. Neena Nejad, Xoel Pamos), focused on Sarah and Amina Said. The teenage sisters from Texas were killed in a premeditated manner by their father Yaser Abdal Said on New Year's Day 2008. The father was angered as the girls were dating non-Muslim boys. The killing had prompted the Fox News Report *Honour Killing in America,* aired on August 6, 2010.

Women of Freedom (Israel, 2016, dir. Abeer Zeibak Haddad) follows the stories of women murdered in the name of honour. Here are snippets of dialogue from the documentary:
'Suddenly my father grabbed the knife and attacked me.'
'A gang came up and murdered Alaa.'
'Any Arab woman that is killed, they say, it was an honour killing. As if to say, '"It's their culture."'
'It's an excuse for the law to be lax when it comes to the murder of Arab women.'

Blood Honour Bleeds (India, 2016, dir. Samik Roy Choudhury) turns the camera's gaze on the people who spend their lives with the burden of guilt after killing their loved ones for the sake of family honour. 'UN statistics say that more than 5,000 women have been killed by their own family members for westernizing, choosing a partner outside their caste or religion, engaging in homosexual acts...That happens worldwide. But what happens to those who kill?'
Bollywood has time and again taken a stand against the crime—and been blessed with critical and/or commercial success.

Khap (India, 2011, dir. Ajai Sinha) had its seed in the Manoj-Babli case wherein a Khap panchayat ordered their killing to prevent them from tying a same-gotra knot. This case, as detailed elsewhere, led to the landmark judgment against the perpetrators. The socio-political screen drama garnered praise for showcasing a brutal reality of Haryana, Rajasthan and Uttar Pradesh.

Aakrosh (India, 2010, dir. Priyadarshan), based on real life incidents from Uttar Pradesh, showed how police are hand in glove with powerful killers who ruthlessly eliminate every witness, every proof of their misdeed. Even central agencies sent to investigate the matter fail to crack the case as locals refuse to cooperate.

Honour Killing (India, 2015, dir. Avtar Bhogal), a lesser-known film, showed the practice prevailing among Non-Resident Indians (NRIs) who have given up the citizenship of their country but not the evil custom.

NH10 (India, 2015, dir. Navdeep Singh). A city couple on a trip witness an honour killing and are caught in a web of intrigue. The film portrayed the stark contrast between cities and villages in India, and how women who know their mind scare men, who try to crush them using physical aggression.

Sairat (India, 2016, dir. Nagraj Manjule), made in Marathi and remade in Hindi as *Dhadak* (2018, dir. Shashank Khaitan), in Punjabi (*Channa Mereya*, 2017), Kannada (*Manasu Mallige*, 2017), Odia (*Laila O Laila*, 2017), Bengali (*Noor Jahan*, 2018), and other Indian languages.

Sairat premiered at the Berlin International Film Festival. It got a Special Jury Award at the 63rd National Film Awards (in India). Made on a budget of Rs 4 crore, it raked in Rs 110 crore. Classes, masses, everyone identified with the plot that revolves, in the Marathi original, around two college friends from different castes—in the Hindi version, a thakur and a baniya from different states. In the Marathi original, the lovers are killed by the woman's brother, leaving their infant alive. In *Dhadak*, the husband and the child are killed in front of the girl 'to teach her a lesson'. Either way, young lives must pay for daring to love!

Pagdi: The Honour (India, 2014, dir. Rajeev Bhatia), a Haryanvi film, also won a National Film Award, for underscoring that honour lies not in humiliating and shaming the not-so-well-placed parents of the groom in an unequal marriage, but in accepting the happiness of the children truly in love.

* * *

In most of the films described here, the protagonists confront their families. Some find a sensible solution, some succumb. Nevertheless, they all mirror life. The most significant of these tales probably is of *Khap*, the 2011 movie rooted in the tragic murder of newlyweds Manoj and Babli. They married despite the diktat of the Khap panchayat in the Karora village of Haryana which had decreed their marriage incestuous as both belonged to the same gotra of their Jat community, Banwala. While the groom's mother defended the marriage, Babli's relatives abducted and killed them. The sad tale got a happy ending in 2022 when, in a historic first, a sessions court in Karnal awarded the death penalty to five men from Babli's family and life sentences to the panchayat head who had ordered the killing. The driver of the car used to abduct the couple also got a seven-year term. This exemplary punishment should augur well for a course-correction in the practice of honour killing.

Women's rights movements in India have long been campaigning for stronger laws. The Karnal court showed that if implemented with an iron will, the existing laws are sufficient to punish such murders. Others demand more stringent provisions to tackle the menace of honour crimes. Some want to do away with the clause in the Special Marriage Act that requires couples to publicly announce their marriage plans a month before the wedding. This waiting period, they point out, gives angry parents and politically-motivated outfits time and opportunity to organize violence to stop the marriage.

Experts may be divided on the laws required to end the crime. But all agree that multipronged measures are needed to combat the feudal mindset fuelling these patriarchal crimes. Activists know that no law can work unless people strongly condemn these crimes. Advocating a change of perspective, they now say, 'Reverse the way of looking at honour. Make the community feel that such killings bring dishonour rather than restore honour.' This will eradicate the crime over time, they believe.

In this context, Pakistani activists advocate collective shaming as a strategy to pressure governments to act against honour killings. They used it effectively when Safia Bibi, a visually impaired maid of thirteen, got pregnant following rape by her employer's son. Public attention was focused on her by an international NGO. The law at the time required a victim to visually identify the perpetrator in order to convict him. Since Safia couldn't do that, she was subjected to the relatively lenient punishment of thirty lashes! But the international shaming this sentence entailed forced the court to reverse its decision.

That a strong administration can be an effective deterrent is exemplified by Malaysia. It is a Muslim-majority society that is also traditionally patriarchal. Yet it does not seem to suffer this ignoble phenomenon. It could well be because it is a multi-confessional state with a determinedly modernizing mindset and strong secular law enforcement. Regardless of the religious traditions continuing from their rural roots, the State refuses to cede any space to non-state actors—unlike India, Pakistan or Afghanistan.

Perhaps aware of the loopholes and laxities in the laws of these lands, international bodies like the United Nations have repeatedly urged action against such crimes. A major landmark in redressing the recognized gender bias in human rights legislation was the 1979 Convention on the Elimination of All Forms of Discrimination Against Women (CEDAW).[89] Held under the auspices of the Directorate General, External Policies of the

European Union, the strategies it suggested to the European Parliament are often called the 'International Bill of Rights for Women'. CEDAW specifically recognized that violations in both public and private spheres are equally violations of women's rights. And it recognized the negative impact of social customs and cultural practices that are based on the false idea of the innate inferiority or superiority of either sex or stereotypical roles for men and women.

CEDAW has frequently taken up the issue of honour killing in its observations in National Reports. Its recommendations outline paths that can lead to the eradication of the crime. But again, given the weak enforcement mechanisms, and the fact that ratifications are accepted with reservations, it underscores: 'It is paramount that national legislation with respect to honour killing be reformed by all State parties.'

Prime among CEDAW's suggestions are the following course corrections:

1. Support strategies to address honour killing as part of a holistic approach to the promotion of gender equality (in line with the European Parliament Resolution).
2. Support comprehensive programmes of public education in Europe and third countries—through mass media, schools, women's groups, community groups including at places of worship—to change social attitudes. In all these forums, include men to debate alternative ideas of masculinity.
3. Provide support to parliaments of third countries so that the legislators can ratify and accede to key international declarations so that reforms are carried out in penal codes that condone honour killing.
4. Join action of bodies such as the United Nation's Commission on the Status of Women, UN Commission on Human Rights, and the UN Development Fund for Women.
5. Identify, mobilize and support internal forces for social change.

6. All cases of honour killing need to be registered, investigated and brought to justice. Police and other officials found guilty of neglect, concealing, or condoning cases should be removed.
7. Penal sanctions need to be put in place for offenders, be they family members or community groups that encourage it. These could range from, say, suspension of voting rights, health insurance schemes, or economic grants.
8. Train the police, prosecutors, magistrates and judiciary to see the illegality and indefensibility of honour killing.
9. Support access to legal aid, psychological assistance, and social assistance.
10. Provide shelter to those threatened.

* * *

What the combined story of the facts and fiction unfolds is a crying need to be human above all. No legislation can put an end to any crime until people at the grassroots despise such killings. But legislations to end kangaroo courts and dissolving their powers will certainly help. Police protection for such couples can also go a long way in dissuading the killers. Registering FIRs could help. And, yes, the punishment for such killers has to be exemplary—and should not be restricted by borders.

Love of kin for their own kind is, after all, a universal truth.

Note: *Opinions have been given based on multiple conversations with directors and activists and travels around the world as a film critic and journalist. Not all of it can be sourced to books and papers.*

DO YOU WANT TO DIE YOUNG?

Farah Ahamed

I. This moment is your life

Lost in his dreams, your husband is next to you on the bed, snoring. Your daughters are away at a girls' hostel. The elder one has just received acceptance into college. The younger one is finally speaking to you after many years of angry silence. You have a job. Your husband is back after fifteen years in prison.

What more could you want? Your life will never be better than what it is now.

The father of your children sighs in his sleep. He shifts on the bed and reaches out to touch you. You move and face the other way. Your elbow still hurts from when he slammed you against the wall.

In his dreams, your husband mumbles your name. You shudder. Earlier, he'd asked you for money. You said no, you needed it to buy food. He laughed and showed you the notes he'd found, which you'd hidden under the mattress for your daughter's college fees. I don't need your permission, he said. I'm going to meet my friends.

Now, several hours later, he's lying next to you, drunk and drugged up. Just like the old days.

You want to leave him, but you can't.

You remember his words. *Do you want to die young? If you ever leave me, I will kill you. The next time you cheat on me,*

I will kill you. I won't kill your lover. But you never cheated on him.

Your husband is lost in his nightmares on the pillow next to yours. At the trial, he convinced the judge it was all your fault. He said you provoked him to murder a man. Which husband could tolerate his wife cheating? What choice did I have? Should I have killed myself? Or her? Then what about my children? I had no option. I had to kill her lover. The judge said to him, I sympathize with you. I understand the situation perfectly. I've seen it many times before. Cheating wives ruining their families. To you, the judge said, you deserve to go to hell, not just to prison. There's a special place reserved there for shameless women like you. It's better if women like you die young. You're a menace to society.

The judge sentenced both of you to fifteen years. You, for cheating and provoking murder, your husband for killing his best friend, the one he alleged had been your lover but had actually been his.

In the kitchen, the tap drips. From the flat above, you hear strains of a qawwali. In his sleep, your husband pulls you to him. He fumbles with your clothes, his hand cups your breast, and he squeezes hard.

After fifteen years, your nightly terror has returned.

II. There was a time when you were happy

In the Kasur prison,[90] fifty-two kilometres away from Lahore, you shared a cell with thirty-nine Muslim women. You were the only Christian. The cubicle was a long room with a common washing area. Sometimes, the lines for the toilet had been so long that there would be fights between the inmates about who was more desperate to use it. The cell is damp and smells of mold. Most days, there is no electricity. The toilets are dirty and often there is no water. At night you hear the rats scratching, during the day you see cockroaches climbing the walls. You refused to cry.

At night you would lie on the ground and cover yourself with a thin blanket. The vermin would run over your body. No one ever spoke to you. Chura, they said, mocking your low-caste birth. Don't come near us. You'll contaminate us. So, you passed your days sitting in the corner on your own. Until one day you met Z. You can't tell anyone her real name. She saved your life. She didn't care about religion. I don't believe in God, she said. What has God done for me? Z was from Multan. You've never been to Multan. When we leave this place, you must visit me, she said. For the first time in your life, you trust somebody. You told Z about your daughters living in a hostel because you and your husband were in jail. You showed her the torn photograph which you kept hidden under your clothes. You told her about the lover you never had. The husband who raped you every night. The man who had been your husband's lover, and who your husband had murdered. Your husband's drug and alcohol addiction. And the judge who didn't believe you were innocent and found you guilty of provocation and cheating. You showed her the scars on your back where your husband had burnt you with a rod. The marks had still not faded where he whipped you with his belt. Z stroked your spine, and said, it's going to be okay. She whispered, don't worry now, it's going to be fine. She kissed your forehead and said, please, don't cry. She held you in her arms and caressed you. You're safe with me, she said.

One time, you had your period and you didn't have any rags. Z offered her dupatta. Use this, she said and tore it up into strips for you. After your period, you heard another woman complaining she was on her period and had nothing to use. You offered her your rags. I'd rather bleed to death, she said, than be polluted by your chura filth.

Z said she was in jail because she had reported her husband to the police when she found out he had raped her eleven-year-old daughter. The police said, bring proof. The doctor who examined her daughter refused to write a medical report. I don't want to be involved in a police case, he said. I've got better things to do. Maybe your daughter encouraged it, he said. Finally, after she offered to pay him a huge sum of money, the doctor agreed. In his report he said: I examined this eleven-year-old girl and found she was not a virgin. There is no apparent or obvious reason for this condition. The police said, this is not proof. They told Z's husband and he beat her up. He told the police to arrest Z because she was mentally sick. He lied that Z had tried to poison and kill him. At Z's trial, no one believed her when she told them about her daughter's rape. The judge believed her husband and a doctor who said he had checked Z and found her to be medically insane. The judge sentenced her to five years imprisonment. I don't believe you are insane, he said, but just evil. A she-devil. I pray God protects the public from women like you.

In jail, Z had lost contact with her family. She hoped her daughter had run away from home.

Z and you ate together. The other women taunted her—the chura has polluted you. One day when you were getting some dal and rice from the serving table, a woman screamed. You bloody chura, she said, and threw down her plate. You've contaminated our food. Now we'll have to starve because of you. All the inmates gathered around you. One woman slapped you. Chura, she said, go to hell. Another woman punched you. Chura, bloody chura. Stop, Z said. Stop. She tried to protect you, but the women hit her also. They pushed both of you onto the floor, jumped on you, and pulled your hair. Later, the warden found you with your head in Z's lap, she was wiping the blood off your face with her hands. The inmates had told the warden you had abused their prophet and committed blasphemy. The warden said, you churas are all the same, filthy sinners.

Your shoulder was dislocated. They sent you to the prison hospital and no one was allowed to visit you. After a few days they sent you back to the cell. You better behave yourself, chura, the warden said, or you're looking at solitary confinement. Sometimes the pain in your shoulder was unbearable and you'd cry. Z would bang on the doors and shout to the warden, give her some Panadol, don't you have any pity? The warden said, stop lying for the chura. She likes to exaggerate. Z swore at her and the warden slapped her. Watch your tongue, she warned or I'll have you put in solitary confinement.

You know your family is too poor to travel from Lahore to visit you in the Kasur prison, so the years pass and you don't see your daughters. You pray they are safe and happy. Maybe God will answer a mother's prayer? There are three babies born inside the prison while you are there. They will not be able to leave until their mothers have served their ten-year sentences. Z said, maybe they are safer inside here, than outside?

Every Sunday, the bishop visits the prison. God has a plan for you, he said. Be patient.

Plan? Z said, which plan? To die here in hell, or die and go to hell?

Z shared her cigarettes and sweets. Don't eat the porridge on Fridays, she said. It has medicines in it. You were curious so you drank the porridge. It tasted bitter. You didn't understand. Which medicines and why? I'll show you, Z said. This is what they are afraid we will do, she whispered in your ear. She stroked you between your thighs, under the rough blanket. They want to kill all your desires, she said. Don't let them. You deserve to be loved.

Five years passed in the Kasur jail. Then one day the bishop said, God is merciful. He did not want you to die young. You're being released for your good behaviour.

When you say goodbye to Z, a part of you dies.

III. You will not die young

You returned to your village, Noor Pur in the Kasur district, a hundred kilometres from Lahore, back to the very house where you were married. Where else could you go? The men in the village jeered at you. You're back? We thought you'd died in that hell.

I'm not dying young, you said. Slut, they said. Are you ready for a new lover? You ignored them.

The women in the village whispered behind your back. You heard them saying, she deserved what she got. What did she expect, cheating on her husband with his best friend? Many cheat but she was stupid enough to get caught.

You wondered about Z every day. You have no friends in Lahore. Your husband was still in prison. You were relieved.

You visited your children at the Salvation Army hostel. You told the woman at the front desk you wanted to see your daughters. You told her their names. Are you lying or a ghost? she said. Those girls don't have a mother. She died in jail many years ago. I'm their mother, you said.

Please go away, she said, or I'll call the police. You showed the faded and torn photograph. Your daughters think you are dead, she said.

Your daughters did not recognize you. They told us you died, the elder one said. How come you look so old? the younger one said. Where were you for so long, and what were you doing there? Why have you come back now? You did not know what to say, so you kept quiet. After that you visited them every week. Sometimes, they made no time to talk to you. You never told them what it was like in prison. They never asked. The elder one said, I want to go to college. I want to work in an office and earn a salary.

You promised her you would save money for her college fees. Her eyes tell you that she does not trust you.

With the help of the priest at the church, you started looking for work. One day he said, a well-to-do Muslim family needs a cook. They will pay well. Can you do it? No, never, you said. They'll call me a Christian chura, they'll accuse me of contaminating their food, and of blasphemy. I'll end up in jail and be hanged for something I never did. I don't want to die young. The priest said, trust the Lord. He works in mysterious ways. I don't trust anybody, you said.

Forgive your husband, forgive the Muslims, and forgive yourself, the priest said. I cannot, you said.

After some time, you found a job looking after a Christian man who was sick and old. Sometimes you were angry with him for no reason. You shouted at him and threw things around the kitchen. Why are you punishing me? he said. I haven't done anything to you. You did not understand your fury but sometimes you felt like you could implode. At the end of the month, you hid your salary under the mattress. *How many months would it take to save for three years of college fees?*

Once when you were waiting at the bus stop to go visit your daughters, a policeman stopped you. Where are you going? he said. Before you could answer, he said, I know you are going to meet your lover. I don't have a lover, you said. I've never had one. Where's your husband? he said. In jail, you said. You're a chura, he said. I'm arresting you for adultery under the Hudood Ordinance.[91] Unless of course, he said, you are prepared to make a deal. You showed him your empty wallet. You know exactly what I want, he said. Don't be smart. It will be over in a few minutes. You refused to sleep with him. He slapped you. You can't leave here until you change your mind. You waited at the police station the whole night. The police officers called you a bitch and a whore but you refused their demands. It looks like you want to die young, the policeman said. After eighteen hours you slept with three of them and they released you.

IV. You will not die

One evening after work, you decided to look for Z. You went to the station and boarded the night bus to Multan. You thought of the journey ahead, the winding roads, and how each mile would bring you closer to Z. You remembered how you used to laugh together on the cold, hard floor, sharing a single, rough blanket, and how she used to stroke your face every night until you fell asleep. After many months, you felt happy. You were going to see Z, you would stay with her for a week, or ten days. The bus started moving, and your phone rang. I hope you're coming to the hostel tomorrow, your daughter said. I've been accepted into college. This is the happiest day of my life. You shouted to the driver to stop the bus. He cursed you as you got off.

You walked home. You found your husband waiting for you by the door. After fifteen years, he was finally released. I'm back, he said. If you ever try to leave me, I'll kill you. I killed a man because of you. I'm not afraid to kill again.

You thought of the bus on its way to Multan.

V. You will not

You are lying in bed next to your husband. He climbs on top of you. You try to push him away. Don't move, unless you want to die young, he says, forcing you back. He pushes your legs apart. All you see is the pinprick of light fading in his eyes. You will not surrender to this. One day you will kill him.

Note: *This story is based on facts, with some parts embellished for the sake of narrative, without changing the intent of the woman's testimony. The 2020 report,* Plight of Women in Pakistan's Prisons[92] *found that the country's prisons did not meet international standards and that laws meant to protect women prisoners were being flagrantly ignored. Overcrowding was a major problem; 66 per cent of the women in prison were not convicted of an offence but awaiting the conclusion of their trial in prison. Many of them had been falsely charged. The majority of the prisoners suffer from diseases such as hepatitis, HIV, and tuberculosis. There were inadequate medical facilities and insufficient healthcare workers to care for the prisoners.*

MONSTROUS

Sohana Manzoor

The girl in her sky-blue frock and white shalwar said with a beaming smile, 'Don't you dare watch the Thor movie without me, Bhaiya. I want to know what happens to Loki.'

Her brother laughed out loud. 'We all know what happened.'

'Yes, but we've not seen it yet,' she replied while shaking her head vehemently.

'All right, all right, I'll wait.'

'Yess! I'll bring Maliha Apu too.'

'Ranu Khala will kill you. Maliha has SSC exams coming up.'

'Bah! I'm sure she would love to take a break for Thor.'

The siblings laughed.

* * *

'Ranu Khala said she cannot come over.' Noyon's face was colourless—a mixture of sorrow, anger, disbelief and unnamed emotions.

Nazneen looked at her son uncomprehendingly.

'What does that mean? Are they going somewhere?'

Ranu was Nazneen's oldest friend in this small town in Bangladesh. When she came to live in Shukhia, twenty years ago, right after her marriage, Ranu had taken to her like a sister. Many others came and went out of Nazneen's life, but Ranu had always been there. Their children had grown up together, and they had shared their lives like two branches of the same tree. Now, when Nazneen's daughter was at the hospital, fighting for her life, Ranu would not come? What had happened?

Noyon did not say anything right away, as if he was lost for words. Then he whispered hoarsely, 'Mahbub Khalu said they cannot come to the house of a girl who has fallen in the eyes of society. It would affect Maliha. People will think she has gone bad, too.'

Nazneen just gaped at Noyon.

'Fallen? Bad?' The words rolled off her tongue like curse words. 'Mahbub bhai said that?' Her voice was like coarse paper rustling in the wind. 'Is that what Ranu said, too?'

Noyon shook his head, 'She was just crying, and after Khalu went out of the room, she said, "Tell Nazu your uncle has forbidden me to go. I would have come, but I have a daughter to think of, too."'

Nazneen stared at the space in front of her blankly. It had been three days since Kona had been in the hospital. The doctors had not even been able to assure that she would live. Since then, Nazneen's mind had gone blank. Her daughter—her thirteen-year-old daughter—how could anybody do something so terrible to a mere child?

And someone like Mahbub, who had known them for decades, called Kona 'fallen'?

The room suddenly started to spin, and Nazneen swayed. Noyon sprang forward and caught his mother, 'Ma! Are you okay?' He helped Nazneen sit on the single sofa in their dining room. Nazneen grasped Noyon's hand and said, 'Where is your father, Noyon? Is he still at the police station?'

'Yes, they have some more formalities to complete.' He paused and then said, 'Apparently, they have arrested some young fellows who might be responsible.'

Nazneen whispered, 'My child, my Kona! How could anyone do such a terrible thing? What did we do? What wrong did my poor girl ever do to reap something like this? Allah!' She broke down. 'And how can people say such monstrous things! And if

Mahbub bhai thinks this way, what would others say? And when Kona comes back home…' she could not finish the sentence, but a fresh bout of sobs wracked her being.

Noyon said bleakly, 'I am learning too, Ma. Something is very wrong with our people.' But he certainly did not expect this from his Mahbub Khalu, whom they regarded as part of their family. As a doctor, wasn't he supposed to be an enlightened and progressive person? Noyon used to think highly of him.

He refrained from telling his mother that, in all probability, Kona would not return home. With 80 per cent of her body having been burnt, she had only a slim chance of surviving. And what would she see and experience if she survived? A society that would point fingers at her. 'There goes Kona—the girl who was gang-raped. They even burnt her, and she still survived.'

Noyon's eyes stung. He had not been able to shed a single tear since seeing his sister at the hospital. Something cardinal in him had died when he first saw the body. He knew that life was over for them—in the coming days and nights, he would only see a ravaged body; the lovely face of Kona had turned into a charred mask. All the joys of life had been taken from them forever. He did not even know how to react. People around die and have accidents, but how can one prepare for such atrocity?

* * *

The front door opened, and a tired Khairul Islam entered the house. Noyon looked at his father, and his heart almost stopped beating. His face had a greyish pallor, and his hair seemed to have more white in it. Things had indeed changed drastically within a span of four days. First, Kona went missing while on the way back from school one afternoon. They looked for her at all the nearby houses. Then, a half-charred body was found near the Kumudini Pond, half a mile away from their house. And then pandemonium broke loose.

Initially, everybody came. Everyone looked for their missing Kona. But ever since the doctors proclaimed that she was sexually assaulted before being burnt, people started to act strangely. Mahbub Khalu was one of the first people to leave. Then, he called his wife to return home immediately. Since then, they had been shirking. And today, Noyon learnt that his sister was a 'bad' girl because someone saw her talking to a group of boys after school. Some people even assumed that she went with the boys willingly and had fun with them. Noyon could not help wondering what they meant by 'fun'. Kona was only thirteen years old!

He shook his head and advanced toward his father.

'What did the police say?'

His father stared at him for some time before replying. 'They have caught a group of local hooligans—the mastaans of Ajmot Matbor.' Noyon knew it already. Then Khairul Islam added, 'One of them has admitted to everything.' He could not say more. Slowly, he lowered his body on a chair and looked at his son like a dumb animal.

Nazneen let out a piercing cry and fainted. Rohimon's ma came rushing in from the kitchen, and Noyon and the maid raised Nazneen and carried her to her bedroom. Khairul just stared at them vacantly; he did not even have the strength to get up.

Nazneen's sister, Nazma, had arrived two nights ago. She was the one who had been practically handling everyone and everything. She was exhausted from the journey and the unusual flurry of activities and was asleep in another room.

Shahed, Nazma's brother-in-law, was a well-known journalist and had assured them that he would do everything in his power to bring the criminals to justice.

From the next day onwards, the Kona rape case started taking the shape of a media sensation. Journalists and TV cameras started pouring in. Someone called it a 'high-profile' case since the criminals had connections to the ruling political party. Ajmot Matbor has washed his hands off already, proclaiming that no rapist could be a part of his party. If it were proven, he would personally see that the criminals were hanged. The only problem was that one of the accused was also his nephew, and Mr Matbor maintained absolute silence on this.

Two days later, Kona died. She never regained consciousness. The people who worried about what to tell her about her burnt face had nothing more to worry about. The bouquets, the teddy bears, and all the other nice things fit for a girl in her early teens, heaped at the hospital and her home, never made it to her. A representative from a women's organization came to ask if they could have their expensive bouquets back as they could be used for some other case. Noyon's aunt was about to flare up, but Noyon stopped her. Yes, she could have those back. And then he said, 'The flowers have all dried. But would you care to have the other gifts, too? They might be useful for you.' The woman was surprised and asked, 'Are you sure?'

'Yes,' he nodded, 'Take them.'

The news spread like wildfire. Headlines ran in all major Bangladeshi newspapers: 'Kona, the thirteen-year-old girl from Shukhia of Khulna, Succumbs to Death' or 'Death Brings Peace for Kona, the Unfortunate Girl from Khulna.' Organizations of all sorts came forward with demands for justice. Human chains were formed across the country. Noyon saw people around him change once more in a span of two days. The 'fallen' girl became 'The Martyr of Shukhia'.

'How do you feel about your sister's death?'

'We would like to interview your parents.'

'Oh, the bereaved parents. They must feel awful. But could we have a few words with them? Just want to ask them what they are thinking.'

Questions poured in from women activists and journalists, too.

'Don't you want justice?' One of the journalists asked Noyon.

Noyon did not know what to say. Did the woman realize what she was asking? They were all in a frenzy for justice. For them, the punishment of the rapists and murderers would bring justice. Kona would be avenged. Yes, Noyon wanted the monsters to be punished. But he was overcome by such deep sorrow and frustration that he could not even voice his feelings. His sister, his only sister, whom he had carried on his shoulders as a child, had been killed in the most terrifying manner possible. They had practically dehumanized her. He could not find his young sister in the girl who had been raped and razed. And in what she had been transformed into after death.

'Oh, what an amazing girl she was! So bright! So innocent! Can't believe it happened to her.'

'She was too lively, always running and jumping around. Maybe that's why it happened to her.'

'She had a boyfriend. Maybe she went out with him, and they caught them at some secluded spot, and this happened.'

'Girls should be more cautious. Their parents, too.'

'I would not send my teenage daughter alone to school.'

'Get those bastards and hang them. Hang them before they do it to another girl.'

'Punishment should be exemplary. Castrate them.'

'Poor Kona! She hated men, you know. And this happened to her!'

'She was pretty but very proud.'

'She was loving and caring.'

Where was his sister in all this, Noyon wondered. Her pictures were in the newspapers and the electronic media, but it was not really her. One newspaper even went as far as to claim she was 'our failed Malala, who claims justice from beyond her grave'.

Thankfully, Noyon's friends left him alone. His two best friends, Topu and Ashish, were grim and quiet and did what they could to shield him from the media. But people were curious to learn how they lived and what they did now that their little girl was gone.

***

One evening, when Noyon came home from college, he saw a familiar figure in the drawing room. His heart froze as he recognized Mahbub Khalu. What was he doing at their house?

Noyon's father had not been well lately, and he was reclining on the small cot. Mahbub Khalu's face took on a guilty look as he saw Noyon.

'Baba Noyon,' he spoke slowly. 'I'm sorry about everything. I know we should have come earlier. But we had to think of our daughter...'

Noyon said gratingly, 'Is she dead now?'

'What?' Mahbub Khalu blinked.

'I'm asking if Maliha has died.'

'W...why should my girl die?' Mahbub Khalu was horrified.

'Then why are you here now? I thought you were worried about your daughter's reputation. So, I assumed that since you came, your daughter must be dead.'

Mahbub Ahsan looked helplessly at the lean young man he thought he knew so well. He reached out to touch Noyon, but the young man moved away. When Noyon spoke again, his voice was brittle, 'You're not welcome here. I don't want to see anyone who thinks ill of my sister.'

'Maliha wanted us to come, and so we came,' mumbled Mahbub Khalu. 'She is inside with Ranu, talking to your mom.'

Noyon touched his forehead with three fingers and said wearily, 'I'm leaving for now. But please, go away. You can only bring pain and sorrow to us. And considering everything, perhaps it's better for Maliha not to brood over this.' As he turned to go, Mahbub Khalu's broken voice drifted out to him: 'Forgive us.'

Noyon walked through the silent streets. The single lamppost near the turn leading up to the marketplace created an eerie ambience. The sky was dark, and the air was damp. It would surely rain. But he was not afraid. He was thinking of Kona, who had gone down a far darker way than this. His thoughts turned to Mahbub Khalu and Ranu Khala as he wondered about Maliha. She would come again, Noyon knew. But it would be better if she did not.

The face of Ajmot Matbor, who had offered 20 lakh takas in compensation to leave his nephew's name out of this, drifted into his conscience.

Noyon's uncle, his father's only brother, had asked Matbor, 'Would you make this offer if this was your daughter?'

The leader had left with a darkened face and a veiled threat.

Considering the attention Kona had garnered, in all probability, the criminals would be punished. Then what? He thought of his parents. How would they live? The hullabaloo would quieten after some time. The world would move on. Where would they go, the two maimed parents and an eighteen-year-old brother? He wondered about all those other women whom life had cruelly deprived of all they had and all those brothers and fathers and mothers around the world who suffered. It was strange, like he had never thought of them before. Why did he feel so helpless that nobody really thought or cared?

Thunder clapped in the distance. It seemed Thor, the thunder God, had finally awakened.

Where was he when Kona was violated and mutilated?

Noyon and his sister had lived in a world of fantasy and myths. The fantasy was finally gone now, and all that was left was this monstrous reality.

He thought of going back home. But that usual leap that the thought of home brought with it seemed missing. The bright face of his sister that always welcomed him home was now gone forever.

The lonely young man stood alone at the bend of the road and felt a never-ending darkness engulf his life.

Note: *The names in the narrative have been changed at the request of the brother, who related the story to the writer.*

WHEN FIGHTERS WRITE: THE LITERARY LEGACY OF SRI LANKAN WOMEN

Simran Chadha

On the island nation of Sri Lanka, formerly Ceylon—a land known for cultural and racial cohabitation—post-independence nationalism came to be singularly defined in terms of a Sinhala-Buddhist identity, the ethnicity of nearly 80 per cent of the island nation's population. To perpetuate democratic republicanism, it was necessary for this community to see itself as one people sharing their origin, history and goals. Hence, the varying strains of Sinhala-ness, or ways of being Sinhala, were downplayed, even erased in the former colony. Sinhalese women now came to be defined through definitive brush strokes that set them apart from women of all other races, ethnicities, and hybridities, though all of them had lived in comparative harmony on the island. Chastity and modesty took pride of place in the construction of a new Sinhalese womanhood, with these 'virtues' increasingly portrayed as racial traits, the result of being born Sinhalese. The scholar Niloufer de Mel describes in her book, *Women & the Nation's Narrative: Gender and Nationalism in Twentieth Century Sri Lanka*,[93] how women from the Burgher community, who also share Sinhala roots, bore the brunt of this racial profiling. Though Burgher women were mong the leading doctors and educators in Sri Lanka, they were portrayed as the sexually promiscuous counterparts of Sinhala womanhood, mainly on account of their racial commonality with the European colonizers. Similarly, the Tamil community as a whole was decried as invader and outsider, while Tamil women were mainly seen as interlopers.[94]

The need to reinforce belief in the uniqueness and apartness of one's ethnic community became paramount when ethnic collectives acquired political resonance as potential vote banks. Communal majoritarianism then became a tool to acquire political power, and it strived to cement inter-community differences in language, religion, and rituals, while ignoring the similarities. Cultural hybridity, once a hallmark in the island nation, was decried as 'contamination', something that must be done away with.

In her essay, 'Forced Identities: The State, Communalism, Fundamentalism and Women in India',[95] Amrita Chhachhi, a visiting fellow at the International Institute of Social Studies, points out how the behaviour, even the dress codes of other traditions are deemed ethnically or culturally (in)appropriate to create boundaries to enable men to define 'our' women as opposed to 'their' women. In Sri Lanka, to establish a common Sinhalese/Buddhist identity, the Kandyan style of wearing the sari became the national dress of Sri Lanka (when it was still Ceylon), excluding women from the Tamil-dominated regions and Burgher women.

It is a feature of most nationalist discourses to value women as the carriers of ethnic identity, embodying the cultural apartness of their communities. This translates into stringent control over women, exerted by imposing norms related to modesty, chastity, and respectability on them.

And yet, even after Sri Lanka's post-indenendence civil war, in new and altered circumstances bloodied with violence, women continued to negotiate their ethnic identities. This is demonstrated in the poetry written by women from the conflict zones, including the women cadres of the Liberation Tigers of Tamil Eelam (LTTE) in Jaffna, and women connected to the Sri Lankan armed forces.

By the eighties, Jaffna, located on the northeren tip of Sri Lanka, had become a hothouse of violence, a phenomenon that originated as resistance to an increasingly monolithic Sinhala

State. The civilian population of the peninsula bore the brunt of State violence and mounting ethnic tensions eroded the fragile cosmopolitanism base that had held society together. Across the country, hybrid unions became suspect in the light of the dominating ethnic discourse, and women were seen as 'belonging', first and foremost, to their ethnic communities.[96] The July 1983 anti-Tamil riots in Colombo culminated this process. With a civil war that lasted over three decades, gender demarcations on the island, particularly with regard to labour and space, were bound to undergo redefinition. But what also complicated articulation of resistance or 'difference' among women members of such a group as the LTTE was the growing belief in Sri Lanka that the conflict itself resulted from the ethnic apartness of the Sinhalese and Tamil communities. Indeed, the conflict in the country has been classified as both a civil war (from the right-of-centre perspective) and as a war of liberation from the Tamil resistance point of view. In the former view, 'terrorism' features as a prominent classification of the non-State fighting forces, who are seen to weaken people's faith in the State and its institutions. In turn, 'the terrorists' see these institutions as oppressive and opposed to their ethnic denomination. Further, terrorism earns its unethical moorings from attacks against civilians, a definition of the LTTE which the Sri Lankan media popularized, further complicating the act of writing by women members of the group.

Let us, therefore, see against this backdrop how this the civil war redefined the stereotypes of the heroic male warrior as well as the victimized, silently suffering, home-bound woman. The latter was replaced with woman-headed households and the combat-ready women fighters of Illivar—the LTTE's women's brigade—fighting for a Sri Lankan Tamil homeland. The idea of Eelam thus introduced a new image of Tamil womanhood, marking a radical transformation and even a break from the (Tamil) population's epic past. In 'Gendering Tamil Nationalism: The Construction of "Woman" in Projects of Protest and Control', Sitralega Maunaguru, [97] drawing from *Puranaanuru*, a 1st century A.D. anthology of Tamil heroic poetry that elaborates the qualities women must cultivate as mothers, points out that the LTTE created an equally iconic image of a dutiful woman—first as mother, then as warrior for the motherland—and in both, actively pressed women into service.[98] Simultaneously, on the Sri Lankan peninsula, women-centric protest movements such as the 'Mother's Front' also started taking concrete shape. Staging these movements required immense courage, for the women had not to overcome just the sheer terror of the times but also the stigma of transgressing the strictures of passivity and silence traditionally imposed on women.

While the woman-as-mother is a key construct in nationalist imaginaries, which see women as the creators of a new generation of ethnically hardy children, the Mother's Front enabled women to carve out a space to speak out against both State and LTTE atrocities. And it attracted tremendous mass support, for it was founded upon the image of the grieving mother, who already commanded social respect and moral weight as mothers. This enabled the Mother's Front to stage protests when civil society networks were in a state of near-complete paralysis.[99] The movement also overrode constrictive stereotypes. For instance, grief was no longer a disabling condition that would force women to isolate themselves within their homes. Instead, women transformed their loss into an empowering act of collective and public protest against those they held responsible for killing their children.

The Mother's Front would heap curses, invoke superstitions—including folk rituals of black magic—undertake fasts at Kaliamma temples, and seek divine vengeance as justice for their murdered kin. The State then responded with attacks on the movement for encouraging irrationality, a stereotype usually associated with women, by encouraging hysteria, gullibility, and superstition,[100] and it accused the Mother's Front of politicizing grief,[101] not to mention 'having failed their duty by their children and the nation'.

However, the United National Party (UNP) government in the South, too, formed a Mother's Front in opposition to what they termed as the Sri Lanka Freedom Party's Mother's Front operating in the north. This politicization, apart from the pressures in the north from the LTTE, led to the eventual dissolution of the movement. However the Mother's Front created much-needed space for women to reach out to one another, swap experiences, and expect to be understood and supported. Its members were 'as much in dialogue with each other as they were with the nation'.

Poetry by women flooded the island during this time of violence and strife. It was poetry of protest written by women experiencing war at its worst. Then came the poetry written by women connected to those serving in the armed forces and, finally, by women cadres of the LTTE, Illavar ('Birds of Freedom').

'A Mother's Lament' by Sanmarga, (the pseudonym of Sarvamangalam Kailasapathy) is part of the anthology, *Women in Wartime* (2002), compiled by the Women & Media Collective. The speaker in the poem is a mother in Jaffna who heads her household, and whose lament discards romanticized ideas of womanhood propagated by patriarchal nationalist movements (whether Tamil separatist or Sinhala). Seeing her son's body rotting by the roadside, she laments:

> *You lie on the road dust*
> *Your body soaked in blood*
> *I bend down to see your face*
> *Yes son it is you...*[102]

Her words reach out beyond the personal purview of the speaker to articulate the vulnerability of the majority of the civilian population living in Jaffna, at the time caught between the violence of the State and militant forces. She writes:

> *You went away for six months*
> *unable to bear the oppression of Ravana*

Ravana, the mythical demon-king of the epic the Ramayana, signals oppression. It could be a reference to the head of the LTTE, Vellupillai Prabhakaran, or the president of the elected party governing the nation, or the head of the military unit stationed in Jaffna to wipe out the Tigers.[103] She writes:

'Do you know the boy'
Threatens the man with the gun
'No I don't.' I shake my head
Denying you my first born

The 'man with the gun' is just that—an armed threat—it is irrelevant to her whether he belongs to the Sinhalese armed forces or the LTTE. Was her son killed as punishment meted out to deserters/traitors as per the LTTE's idea of justice? Or was it a staged encounter by the armed forces protected by stringent anti-terror laws? It does not matter.[104] The violence of war is the point of these lines, and that nothing justifies a cold-blooded murder intended to arouse fear and paranoia among the living. The mother laments:

If I claimed you as my son,
They will come home and take away
your brothers and set fire to my hut
will load my cow on their lorry
and drive away to Palaly...
...who is there to question them?
I am just a poor woman

Despite this reference to the military base in Jaffna (Palaly), the mourning mother is clearly not a Tigers supporter. Indeed, she does not even present her gender as the reason for her victimization, and clearly throws light on her economic status: poverty makes her powerless, ethnicities are immaterial throughout her text.[105] She thus draws attention to the often overlooked class factor in what was seen as an ethnic strife in Sri Lanka. She is 'just a poor woman', but she weaponizes her grief in a powerful message sent by the lines below, which subvert the normative order of nationalist ideologies, wherein a son must further a woman's sense of agency,[106] marking her out as a producer of future soldiers and protectors of the motherland:

...My grief will one day destroy those
Who have been so cruel.

While those who advocate a separate state
On platforms endlessly
Are guests in neighbouring country safe and secure,
You who gave your life for the country
Are dead on the road-side
I am a sinner who cannot even claim
My son as my own.

To be clear, Sri Lankan women also produced much poetry that was in tandem with the nationalist discourse, where the veneration of the mother figure is extended to the nation as motherland, and then, protecting the motherland is equated with the service of a dutiful son for his mother. This is usually the case with poetry emerging from the families of armed forces. One such poem is 'To My Son on the Battlefield', written by the mother of a soldier stationed on the frontline:

When her son Dutugemunu went to battle
The venerable queen did not shed tears
I cannot do likewise my son
For warm tears are cascading down my face

The legend of king Dutugemunu, the founder of the Sinhala race, and his mother, Queen Vihara Mahadevi, as recounted in *The Mahavamasa*,[107] was a foundational text during the post-independence phase of mounting (militant) Sinhala nationalism. With the ascendancy of Sinhala-Buddhist nationalism, the legend of the venerable Queen acquired vital importance. As a young princess, the Queen had put service and duty to her people before personal safety and, displaying exemplary courage, set out for a sea voyage on a tiny barge. During the ethnic conflict, the circulation of this mythology about a young king's desire to wage war—the Queen was his chief advisor in matters of war and statecraft—against the Tamils helped legitimize the boundaries of a national imaginary of a Sinhala-Buddhist land.

The noted anthropologist, Gananath Obeyesekere, presents in his study, 'Dutthagamini and the Buddhist Conscience: Religious and Political Conflict in South Asia', his version of a dialogue between the queen and her son, young Dutugemnu:

> The queen came and caressing Gamini spoke thus: 'Why dost thou not lie easily upon thy bed with limbs stretched out my son?' The son replies: 'Over there beyond the Gange (the river Mahaveli) are the Damilas (Tamils), here on this side is the Gotha (ocean), how can I lie with outstretched limbs?'

The internalization of this myth by Sinhala women, especially the wives and mothers of the members of the armed forces, is illustrated through another poetic utterance of the soldier's mother:

> *Even if you die in the battlefield, beloved son*
> *Lay not your rifle upon the earth, hand it over to another*
> *This is the way I know you are my eldest son for sure*
> *Tomorrow I'll send my heroic younger son to battle*

While the mother in this poem is distraught over death possibly awaiting her son, never does she question the legitimacy of the battle or imply that it is a waste of human life. The glory accorded to the warrior overrides the thought of death in battle. Sinhala nationalism needed women/mothers who could amply illustrate the Dutugemunu myth at work. Indeed, what the body politic of the State needed then was not only the reproductive capacities of the woman but mothers who extol duty, honour, and nationalism.

The late Malathi de Alwis, a Sri Lankan anthropologist, notes in her essay 'Moral Mothers and Stalwart Sons'[108] how images like those of 'warm tears', invoked amid talk about preparedness to sacrifice one's life in battle, became familiar tropes during the armed conflict. These imageries even found their way into the popular discourse, such as in the 'war songs, political speeches and statements to the press by bereaved parents.' She writes:

> In times of crisis such as war...the heroism required of her male citizens [is] foregrounded against the sacrifices of her female citizens. In addition, the female citizen is often perceived to

embody the Motherland (they are both nurturant yet vulnerable); her rape or capture symbolizes the very desecration of the community/nation/land.

In this equation, while the man, as protector, is duty bound to defend the nation, the woman, as mother, must order her sons to battle and not mourn their killing. However, this national deification of motherhood—much like the mother goddesses in the Indian pantheon—did little to alter the lives of real women. Moreover, this so-called power was exercised within the confines of and in the service of a clearly patriarchal nationalism, so it did little to improve the gender inequilibrium. In most cases, any ascendancy that women achieved in the power hierarchy was not through choice but an enforced reality—another form of disempowerment—and only in the absence of the male head, a not infrequent occurrence during wars and conflicts. This lack of choice also became evident in the strict monitoring of sexuality within the LTTE, which made the very idea of freedom debatable.[109]

Seen another way, the valorized motherhood trope predominant in Tamil Tigers texts also displays the cultural similarities between the two warring ethnicities despite their avowals of difference. The historian R Cheran writes in his book *The Sixth Genre: Memory, History, and the Tamil Diaspora Imagination*[110] about an ancient Tamil practice called Maanam, which contrasts the self-image of Tamils against the actuality: 'The concept of Maanam, coupled with pride and valour, constitutes a self-image of Tamils as proud and valiant people who would not tolerate any infringement of their honour and who would, if need be, redeem it by courting death. In the current dominant Tamil nationalist discourse, the Tigers are treated not only as a symbol of pride and honour but as the warriors, who reclaimed these qualities for the Tamil "race". It is not surprising then, that the motto of the Muzhakkum is "pulikalum innaal illaiyel elikathaan thinnum thamilarai" (if it were not for the Tigers the rats would have devoured the Tamils).'

Clearly, when communities take to arms, discourse must

comply. In fact, discourse must be tailored to render life dedicated to the community as the most desirable.

That is what Adele Balasingham may have had in mind when she wrote the manifesto for Illivar, which claimed to reset the gender binary associating men with armed combat and women with the victimization of familial spaces. Balasingham hailed in this manifesto a 'new image of Tamil women', distinct from one serving the needs of patriarchal and traditional Tamil society. Exploring further, we find Captain Vaanathi, who died in the First Battle of Elephant Pass, writing in her poem 'She, the Woman of Tamililam', about a battle-hardened all-woman force engaged in combat with the Sri Lankan Army. She writes:

> *Her forehead shall be adorned not with kumkum but with*
> *red blood*
> *All that is seen in her eyes is not the sweetness of youth*
> *(but) the tombs of the dead*
> *Her lips shall utter not useless sentences but firm declarations*
> *of those*
> *Who have fallen down*
> *On her neck will lay no tali, but a Cyanide capsule!*
> *She has embraced not men but weapons!*

The turning away from domesticity to take up arms is in sync with what was then being touted as the nobler cause: death by martyrdom, and is in keeping with R Cheran's deification of dying-for-community as noble martyrdom. What defines the life of the woman Eelam fighter is the subversion of traditional domesticity and the symbols associated with it. Earlier LTTE strictures had demanded that Tamil women in Jaffna wear the sari and not ride bicycles, but soon the image emerged of women cadres dressed in belted trousers, loose shirts, rifle holster, and a gun slung over their shoulder. That is why, to say that this path entails just violence would be reductive, as it involves courage and needs the determination of a warrior/soldier, and that, too, in a society lacking such role models.[111]

What is being 'othered' in this discourse is the normative values for which women have been traditionally lauded—softness of temperament, tenderness of heart, nurturing, self-sacrificing, care-giving, motherly, etc. The woman Eelam fighters must embrace a new womanhood as LTTE militants, as frontline combatants enlisted to serve 'Tamiilam'. Apart from reproduction, women had to now be active warriors in the service of an (imaginary) motherland. But did this new manner of being and becoming a woman redefine traditional patriarchal strictures on the female gender, or was it a device tailored just to meet the need of the hour? Captain Vaanathi writes:

> *Her gun will fire shots*
> *No failure will cause the enemy to fall*
> *It will break the fetters of Tamiilam!!*
> *Then from our people's lips a national anthem will tone up!!*

The text does not exclusively refer to Captain Vaanathi's situation but is germane to the idea of Illavar, wherein the value of woman-as-cadre is yet again underscored by her ability to sacrifice herself for others, in this case, the nation-as-community-as-family. [112] So, while the kumkum and tali signify the drudgery and anonymity of domesticity, giving them up is tantamount to embracing another sacrifice, that of martyrdom, for 'then from our people's lips a national anthem will tone up'.

Moreover, these lines were issued by the cultural unit of the LTTE, which renders ambiguous authorship to its cadre, and yet Captain Vaanathi liberates the text from purely subjective underpinnings of one woman, to encompass the idea of a unit, functioning under one ideology, and for one purpose—national liberation. Studying these changes, de Mel accurately pronounces this as a symptom of the intense militarization of Sri Lankan civil society, and questions the freedom that the movement claimed to grant women who were being put in service of violence and war.

This view has also been iterated by feminists such as Francine D'Amico, who have raised questions regarding the empowerment wrought by this subversion of gender norms during wartime. In her article 'Feminist Perspectives on Women Warriors',[113] she states: '...the woman warrior image subjects women to greater manipulation by those controlling military institutions, thus allowing women to be militarized but not empowered. Military institutions and their needs (not women's needs) determine women's role in the armed forces. Women's military participation reinforces rather than undermines the gender structures of the military and the broader society.'

What emerges in the end, amidst the in-your-face senselessness of war, is the fraught notion of female empowerment when it comes from institutions steeped in patriarchy, be they nationalist or separatist.

SATI, A WIFE DIVINE

Sandhya Sinha

Thirty-seven years have gone by since the lively eighteen-year-old Roop Kanwar had to become a Sati. The day was September 4, 1987, the place—Deorala village in the Sikar district of Rajasthan in India. Which present-day, middle-class father or mother can be convinced that their convent-educated, good-looking daughter with a modern outlook on life and only eight months of married life behind her, fell so intensely in love with her husband—after an arranged marriage—that she sprang into his burning pyre? There can be no bigger deception and delusion than this. There is no record of pre-marriage love or courtship between Roop Kanwar and Maal Singh. Her birth in a Rajput family was perhaps the only crime she unwittingly committed a full eighteen years ago. A crime she paid for with her life.

Maal Singh Shekhawat was not exactly a tall, dark and handsome youth. Failing to get past the entrance exam for medical studies, he was suffering from depression. It is a task to try and understand why her parents decided to pack off Roop Kanwar into matrimony with such a groom. They may have decided that the heavyweight antecedents of the Rajput family counted far more than the happiness of their own offspring—especially when that offspring happens to be a girl. Just marry her off! That would be the end of her story. And who knows what tomorrow will bring? Where's the need to be its guarantor? After all, scriptures, too, can be quoted to justify the destiny that befalls her.

Roop Kanwar did visit the haveli of her in-laws in Deorala. Just twice. Attired as a bride, she was a feast for the eyes. But she did not conform to the stereotype of a wife lost behind the veil. Her demeanour, her hairstyle, her body language, her movements—none of it befitted the conservative household of the tradition-ruled village. She spoke of opening a beauty parlour to ensure her own, independent source of income. This was the portrait of an emancipated woman with a mind of her own. A woman who would not falter over doubts or trip on objections raised by hidebound ages. With a bride so pretty and self-confident, Maal Singh started suffering from an inferiority complex. He, his father Sumer Singh, and other members of his family too realized that it would be a job to cage this free-spirited bird—so what if the cage was crafted in gold? This girl had it in her to spread her wings in the rejuvenating blue of the awning skies.

* * *

Did Roop Kanwar play a part in planting the seed of becoming a Sati on that very first visit? Inevitable Yama, the God of Death, only assisted Sumer Singh Shekhawat and company in accomplishing this. On the morning of September 4, while under treatment in the city of Sikar, Maal Singh suddenly expired. Merely an hour before his body was brought back to Deorala, Roop Kanwar stepped into the Shekhawat mansion for her second—and ultimate—visit.

Roop Kanwar's uncle, Arjun Singh, and her paternal aunt, Magan Kanwar, lived in this very village. Apparently her chacha, Arjun Singh, had fervently pleaded with her not to take the drastic step of sahamaran—burning on the same pyre as her dead husband. No one owns up to hearing the girl, still in her teens, express the desire to immolate herself. So why did her uncle—brother of her own progenitor—out of the blue, take it upon himself to plead with her *not* to be a Sati? A simple tactic of brainwashing? The news of Maal Singh's death, too, was tacitly hidden from Roop's parents and sibling. They came to know only through the newspapers that their daughter had embraced death with her deceased husband. Her father and mother lived in Jaipur, less than 70 km away, not in faraway Timbuktu. In the twentieth century, sending a telegram—if they didn't own a telephone—was no big deal.

The prime reason for not doing that was to take advantage of the helplessness of a solitary girl fighting a lonely battle against an archaic Rajput custom: the wife would not set her eyes on her dead husband. Roop Kanwar opposed the practice and 'dared' to see the face of her lifeless spouse. She had sent out the Rudalis—every one of the professional mourners beating aloud their seasoned chests—and shut the room to see for herself how and why Maal Singh had suddenly lost his life—an act that speaks of the plucky girl's sharpness and strength of mind. Alone in a friendless house full of dogmatic in-laws, the just-widowed girl must have been in a traumatized state of mind. Who offered her a mite of solace? Had Arjun Singh and Magan Kanwar fulfilled this responsibility, the horrendous incident would never have come to pass. But they did no such thing and on the contrary, may have fanned the flames of that unholy pyre.

Shame on you, you bigoted zealots of Deorala! Your warped minds could think of only one barbaric rite? In front of your very eyes, encircled by so many Shekhawat heads, decked out in the glory of her bridal finery, Roop Kanwar wended her way through the maze that are the lanes of Deorala and reached the burning ghat. Many of us boast, especially to foreigners, that the indomitable will and community feeling of rural India is a wall against injustice. So, the news of the twentieth-century Sati stunned the world.

Like us, many others must have wondered, what sort of a people were these that could not protect the life of a blameless teenager? What kind of a nation are we? Was there no man present with human blood coursing through his veins? Fie upon you, you Rajputs of Deorala: cowards, mindless herds who raced to the cremation ground to witness with their own eyes the monstrous enactment of a ritual that had been laid to rest a century ago! They not only stood and watched, but also did not utter a single cry to protest this premeditated, cold-blooded, public killing at the hands of an 'established' family. Mutes, they had turned into ignoble affluent lumpens. Alas! Every one of the thirty-two killers led by Sumer Singh, who murdered Roop Kanwar in broad daylight, walked free.

* * *

The deafening clatter of bronze plates, the boisterous sound of conch shells, the frenzied cries of 'Sati Mai ki Jai!' (Praise be to the Goddess Sati) must have drowned every decibel of Roop Kanwar's heart-wrenching howl as the bewildered and drugged teenager was made to embrace the diabolic flames. A set of wrestler-type giants pinned her to the pyre with menacingly long bamboo staves. The girl could not put up any resistance against the lusty fire fed with ghee, camphor and chants. Neither Agnidev nor Vulcan took pity on her. Any amount of sandalwood was stacked to overpower the stench of burning flesh. The heinous liturgy overnight metamorphosed the mortal Roop Kanwar into an immortal Devi, a Divinity. Hail her good fortune!

Bravo, the savagery of the predator called man! This is how the womenfolk of India are kept in place! The Rajput inheritance of 'family pride', which has inspired so much bestiality, is nothing but a false notion of honour. There is not an iota of dignity in consigning Roop Kanwar to the all-consuming fire. And still thousands of Rajputs descended on Deorala, armed with an assortment of weapons, to 'protect the holy site' of the last Sati. Lakhs assembled on her Terahvin—the thirteenth day after her death—for her Chunri, sacred veil ceremony. Let alone mourn for her, their chests swelled up with pride and self-glorification.

What explains the delight in such a depraved deed? That same old story of Rajput queens like Padmini who jumped into fire to preserve their virtue that would be demolished by

Alauddin Khalji, the Sultan of Delhi, and other Turk-Mughal invaders. The chronicles of those resolute acts are still recited by balladeers and cited by these modern marauders. Who will make them understand that the twentieth century is far removed from the thirteenth century and that Roop Kanwar was not Rani Padmavati? The hoary inheritance of Jauhar aided the sinful Sumer Singh and his cohorts in fulfilling an abominable stunt. They knew only too well that the government of Rajasthan would not have the political will or the guts to go against the power-wielding faction of Rajputs. Pulling the wool over the administration's eyes, a sixteen-year-old—the minor brother of Sumer Singh—lit the pyre. Who placed the ghee-smeared Roop Kanwar on that pyre? The answer is blowing in the wind.

The victim's parents must have been devastated by the turn of events. And yet they did not grieve. How could they, when the entire clan was rejoicing at the re-emergence of the ancient custom and ascent of Rajput honour? How could they shed tears when her immolation had glorified them too? Instead, they ought to be grateful to her, cretins! So, a woman is turned into cinders and the thirty-two murderers—down to the last man—go scot-free, acquitted by the courts of the Republic of India.

This reminds me of the shameful moment in the Mahabharata when Draupadi, the Pandava queen, was disrobed in full view of the Kaurava Durbar. One lone woman, the righteous Queen Gandhari had spoken out against her hundred licentious sons in vain. She failed to deter them to desist from the insolent act. Draupadi had to undergo utter humiliation, the ultimate nightmare of being denuded in front of every family elder. It resulted in the battle of Kurukshetra where Gandhari and Draupadi, too, lost their sons. Still, her feisty stand in the royal court carved her place among venerable women down the ages.

In the present century, a woman is no longer alone, in no country of the world. There are mahila samitis, women's councils, welfare associations, rehabilitation centers, so on and so forth. What if these organizations join hands to mete out justice to the men whenever they transgress? An eye for an eye—let there be no exception. A Pati Daha—husband's immolation—for every Satidaha. Where is the harm in men standing around an inflamed pyre to watch a man being burnt alive with his dead wife?

Fear not, no woman will be convicted for this crime. We have a robust precedence in Deorala.

JAUHAR AND OTHER SUICIDES: HEROIC SUICIDE OR MURDER?

Ratnottama Sengupta

(In continuation of 'Sati: A Wife Divine' by Sandhya Sinha)

Roop Kanwar's forced immolation on the pyre of her dead husband in 1987 was an aberration, it was no longer a practice. That is why it became the first instance in the country of a murder charge being levelled in a Sati case.

Coming as it did, more than 150 years after it was banned by the Bengal Sati Regulation Act of 1829, the Roop Kanwar case had seared the conscience of the nation. That is why it was shocking that though thousands were reported to have watched her burn, only thirty-two persons were charged with her murder—in accordance with the demands of women's rights activists—and all of them were acquitted by a Rajasthan sessions court in 1996. As Manoj Mitta wrote in *India Today* in November 1996, the legal debate provoked by the verdict suggested that the outcome might have been different if, instead of Murder (Section 302 IPC) the prosecution had levelled the lesser charge of Abetment to Suicide (Section 306 IPC).[114]

This had a precedence. After the last instance of conviction (Tej Singh *vs* State, 1958)—again, in Rajasthan—the high court in Jaipur ruled that even those who merely joined the Sati procession were guilty of abetting suicide. 'It may be that these persons did not directly instigate the widow to commit Sati, but once she had made up her mind, their actions of applauding her were meant to encourage her and keep her resolve fixed.' This was a kind of instigation, he had ruled, sharply reducing the burden of proving Section 306 in any case of Sati.

The public outcry against Roop Kanwar's death led, first, to state-level laws to prevent such incidents, then the Indian government's The Commission of Sati (Prevention) Act, 1988, which banned 'i) the Burning of the Woman ii) Glorification of the Act iii) Establishment of a Temple dedicated to the Sati.' Ironic, isn't it, that forty years after independence, Parliament had to do something that the imperialist government had done 159 years ago?[115]

When Lord William Bentinck became the governor-general of Bengal in 1828, Sati was pretty much prevalent only among the Brahmins of Bengal and the Rajputs of Rajasthan and, partly, Madhya Pradesh. Going by one account, a total of 834 cases of Sati were recorded between 1815 and 1828, mainly, but not limited to, the upper caste Hindus. In fact, in Bengal, the practice gained prestige as the British officials, then consolidating their hold over India, would also attend the proceedings. However, the colonial missionaries initiated campaigns against it—and the nineteenth-century modernist, and perhaps the first feminist, Raja Ram Mohan Roy, became a force to reckon with as he argued that the Hindu scriptures did not condone or encourage Sati Dahan. His endless efforts bore fruit and in 1829, the Bengal provincial government passed a law abolishing its practice. Gradually the other provinces and princely states followed suit, and queen Victoria imposed a general ban in 1861.

If some historians are to be believed, the rite had been prohibited many a times between the fifteenth and eighteenth centuries by the Great Mughal Akbar, by his great-grandson Aurangzeb, by the colonialist Portuguese and French, too. Quite clearly, Sati could not be eradicated. When the founder of the Sikh empire Maharaja Ranjit Singh, the 'Lion of Punjab' who owned the Kohinoor and was on good terms with the British, died in Lahore in 1839, four of his twenty wives and seven slave-concubines embraced death with him. This, despite the fact that the Sikh gurus condemned the man-made notions of women's inferiority, denounced their subjugation, and argued for their equality.[116] So, why did it happen? Historians surmise that it was because two of the wives were Rajput—a 'warrior community' like the Sikhs—and saw Sati as a martial tradition. So, a Kangra miniaturist commemorated the Sati, as recorded by a European eyewitness, Lt Col Steinbach.

This painting—which might be construed as glorification of Sati—is preserved in the British Museum. But Sati temples, cenotaphs for those who chose to burn alive—or sometimes drown—so that conquerors cannot touch them, flourish in Rajasthan, Gujarat, Madhya Pradesh and Jharkhand. The Rani Sati temple in Jhunjhunu is a pilgrimage site, while the Mehrangarh Fort in Jodhpur displays the hand impressions of fifteen Rajput queens who went the Jauhar way. The annual celebration of heroism by women continues in the Jauhar Mela held in Chittorgarh, also in Rajasthan, where Rani Karnavati, spouse of Rana Sangram Singh, committed Jauhar when Bahadur Shah of Gujarat attacked Chittor in 1567; as Phool Kanwar had done in 1534. Both had emulated the precedence set by Rani Padmini in 1303. And 375 kms away from Chittorgarh, Deorala continues to be an attraction as the site where Roop Kanwar became a Sati.

Although Sati is considered synonymous with Jauhar, two organizations of Chittorgarh—Jauhar Kshatrani Manch and Jauhar Smriti Sansthan—have pointed out a subtle difference. Jauhar was a mass suicide committed by the queens while the kings were alive so that, free of worries about the women, the men would fight unto death in the battlefield and retain their honour even in defeat. They were motivated by the principle of 'death over dishonour'. Sati, on the other hand, had individual women dying on their husband's pyre, mostly under pressure from the patriarchs. The first Jauhar is believed to have happened in 712 AD when Muhammad bin Qasim attacked and defeated King

Dahir, the last Hindu ruler of Sindh, while the first instance of Sati is found in mythology.[117]

* * *

The rite derives its name from Sati, the daughter of Daksha who married Shiva without her father's approval. When she came uninvited to Daksha's palace to attend a yagna, he taunted her and abused Shiva. When he crossed the limits of her tolerance, Sati jumped into the yagna fire and immolated herself, 'unable to bear the insult of her husband'. Shiva was infuriated by this. With her burnt corpse, he went on a rampage: his Tandava was a dance of destruction. 'Sati' thus became a byword for 'a chaste woman' and the original suicide is worshipped in Shaktipeeths like the Kalighat temple of Kolkata, the Kamakhya temple of Guwahati and 106 other sites.[118]

Since Sati had jumped into fire for the love of her husband, the practice acquired a halo and in the medieval era, when India was invaded from the northwest, Punjab and Rajasthan, these first provinces subjected to the warfare found themselves in unequal battles, their soldiers killed or taken hostage. To minimize the bargaining power of the marauders, and to prevent the possibility of the women being taken as slaves, raped, forced into harems and other humiliations, the wives emulated Sati and committed Jauhar. In fact, the Rani Sati temples came up to celebrate the heroism of such queens.

Like every practice, Jauhar, too, degenerated into Sati, a patriarchal imposition on women, due to two possible reasons: one economic, another social. With the husband gone, the widow would be a burden—a non-productive member who would still have a claim on the household property, on subsistence, and so on. Worse, if she was still young and in a reproductive stage of life, she could 'lure' or be used by other men in the family, or neighbourhood, or society. What if she then conceived? It was because of these fears that even the other women in the family rarely objected to the forced burning on the husband's pyre: they themselves had little economic security, and who would want their men to be 'lured'?

When Sati was abolished by the British, the number of women going to Vrindavan went up. It was very convenient to send them off to 'Krishna's land'—it had a religious sanction, the families didn't have to pay for the widows, and if they were subjected to anything unsocial, it was away from the prying eyes of 'family honour'.

Unfortunately, even in the present when travels to outer space are routine affairs, newspapers have reported at least four cases of Sati between 2000 and 2015. Of these, the death of Kuttu Bai in the poverty-stricken Patna Tamola village of the Panna district in Madhya Pradesh is most revealing.[119] On August 6, 2002, the eighty-seven-year-old had taken the gruesome plunge with her nonagenarian spouse because her two sons did not care for them. But this death saw seventeen villagers being booked under the 1987 Sati (Prevention) Act; four sentenced to life imprisonment by the local court; and even circumambulation—Parikrama—of the site being a punishable offence.

But the 'best' part of the impact of the story? The villagers initiated a movement to socially rehabilitate women widowed— or deserted—at a young age. Thus, Pinky Namdev, deserted at twenty-one, was married to a village youth with the consent of the families!

SATHYAVATHI: CONFRONTING CASTE, CLASS AND GENDER

Vasanth Kannabiran

This story captures the violence of the reality of rural Telangana, beginning with joginis, child marriage, poverty, hunger, domestic violence, violence against children and the struggle for survival. I have often in the past visited and criticized social welfare hostels and their lack of basic amenities. The inhumanity of the officials. The critical role played by social welfare institutions in the survival of children on the margins by providing a roof and a plateful of food struck me afresh. We feel these are familiar issues. We have not experienced these as lived reality. Sathyavathi's dogged determination to make meaning of her life, and the pride she takes in her people without being romantic or unrealistic, is remarkable.

Born Hungry

I come from Alampalli village in Vikarabad.[120] I was born during a severe famine and my mother said she fed her children by grinding gram flour and making rotte with it. Maybe that's why I'm so small. We are Madiga[121] and my mother, Anthamma, was the youngest of three children. She had an older brother and sister. My mother's parents died when she was hardly five. Her brother and sister were married off but she was placed in the care of her uncle, Venkaiah.

In our village there lived a man Gorre Anthaiah who was in his late twenties. He was living with a woman in the village and she had borne him four children. The woman was from a jogini[122] family. This meant that she would have to be dedicated to the temple. Her mother, to save her daughter from this custom of dedication, got her married to an illitam (live-in) son-in-law. An illitam son-in-law, since he was financially dependent on his in-laws, was usually sent off for wage labour to bring in some income. While he was busy earning a living, his wife continued her relationship with Anthaiah and bore him children. Seeing these four children, the son-in-law took to his heels and ran away as far as he could.

It was also a custom in our village that a man could not legally marry a woman who had borne him illegitimate children. He had to first marry another girl traditionally and then go through a seeraraika ceremony with his mistress—a gift of a sari and blouse presented ceremonially—which would then give her some social recognition and acceptance though not the status of a wife. This meant that she could take part in village ceremonies and feasts without the fear of being an outcaste.

So Anthaiah went to my mother's uncle, Venkaiah, and asked for his niece's hand in marriage. My mother, Anthamma, was all of five years old then. Venkaiah flatly refused at first but soon when he was drunk, he was made to agree. The rest of the family also realized that this marriage could actually fetch a bride price instead of a dowry, which would have meant their selling the little land they had to get her married. And so, the marriage was arranged for a bride price of one rupee and four annas. This was in the year 1932. On the very same day and within hours, he also went through a seeraraika with his mistress and legalized their union. His love and devotion to her were evident.

The new young bride was the same age as her children. All the decisions in the household were controlled by the older wife and her mother. They had some land, and would lease mango trees, grow vegetables and earn some money. During the lean summer months, they would also cobble shoes and slippers. As a young bride, my mother provided unlimited child labour and was shamelessly mistreated. She did all the housework, washed all their clothes, carried their food to the fields and was given a few scraps of leftovers to eat. There was no one to look after her. Nature taking its course, she matured at twelve and had a child at thirteen. The other wife had just died, so young Anthamma had to bring up her stepchildren as well as her own. She continued to bear a child every year till she had eleven—I was the seventh child.

* * *

Sathyavathi's father [Anthaiah] worked in the Crawford Memorial Mission Hospital in Vikarabad as a construction labourer in 1907. It was during this time when he worked at menial tasks for the hospital, carrying stones and bricks, that the missionaries held prayer meetings for the workers and preached Christianity. According to Sathyavathi, the material benefits of belonging to the church are what made Anthaiah convert to Christianity. Part of the family now became Christian. Anthaiah became a class four employee and got his older wife a job. After she died, Sathyavathi's mother began to work there. Sathyavathi's father was paid Rs 18 and her mother Rs 15 a month. In addition to this, they would get rations—rice, wheat, milk powder, soap and talcum powder. The father promptly sent half his share to his elder daughter Lakshmamma, although she had plenty. She dominated him completely. Sathyavathi says that although Lakshmamma had only studied till the third form, she was shrewd and calculating and often planned her manoeuvres to harm people well in advance, sometimes three years ahead. In those days, there were huge hybrid chickens in the hospital. Anthaiah bought a few and gave them to his eldest daughter. Whenever her brothers came visiting, she would slaughter a couple and Sathyavathi and her siblings had to collect all the feathers and waste and throw the rubbish away.

How we longed to taste a bit of that chicken! We would hide behind the door and look in just to see that delicious food. We would sniff and draw in the smell of that spicy chicken curry, our mouths watering. But she would scream at us and tell us to go home and eat our meal and come back. We would go home to eat, returning to clear the leaf plates after the feast, sweep the floor, wash the pots and pans and then clear up. Not a scrap of leftover chicken did she ever give us to taste. Never.

There was plenty of work to do. Lakshmamma had lime trees, vegetable plots, banana plants and coconut trees on her land. The children had to collect dung and pile it up in the dung pit for manure. There were plenty of pigs in the village and they roamed about the village and collected pig shit to throw into the pit for pig manure. They also collected the carcasses of animals in the village on a piece of sacking, dragging it all the way home, then dug a deep pit and buried them under the trees. They also collected cow dung for manure. Sathyavathi always fumed at this labour. Her mother and sisters, however, were more patient and worked quietly.

* * *

Sometimes when the older women in the village were going to work, the ones who were old enough to be Sathyavathi's grandmothers would call out to her to come and work amidst them. That work was mostly picking onions, plucking green and black gram. They were not paid wages but given something in kind, grain or beans to take home. Landlords would give adult women more and children fewer beans. Then the women would protest, saying the children had done more work than they had and should be given more. So, the variety of grains collected would add to the family's food pot. Once, Sathyavathi went to work when they were laying a slab for a building. At the end of the day, after carrying cement in iron baskets, her hands were completely sore and covered with blisters. The wage she got for the day's work was four annas. Her mother had to spend one rupee to get her treated by a doctor. After this, she went with a couple of friends to work in Singarapu Rangayya's dal mill, where her job was to stand ready and fill the chaff that flew out as the dal was husked into sacks. After inhaling that dust the whole day, Sathyavathi developed a chest infection and breathing difficulty. She had to be admitted into the Mission Hospital where her mother worked for three days. After she got better, she went to the owner of the mill and asked him to pay her for the day she had worked. He flatly refused. The next day, her mother went and told him how sick she had been and he reluctantly paid six annas.

Born to Rebel

When Sathyavathi was in the sixth class, her older sister fell in love with a boy in the village during her holidays and married him. Their father and older sister caught them, brought them home, hung them from the wooden rafters and thrashed them mercilessly. The couple escaped and ran away to Bombay. Unable to do anything there, they returned to Hyderabad. Satyavathi happened to be on the same train, returning to Vikarabad. The boy got off at the next station and she took her sister home. She was stinking and dirty. Caked with mud and filth. Sathyavathi scrubbed her down with some warm water, bathed her and gave her clean clothes. When her father came home after work, she told him that her sister had returned to the hostel. She came to know later that both father and daughter had called a panchayat of elders and thrashed the young couple on their advice. Furious, she got a friend at the hostel to help her draft a letter and sent copies to their brothers and other elders. This probably marked the beginning of Sathyavathi's campaigning. Her sister promptly warned their father that this girl was extremely dangerous, her education should be stopped immediately and she should be married off. Within a week, they had found a match. The man worked in some company but was suffering from leprosy. Sathyavathi refused to marry him and they slippered her mercilessly.

* * *

After they [the prospective groom's family] left, their father turned on Sathyavathi and said angrily, 'You are no bigger than an onion and you dare to defy my daughter? You should be driven out!' He then pounced on her and thrashed her till the neighbours rushed in and stopped him. 'Is this the way to behave with your children? Do you think you are living in a jungle? No village? No elders?' So, he had to stop. But he started again at night, saying that if she didn't agree to the marriage they had fixed, she could get out of the house. Sathyavathi then wrote to her sister, Sarojini, telling her about her troubles. Her brother-in-law, Christopher, was a clerk in the Zilla Parishad School in Gommaram in Narsapur. She begged them to rescue her and place her in a social welfare hostel somewhere. She would not be a burden to anyone; she just wanted to escape from her father's house. Her sister and brother-in-law came the same evening and told her father that it was a bad idea to stop her education and get her married. He replied that he didn't have the money to educate her further. Besides, he added, the more she was educated the more cunning she became, turning against them and questioning them. Marriage was the only way to tame her. The sister said they would take her with them. He was silent. They told her to be ready to leave in the morning. Their father abused her as they left, saying she would get no schooling, she would only be made to sleep with her brother-in-law.

Learning to Survive

The next morning Christopher found her accommodation in the social welfare hostel in Sangareddy and a seat in the Zilla Parishad Girl's School. This was 1968. The Telangana agitation had started again, and no buses were running. Her sister packed four jawari rottes and sent her off to the Sikindlapur Railway Station with a chaprasi. The station was about ten miles away. They left home at 4 a.m. and reached at 6 a.m. The chaprasi left as soon as they reached the station.

I had not eaten for two days so I sat down and ate two of the rottes and waited for the train to Secunderabad. After I reached Secunderabad station, I had to go to Ranigunj and take a bus to Sangareddy. There were no buses running because of the agitation. So, I picked up my bag and walked all the way to Ranigunj. There I got a ride on a lorry and reached Sangareddy.

She had her admission letter with her and she met the warden Devaprabha, who admitted her to the hostel. She had a few saris, some oil and soap that her sister had given her. There were very few girls in the hostel as the school was closed because of the agitation. Sathyavathi was about fourteen then.

Meanwhile, Christopher sent her a letter. He pleaded that though she had refused to [do as he asked], she should not reject his help. He would send money for her daily needs. The warden, as was customary in hostels, read the letter, then handed it over to Sathyavathi. She broke down when she read it and wept bitterly for two days.

The tears would not stop flowing. My belly was full of grief. For that little timely help, he expected me to pay with sex. My own sister's husband! Why had I thrown myself open to this kind of behaviour? What had I done to deserve this humiliation?

The warden then sent for Sathyavathi and asked her to tell her story, assured her that she could trust her like a sister, as someone who could understand all her troubles. She said she should not hesitate to ask for any help she needed. She gave her two sets of clothes, a notebook and textbooks. Sathyavathi stood first in the seventh class and again in the eighth. Christopher came to visit her once and she sent him away brusquely, saying she did not need his help. In the hostel she had one friend, Lalitha, who took care of her, gave her clothes, slippers and helped her with other simple needs.

In those days, there was a severe shortage of rice. The first item in their hostel meal was jonna gatka, a gruel made of broken maize, which they had to finish before they were given a small helping of rice. The moment the tamarind pulusu was ladled on the lump of gruel all the worms came crawling out. No food could be wasted or thrown away as the warden stood watching. Rice would be served only after the gruel was finished. Sathyavathi, though famished, could not bring herself to eat that worm-ridden gruel. She quietly threw her food away. The warden sent for her and told her that the hostel rules were strict, that she could not violate its discipline and set a bad example. She could not go to the dining room in future but could go to the warden's room where she would be given rice. She told her to eat her fill. She was like her sister, there was no need to feel awkward. And so Sathyavathi had her afternoon meal. The night meal was a phulka with some watery dal. The dal was insipid without chillies or tamarind. Sathyavathi was accustomed to hunger but when she ate, the food had to be spicy. So, when she chewed on the dry phulkas tears rolled down her cheeks. A few girls had brought pickles from home, but the hostel rule was that no outside food was allowed into the dining room. The girls would sometimes sneak in a smear of pickle on a piece of paper and eat it secretly. One girl would bring her bottle of mango pickle to the library. They would lick the pickle, followed by big gulps of water, to kill their appetite so that they could chew their phulkas without the added torture of gnawing hunger!

* * *

When I was in the Sangareddy hostel, my friend Lalitha used to buy me a pair of rubber chappals every year. Some of us girls shared a room. Then one friend of mine said, 'Look! Don't wear your chappals every day. Wear them once a week when the Monday market is on. They will get spoilt if you use them every day! That day people from different villages come here. The rest of the days just wrap them up and keep them carefully!' We would go around on the market day, my friends would buy five paise of pattane [dried, salted peas] give me two peas in the afternoon, tell me to keep them in my mouth and enjoy the taste till the evening. Then I would chew and swallow them. This way we would have two peas to snack on daily till the next market day.

* * *

Soon, Sathyavathi had to appear for her Secondary School Certificate (SSC) exam, and the fee was Rs 25. She did not have the money and none of her friends had the means to help her. Borrowing seventy-five paise from a friend, she came to her village, stayed with a relative and asked her mother for the money. This was 1973. Her mother's salary at the time was Rs 15. She wept bitterly and asked how she could raise so much money. She took Sathyavathi to her brother, Bhimaiah, saying that she did not know where to get the money for Sathyavathi's fees. Her brother's situation was not much better. He cobbled shoes for a living, and people always paid in kind. No one paid cash. He thought for a while and then, pulling off the silver buttons on his shirt, he gave them to her and asked her to sell them. Sathyavathi took the buttons to a goldsmith who paid her Rs 35 for them. She paid her fees and with the Rs 10 left over, bought a new pair of slippers.

She worked hard and when she passed her exams her mother and uncle were happy. Her mother wanted her to do a nurse's training course but Sathyavathi did not like the profession. She began the intermediate course with the help of the collector in Sangareddy.

THE WOMAN IN EVERY STORY
I HAVE WRITTEN

Anuradha Kumar

For nearly two years of my life, I lived with a ghost. Or rather, the ghost lived with us.

At that time, my father was posted in Sambalpur. He was with the government, and the bungalow we came to live in was by the river Mahanadi. It was an old British-era bungalow with a slanting asbestos roof, huge rooms, doors with panels that folded, old-fashioned bathrooms, and a hallway that led off to the storerooms and an old kitchen, and out towards a courtyard, a well, and at last, the garage. A wall separated us from the river.

The ghost lived in the well. At first, I wasn't sure how to refer to the ghost. But the orderlies, once they became familiar with us, revealed more. In hushed tones and with eyes round like saucers, they told us how the ghost—the 'bhoot'—lived in the well. That the ghost had thrown herself in there. And that was why the well wasn't used anymore.

I never believed them. For one thing, wells weren't really used anymore, in any case. The bungalow had running water, though sometimes, our mother complained of 'low pressure' and the electricity, which went off whenever there were storms. In the two years we lived there, there were some bad ones.

Later, of course, everything was blamed on the ghost. Not just the storms but everything that happened to us in those two years. For those were the years in which my family changed in certain ways. I feel that time in Sambalpur mattered. And maybe how we dealt with the ghost had something to do with it.

I remember the first time I went to look down the well. I remember, too, that I was bored, for there would be times later when I would tell myself that I had been drawn in some manner towards the well, but this was never the truth. It was one of those long, sultry summer afternoons that sometimes came upon the town with a heat so thick it turned things dry, dull, and slow. Everyone was dozing while I walked down the hallway with the storeroom doors to my right and the barred windows to my left through which the sun came in, making slanted, unmoving, dark shadow lines on the floor.

I thought I might head to the garage—an outhouse that lay beyond the well, where my father's official car was parked. The car was a rather stunted-looking sedan with a low roof that always caught the head, no matter how careful one was getting in or out. It was a sort of yellow. There did seem to be a lot of yellows everywhere—I even imagined the summer in Sambalpur as a glaring shade of yellow. But the car had a radio that could easily catch short-wave radio stations. There was a test match on, and I sometimes listened to the commentary, imagining myself in a place as far away from Sambalpur as possible.

I remember that I had to really crane my neck to look down the well. The water lay at a great depth and looked limpid blue, a contrast to the hot glaze around. And in place of the dull buzz of the heat I felt around me, the water exuded quiet, even calmness. I must have stood there for seconds, not more, and then I headed to the garage, unbolting the wooden door before I slipped into the car. The driver never locked it, and the station broadcasting the commentary was easy to find on the dial. In moments, I forgot about the well and the ghost in it as I was transported to Lahore, where India was doing badly in the cricket match against Pakistan.

I did not think much about the ghost. No one asked me either. No one asked me much about anything in those days. My mother and grandmother had warned me not to go near the well. All I knew about the ghost was from a conversation I had overheard. That a woman had thrown herself into the well. Sudden deaths were, as I knew from countless stories, a certain way to turn into ghosts.

I did not think more about it. Wells were dangerous places, anyway. That a ghost had made this particular well her home did not scare me.

If my brother had not gotten the fright of his life one dark night when there was an unexpected power cut, I suppose my grandmother might not have persuaded my parents to have a puja, a supplicatory worship, to appease the ghost who resided in the well. And other ghosts, too. For that night of the power cut when everything for miles was plunged into a coal-black darkness, broken only by the flitting fireflies and the garland of forest fires across the river and perhaps the light of a boat far out in the river at an untimely hour, the orderlies told my brother stories. There were two of them that evening, one on 'regular' duty and another on the night shift, and, between them, they told him stories: of animals that suddenly appeared in the dark, cows with glinting fires in their eyes, a dog that appeared faithfully for nights on end and then vanished, and, of course, about the ghost in the well.

My brother later mentioned that what had scared him the most was how the orderly Shahu's teeth had glinted in the dark. It made him look like quite a spectre himself, but clearly, the ghost story, too, made an impact.

One morning, she gave her boys their breakfast and then jumped into the well. That was how I knew the story began. From that one statement, I realized she must have been young. That like every mother, she had ensured the children didn't go hungry for some time before help came.

Her husband, so the orderlies said, was a doctor, and he travelled often. That morning, or even the night before, he wasn't there.

She was in that house, the same house we now lived in, with her two sons and her father-in-law, one of my father's predecessors as the most senior police officer in Odisha's northern districts.

At that time, I did not think or ask why she had jumped into the well. All that I had to say to counter my brother was that she wasn't really harmful. The ghost hadn't scared us in any way. In fact, I added in a fit of bravado that there was no ghost at all. And out came the story of how I had peered into the well and seen nothing.

A stunned silence followed my declaration. My grandmother warned me that I must never do such a thing again. Considering the awe ghosts commanded and the distance we were expected to keep from them, I was surprised that nothing more was said, and I was reprimanded no more. But I guess they were already thinking of the puja doing something that would appease the ghost, making sure that she stayed in the well and did not stray anywhere else. The puja was a way to assuage my brother's fears, and, as I realized years later, it was also to keep my 'wild ways' in check.

Those days, as my grandmother and mother planned for the puja, school went on much as usual, but the ghost came to exercise a greater influence. She was blamed for my brother's fears that had, since that evening, grown in quantum leaps. Suddenly, he would run out of his corner room, unable to express his fear. At night, to assuage his fears and help him sleep, a lamp standing on three rickety legs always had its light on. My parents started noticing the ghost's presence, too. Some nights, when there was silence everywhere, they said they had heard a woman's high-pitched laughter. The tinkle of bangles. And though I did feel a shiver of fear at this, there were other fears that haunted me more at that time.

School had become difficult for me. There was only one missionary school that everyone attended. And my brother made up stories about me and got me into trouble with the teachers. I think now that he always resented the many differences between us, especially the fact that, unlike him, I wasn't afraid of the ghost and had actually been disdainful of his cowardice. I remember laughing when he ran out of his room in utter fear.

Yet, I did nothing to contradict my brother's made-up stories because his creativeness surprised me. I apparently criticized, mocked, belittled my teachers before my parents as a matter of routine. Everything about me, in turn, was made over into a joke. In school, classmates learnt that I mugged things up, was given to strange eating habits, and that I was fat.

This was something I hadn't realized about myself. But now, I knew why my father looked at me with hopeless pity. My mother mocked my body shape, and so I retreated into myself. There were long evenings when, as the sky greyed slowly outside, I sat at my desk, feeling a boulder-like heaviness in my chest. That stone was something I couldn't dislodge, no matter how much I shifted, took deep breaths, or stretched. The stone moved, but nothing could shake it away. I never told anyone this for fear of being laughed at and ridiculed. In any case, there was a bigger problem that haunted the family: the ghost.

And so, the puja preparations only gathered force. My grandmother looked up her 'paanji' (almanac) for an auspicious date, my father made inquiries for a suitable priest, and I learnt more about the woman in the well.

Her father-in-law, the man who had been in the house with her, Narayan Chand, was a police officer who had served in the district some years ago. When his name was mentioned, I saw my mother and grandmother exchange quick looks of comprehension and warning. This meant it was a matter that couldn't be discussed openly. The orderly looked disappointed. And I persisted. 'Who was he?'

'He's a very corrupt man. And rich too,' said my mother with some finality.

And she said nothing more. Only a flat no when I asked, 'The son never married again?'

The house fell into a quiet then. The red gravel driveway was lit up a ghostly blue with neon lamplights. And the jackals howled across the river, and, as before, the forest fires rose high in the sky. The river that otherwise looked sluggish blue now appeared dark and menacing, almost as if a curtain had dropped, sheathing us, apart from that red fire ring, from the rest of the world. The crickets chirruped, and the moths fluttered around the lamplights. The jackals called. Sometimes, affected by the direction of the wind, they sounded very close. When everything fell really quiet, like the times my father was on tour, we felt marooned looking out through the netted bay windows of the verandah, watching the dark river. Then, my mother sang songs and, for some moments, dispelled any fears we might have. It was at those moments, for those songs, that I really liked my mother. And I wanted her to like me, too. I would be good. I would try and be thin. I would not be wild. And I would stay away from the ghost. And not argue about her.

So, I quietly absorbed all that was said about the woman. She had done a selfish thing. How could a woman jump into a well, leaving behind two young sons, a travelling husband and an old father-in-law? But she had given them breakfast in the morning. That was the detail the orderly always ended his story with.

My father's office was just a short walk away. The bungalow and the office were within a walled compound with the river on one side and the Cantonment Road on the other. The post office and the vigilance headquarters flanked us to the left and right. My father sat at one end of a green-topped table with wooden outer bands. The table was always packed with files, but I liked the pen stands and the prismatic paperweights. Behind him on the wall hung all the photos of his predecessors—over thirty-five of them, right from the 1930s till the one he had succeeded. Men, passive and stern, unsmiling, wearing their uniforms and sitting a bit sideways, their heads turned left as they posed for the mandatory official photo taken just before they handed over charge to their successors.

Narayan Chand was somewhere in the middle. His bespectacled, lantern-jawed face loomed over my father's head. He looked unrelenting and glowering, with a certain look in his eyes. The first time I saw his photo, I was afraid. He looked like all the men I have known since then, who appeared distant figures to be feared and respected. The only time they acknowledged you was when you greeted them in a whisper and with hands folded in a namaste.

Even though there was little likelihood of my meeting Narayan Chand in real life or of him stepping out of the photo and standing over me, fingers crooked into his leather belt, I knew what he would do. Acknowledge my greeting with a clipped nod, and then let his eyes—bulbous and all-staring through his thick-framed glasses—rove over me. Had his eyes moved like that over his daughter-in-law, too? Had she, too, understood the things in that look that all women and girls learn almost always too soon in life?

The priest who was recommended worked in an insurance office. One afternoon, on our return from school, he was sitting next to my grandmother on the cane chairs on the patio. My father trusted my grandmother about such things. By testing the priest on things like how much he knew about the Gita, some other holy texts, the fasts he observed, the occasions he had officiated, she could tell if he was a charlatan, a bits and pieces 'purohit' or someone really authentic. He looked a bit dishevelled with his unkempt grey hair, tobacco-stained teeth, and his off-white loose kurta and dhoti. He wore mud-streaked black sandals. Maybe he saw me assessing him and read it as disdain. But back then, I was curious about anyone who could look as wretchedly attired as I did those days. I was quite awkward and gawky and felt I looked good in nothing I wore. The girls in my class were slender and delicate and looked well turned out even when they wore the simplest of clothes. Not me. I always looked frumpy, an object of scorn, and, for my parents, a source of despair.

The priest did have his revenge. My grandmother asked him to read my palm and tell her my fortune. He took his time, frowning as he held my hand gingerly. He peered through his glasses, tut-tutted in concern, and then told my grandmother that there was going to be trouble in my life, for I was much too stubborn. 'Ziddi,' he declared. I dared not look at my mother, who stood nearby. That would be the last nail in the coffin of my mother's meagre expectations of me. Grandmother attempted to shush him, telling the purohit that such things should not be mentioned before the young. And I, my voice strangled, asked if he saw anything even a little good in my lines. 'You will live till about sixty-five.' And studies? For I knew I wanted to go on to college and beyond. Shaking my hand off, he said dismissively, 'Oh, maybe a BA.'

With my brother, he was effusive and generous. He would go far and be brilliant in whatever he did. Looking at my now-beaming mother, he went on, 'Your son will either be a doctor or an engineer.' It added to my distress, for my brother shot me a triumphant look. Not only was I a failure in the present, but even my future posed problems. Yet, the predictions he made about my brother cheered my mother up considerably, and my grandmother set about making the puja arrangements.

The puja to appease the ghost was almost over by the time we got home from school. There was an array of inviting food in front of the deities. The fragrance of sandal and the cloying smell of incense pervaded the air. We heard the tinkling of cymbals and the blowing of the conch shell. Then the priest, followed by my grandmother, my parents and the orderly on duty, moved from room to room, holding the prayer plate with smoke billowing out of flaming coir strands. This smoke, enervated and blessed by the various deities arranged in my grandmother's prayer room, would dispel every evil, every malignant influence in the house. It made me cough and brought tears to my eyes. But I was forced to inhale it in deep so that no trace of wickedness was left in me.

The priest took home lots of food wrapped in a gamchha. He was given silver utensils, a new set of clothes, and money. All this was kept in neatly arranged packages before him as he was served lunch on a king-size plate with small bowls holding vegetables and sweets that I could never name. The very sight of all this food made me hungry.

The priest, who seemed rather prescient where I was concerned, asked me why I was not lending a hand to my mother and grandmother and serving food to the men. I bristled inwardly. It always angered me when such assumptions were made. That women cooked, served, cleaned up, and the men lorded over everyone. I saw my father and brother take their places next to the priest—the same king-size plates were placed before them.

The priest told me, 'Try to be a good girl.' I knew then that he saw me as quite the opposite. He looked at me long and hard. But, to my relief, he said nothing. When he rode off on his moped, I had my doubts about the puja. A bad spirit had been dispelled, but I was still around.

Some months later, we travelled in my father's car to the neighbouring town of Jharsuguda. It was an old industrial town, where a hundred or so years ago, the Marwaris had settled to trade in timber and minerals that the area was rich in. The town was also an important station for trains crossing the country, moving to Calcutta, or travelling west and south. We were on our way to see a guru. My parents had suddenly begun to have immense faith in this guru, who was tall and strapping and travelled the world with an entourage of disciples. What fascinated us, my brother and me, were the foreigners among his disciples, a sprinkling of Germans and some Japanese and Americans too. We liked to practice our English on them. This usually happened when we had to describe things like some local food items to them or especially warn them if things were likely to be too spicy and hot to their liking.

We had met the guru before. In Delhi, my brother and I had gone with our father to pay him a courtesy call, and then again in Calcutta, where the guru, returning from one of his foreign trips, had stayed at my aunt's place. This time, though, the visit was serious. My parents were to be initiated as his disciples. It seemed to be the next big step after the puja that the ghost had prompted them to do. Being his disciples meant that my parents would have to meditate and do yoga stuff for an hour—all kinds of contortions mingled with heavy breathing. They would also have to host the guru and his disciples whenever they came by, back from their foreign jaunts and sojourns to other places in India.

The Marwari businessman who hosted the guru this time in Jharsuguda lived in a huge house. It was twice the size of the government bungalow we lived in. Rooms on two levels overlooked a courtyard, almost like a respectable-sized basketball court. Once we stepped through the door, we encountered a soothing quiet and emptiness. Apart from an empty bench in the courtyard, there was no one and no other bit of furniture.

But on the first floor, we saw silent, moving figures. It was clear that the guru was somewhere near when we saw some fairer-skinned people dressed in long, colourful kurtas float around aimlessly, looking ethereal and disembodied. 'His foreign disciples,' my mother exclaimed in a whisper. To my brother and me, they looked like creatures from another world, which indeed they were, for one rarely encountered the likes of them in small-town Orissa.

The Marwari businessman's name was Singhania, and what I remember before we were ushered into the room to pay our formal respects to the guru was how amused he was when our father told him that my brother and I were confirmed disbelievers. I did not know then what my father meant—parents did not usually hold their children up for the world's mocking scrutiny when other conversational tactics had failed—but Singhania, bald-pated and rotund, threw back his head and laughed, dazzling us all with his gold-topped incisor. We trooped in to touch the guru's feet and then, as was protocol, sat on a carpet amongst others who looked on with suppliance as the guru stretched out on a low bed, his legs and arms massaged by two sets of people regularly changing places with those seated on the carpet.

I saw how their hands moved from his rose-pink feet, up his ankles and knees, where his saffron robe flapped open in places to reveal saffron tights, to his thighs and waist. The masseur's partner focused on the guru's hands, replicating the same moves from fingers to hand, wrist, elbow, upper arm, and shoulder. Yet the guru did not squirm in the face of this sustained pummeling. His skin turned pink and red, and he moved his fingers through his beard as he stared down at us, his eyes behind gold-rimmed spectacles moving from one face to another. I hid behind my father's broad back, afraid to be singled out for attention. I was sure I would be spotted for the bad girl I was and forced to confess, atone for my disbelief, before this suppliant and all-accepting audience.

It was as I skulked in some desperation, trying to fit myself behind my father's back, that I caught the eye of another saffron-robed figure. He sat on the carpet like us, but close enough to the guru so that he could hand him stuff like a pen, or water, or read out things he wanted. There was also a telephone close at hand. He was much younger than the guru and did not have a long-flowing, wispy beard. He looked back at me, stern and unsmiling. When I folded my hands as I had seen the others do in the face of similarly robed figures, he did not respond. He glowered at me instead, his black beady eyes and bushy black eyebrow giving away little else. But there was something about his wide jaw, his square forehead, that seemed familiar.

I would soon know more on the drive home towards Sambalpur. As we dozed in the back seat and the Ambassador hummed its way down the narrow highway, it was Mother who said, 'That Chand's son looked a bit at peace.'

Father nodded in agreement. 'After all these years,' Mother said, and Father agreed again. And when silence prevailed, I had little option but to pipe up and ask who they were talking about. When they didn't reply, I persisted. 'Is that the man whose wife died?'

Now, she was forced to nod. 'Yes, poor thing.'

'Did he kill her?' Father and Mother exchanged glances, and then Mother said, the things I already knew.

'No, she killed herself. She left behind two small sons and threw herself in the well.'

Poor thing. We mustn't talk of her like that.

But he looked calm.

People adjust.

My parents spoke over my head while I thought this was the most terrible thing of all: adjusting to things. It meant an acceptance when you could do nothing. When you were forced to hide things, to live on calmly. But the saffron-robed figure hadn't looked calm, I thought, in fact he looked angry. But I did not tell my parents this. I knew I could be wrong, and maybe the man I had seen, seated by the guru, was angry with me—people always were; something about my ugliness and stupidity inevitably drew people's anger—and I knew I would not be believed.

But I thought of that angry face and wondered if there was a great storehouse of unexplored and unvented anger in him. Maybe he was angry he wasn't there when his wife had gotten up that morning, knowing or not knowing that it would be her last. Perhaps she had already decided what she would do a few hours into that morning, and perhaps he blamed himself.

Maybe he was angry the boys had been left alone, well-fed so that they wouldn't cry for some time, but still alone. And why hadn't she taken permission? Why hadn't she told anyone, as women were supposed to do? Maybe he was angry with his father, who in his own photo had looked like an angrier and meaner version of his son. Two angry people never got angry with each other and not at the same time, especially when the object of their anger was the same.

By the time we reached home, and in the weeks that followed, this was what I understood. They were angry. Maybe the woman was, too, but her anger was the helpless kind, the kind I knew. The kind I felt when I was made fun of—too angry and then angrier because you knew your weakness. Sometimes, hurting yourself was the best revenge. But she had cared enough to feed her boys before she had done anything.

Now that my parents had seen the younger Chand, they could talk more freely about him. Father said he might find it difficult to visit our home should the guru visit. It would bring back memories.

And the speculation moved onto his motives as to why he had become a sanyasi. 'That's a terrible way to lose your wife. She was too pretty.' The way my mother said this made me go very still. She seemed to suggest that being pretty was terrible when I had always thought it was being ugly that was a sin. One you could do nothing about. 'She was too pretty. Poor thing,' Mother repeated.

It took me some more months to realize what had happened. It was something I worked out on my own. Narayan Chand had raped his young daughter-in-law one night. The next morning, unable to accept it, she had thrown herself into the well. She was pretty. He could not resist her. He was a powerful police officer, and no one would believe her. And he knew, too, that she wouldn't, couldn't, tell anyone. She would be blamed—for being pretty, for being a woman who had tempted a man, even an older father-in-law, a respected police officer. Who sat in his portrait, his bulbous eyes popping out in his all-knowing anger.

It was again some years later that I could get myself actually to say the words. He had raped her. Rape was the worst thing that could happen to a woman, to a girl. I had grown up hearing and learning about this terrible truth. It frightened parents, made them worry about their daughters, place restrictions on their every movement, deny them the freedom their brothers enjoyed. We accepted all this, knowing it stopped us from getting harmed— worse, from getting raped. But the young woman was in her own home, and nothing had saved her.

The last bit of this story that took me years to piece together, most of it coming together accidentally, always remained unfinished. For I never knew her name. Maybe it *was* her ghost that moved around, looking not to assuage her anger—for ghosts were supposed to be dissatisfied spirits—but for someone to know her story. For it did look like, despite the puja and visiting the guru, she was still very much around. Late one night, thunder cracked ominously, and lightning flashed menacingly, too close to the house. It lit up the river, turning it into a grey-purple line, and my usually sedate father shouted the guru's name, calling for relief.

The rainstorm went away in the manner of all storms. Some nights later, the lamp that was always kept on because of my brother's fear of the dark caught fire. My mother spotted it in time, for a few moments' delay could have led to the lamplight falling over and setting the mosquito net afire. My parents always talked of this as a narrow escape. And I always wondered if, like the two boys, I might have been left motherless.

After a few months, my father was transferred again. Maybe he wanted to move away, and the government granted his request. When I wrote about this in a fictional form years later, I referred to the ghost as a daughter-in-law, a bahurani. A woman who loved reading and who had killed herself. She became a ghost and lived in the attic of a bungalow, a familiar presence because of her anklets. It was an editor who pointed out, quite by accident, that the bahurani was similar to another haunted character in my book, Ratri, meaning night. At that time, I was haunted by such women who had no one to tell their stories to. But this—my editor's nudge—I thought, gave things an apt ending. The daughter-in-law, the young mother, the bahurani now had a name: Ratri. And everything fitted in.

I was talking to my mother more recently. She is much older now, and so am I, and we live on different continents in different time zones. When I called her, it was midnight, as quiet as the ones I remember in Sambalpur, and she was sipping her morning cup of chai. 'Do you remember anything of the ghost?' I asked. 'Did you ever really hear anything?'

'The gentle sound of anklets on the patio outside. Quiet and insistent. It sounded like a young woman,' my mother said. 'And the sound was always pleasing, like some sweet music.'

A SMUDGED KOHL-LINE

Mallika Bhaumik

*She is a kohl line that carries the deep desire of womanhood,
that becomes the broken fence of defiance; she is that dark
smudged line that defines and redefines the identity of a woman.*

Kajal—that's how she is known to the world

* * *

My frequent train journeys from Kolkata to Bolpur have an
added attraction of listening to some soulful Baul songs on the
way. Bauls or singing minstrels often enter trains and enthrall
passengers with some popular Baul gaan.

The last time, too, as the train gathered momentum from
the Burdwan station, the sound of an ektara string slurred past
me with a high-pitched voice crooning a song by the legendary
Baul singer Lalon Fakir. The lyrics, simple yet throbbing with
an intense passion seeped into my being, flowed freely letting my
thoughts wander.

*Milon hobe koto din e
amar moner manush er son e
chatok prai ohornishi
cheye ache kalo sashi*
(When shall I meet the one my heart craves?
Like the eager wait of a Jacobin cuckoo,
The dark moon stares on.)

The rhythmic motion of the train, the longings of the song rippling within, and the poetry of the changing landscape of red laterite soil outside my window somehow reminded me of Kajal.

Kajal and her indomitable will, her train journeys, her fortitude, her longing for intimacy, her vulnerability, and her return to the place she desired to call 'home'—all rushed through my memory, like frames in a kaleidoscope.

Kajal had tiptoed into the soul of the moment, and putting down her story was but a natural outcome.

Kajal's world spun around the holy town of Sitamarhi in the heartland of India, where she spent her girlhood, and later, some turbulent ones as a young bride. According to mythology, it was in that place that the ever-sacrificing Sita had willed to end her earthly sojourn and return to Mother Earth's lap. An ancient temple stands there with pilgrims coming in round the year.

As a contrasting colour perhaps, Kajal bloomed there, learnt to assert her sexuality, to question and fight back the conventions and established norms, and nurtured an infectious love for life and all its brighter hues.

I came to know about the young, vivacious woman who had been abandoned by people she loved most from the founder of Anjali—Mental Health Rights Organization, Ratnaboli Ray, who has worked extensively on rehabilitating people with mental illness.

She had met Kajal at the Berhampore Mental Hospital in a miserable state and with no clue how she had come all the way to West Bengal. Ms Ray said that what she found remarkable about Kajal was her rebellious heart, sharp mind, and charming looks.

Kajal had been married to Prabhu, who worked outside his native place and earned well. After the marriage, Prabhu left for Indore, and gifted a mobile phone to his young bride. This phone excited Kajal as it carried those special digits that could bring her husband close to her during his physical absence. This delightful gift, however, was taken away by her mother-in-law within a few days. Kajal gradually felt the brushstrokes of harsh reality when she failed to please her in-laws with her share of household chores.

Kajal's romantic overtures to Prabhu when he was in Sitamarhi, and slightly coquettish playfulness, made her a subject of ridicule, even by her husband, who found it 'weird'. Being a romantic at heart and somewhat distanced from reality, Kajal found it increasingly difficult to cope with mundane routine and a lacklustre marriage.

Prabhu's occasional visits and long bouts of absence proved—to her in-laws and the world—that Kajal's womb was an infertile and arid landmass where the hope of a child, especially a male child, would never sprout. She earned the sobriquet 'baanjh' or barren woman. The easiest thing that an Indian woman can earn from society is a label, and Kajal was no exception.

Once, while at her mother's place, Kajal heard that Prabhu was back home. She rushed to her in-laws' place to find him sitting with his mother and another ghomta-clad woman, who she presumed was a relative. Kajal was told that she would be accompanying her husband to Indore.

Kajal boarded the train with Prabhu, her mother-in-law, and the ghomta-clad woman. Train journeys have a strange connection with Kajal's life. Though normally meant to connect people, for her, train journeys mostly spelled abandonment and estrangement, homelessness and desertion.

While Kajal occupied one of the lower berths, she found Prabhu lay snugly with the other woman on an upper berth. It struck her then—this woman was Prabhu's new wife. As a woman who could bear no children, Kajal could not even complain about the cruel way in which the truth had revealed itself to her.

They got down at Delhi, from where she boarded another train with Prabhu, still hoping against hope that she might be able to stay with him. He seated her, asked her to wait, and said he would return with food for their journey. While she waited, looking around for Prabhu, the train started moving. She realized that her mother-in-law and the other woman were also not on the train with her. The train chugged out of the station as she ran through the carriages, frantically crying out Prabhu's name.

A woman with no knowledge of the world found herself on

a moving train with no companion or money, bearing the weight of a deep crater of betrayal and loss within her.

The inevitable happened. She was charged by the railway police near the Burdwan station for travelling without a ticket. The magistrate, finding her completely at a loss, asked her to be shifted to the Berhampore Mental Hospital, deeming it a safe shelter. After recovering from the initial trauma, she was referred to Anjali, the mental health care NGO.

Aditi Basu of Anjali and her team tried to contact Kajal's family with help from the police. They finally went to Sitamarhi to meet her brother, as well as her in-laws. Prabhu was not there; he had settled with his new wife at Indore. Kajal's brother and brother-in-law came and took her back with them.

However, Kajal's journey in search of her identity was not over. She did not like the fact that she had to live without Prabhu in Sitamarhi, engage in hard physical labour, and face sexual advances from her brother-in-law.

Kajal could be anything but a caged bird. She was not one to be 'standing on the grave of dreams'. She was Maya Angelou's free bird, who could claim the sky as her own.

She sneaked out of Sitamarhi to return to the only refuge she had known: the Berhampore Mental Hospital. She was found sitting by its gates one morning.

Kajal was a fast learner, and excelled in thread work (kantha stitch), gardening and other creative activities. Ms Ray's eyes shone as she spoke of how Kajal had recited a long poem of Nazrul at one go. She was loved by all the nurses, but the Anjali team headed by Aditi Basu often had to intervene to ask the doctors to lower the dosage of her medicines. Kajal, too, protested over this issue and once even went on hunger strike. She was a rebel who did not entertain any sympathy coming her way. She wanted her freedom as her right.

One cannot miss the obvious connection of Kajal's life to the brilliant movie, *One Flew Over the Cuckoo's Nest*,[123] which uncovered the tyranny of incarceration by authoritarian forces, institutionalization, and the fragility of social support systems, which, beguiling a person into a strange dependency, rob them of their sense of self-respect and freedom.

Indeed, Anjali even produced a documentary on Kajal's life, filmed by Putul Mahmood, in which she played herself. As I watched the film, I found myself looking at the face of a child-woman, beautiful in its vulnerability and not marred by cruel life. Kajal was a good dancer and she danced merrily with the other patients who featured in the documentary. It was heartening to watch someone who had missed out on the rhythms of life move to the happy, catchy tune of a film song. The fluid movement of her arms, legs, waist, neck was akin to a graceful drift towards light and emancipation.

The film unfolded the pages of Kajal's life like the town of Berhampore was unfolding itself before her eyes. The documentary celebrated her life and showed how she gradually unfurled her wings and learned to fly, how each defeat and humiliation proved to be another step she took towards self-reliance. Reel life breathed hope and optimism into the real life of Kajal.

The crew, however, had a tough time, as Kajal relived her trauma during the shooting and even suffered a severe meltdown. The whiffs of nostalgia and shadows of the past proved to be scary and ghost-ridden for her.

The movie was aptly titled *Love in the Times of Madness*.

Kajal was as candid and confessional as a trusting teenager. She giggled while describing her wedding attire, a Benarsi saree. She elaborated how exquisitely she had been decked up. She expressed how all her happiness and expectations had been tied up in a knot with the person her parents had chosen for her. Through her words, the milieu she grew up in was brought into focus. She said that marrying the person of your choice, or love marriage, was an aberration. It was expected of a girl to marry the man chosen for her and find happiness with him.

The happiness of intimacy that a marriage normally sanctions was another cracked and broken mirror that reflected Kajal's hurt and humiliation. She elaborated how her husband would turn his face away from her when she looked at him, and how, if she went to the other side to face him again and gaze into his eyes, he would still turn away from her. Her romantic advances were thought to be an illness or, more ominously, a madness or abnormality, which Prabhu used as an excuse to abandon her. Her husband had prepared his ground for abandoning Kajal. He had tried to convince her that she needed to get better (read 'normal'), since the children of mentally unwell people are often born with mental disorders. It was pointless for Prabhu to remain in that marriage, for he had understood that Kajal would never be a meek and submissive wife. After all, she was bold and 'weird'—hungry for romance and intimacy. Nor would she produce heirs to carry forward his family's name.

Women, or rather wives, considered the carriers of seeds, could be impregnated for procreation and pleasure, but were not to be pursued or wooed for romance or lovemaking. In a country with such a drastically poor record of gender inequality, it was almost a miracle that Kajal was well-fed by her husband for some time despite not having produced an heir.

Then, very conveniently, Prabhu sealed her fate on the pretext of madness or abnormality. Kajal had longed for a Prince Charming. Instead, she got an ordinary, run-of-the-mill husband and could not reconcile to the fact.

Being a movie buff, I was reminded of a delightful Hindi movie, *Paheli* directed by Amol Palekar in 2005, where two puppets (voiceovers by Naseeruddin Shah and Ratna Pathak Shah) narrated the story of a ghost falling in love with a new bride. When her glum, practical and unromantic husband left for business just after the first night of their marriage, the ghost gladly took the physical appearance of the husband and continued to romance the new bride every night, telling her that he had come back for her.

Alas, Kajal had no such folklore-come-true episodes in her life! Her thirst for intimacy and lovemaking lingered on. While talking to Ms Ray, she unabashedly expressed her fondness for a man who, on finding her alone in the Kolkata-bound train, had hugged and kissed her in a nearly empty compartment. He, too, had vanished at a station after telling her that he would bring her some food. None except loneliness had been her constant companion.

The moment of her ultimate frustration found apt expression in a scene in the documentary in which Kajal, while walking down the steps of an overhead bridge, recounted in desperation why she had wanted to move away from everyone she had known. Her brother, to whom she had turned for help, had asked her to return to her in-laws' place. But her in-laws' place had no husband for her. It did not even have a proper bed for her, so she had slept like a mongrel on the floor through the wet monsoon and harsh winter. Her bitterness and resentment were, in a way, akin to her train journeys in search of love, light and identity.

Train journeys are symbols of her unsettled life and unfulfilled desires. After all, it was during one such journey that she faced the abandonment that changed the course of her life. But even when she was so broken that she did not care whether she lived or died, she was certain that she wanted to flee to some faraway place where known faces would not bother her any more.

> *How far is it?*
> *There is mud on my feet*
> *Thick. Red and slipping...*
> *This earth I rise from, and I in agony.*
> *I cannot undo myself, and the train is steaming.*
> *steaming and breathing, its teeth*
> *Ready to roll, like a devil's*
> *There is a minute, at the end of it.*
> *A minute, a dewdrop.*
> *How far is it?* [124]

The documentary helped Kajal to earn some money. She bought some pretty dresses and a set of black lace lingerie that left her fascinated. She loved wearing her new clothes, her beauty flowering and spreading its fragrance like a frangipani. She had a strong desire to celebrate her womanhood and sexuality like other women. She had been loathed for this self-love and indulgence back home. The milieu she was born into is known to weigh women in terms of the heftiness of their dowry and the fertility of their wombs. Yet, gossamer dreams nestled in her eyes, dreams of a love to lure her.

Sometime later, Kajal left Berhampore with Prabhu, taking all her money and belongings, happy and content, oblivious that he might be using her as an unpaid house help, or nurse for his elderly parents, or nanny for his young children.

The NGO, Anjali, could not object to her departure, since it believes in self-sustenance. Kajal did not look back even once as she crossed the hospital gates. The desire to be accepted and loved by her chosen one had perhaps overshadowed all other doubts, clouded over all her worldly worries.

Ms Ray said that she had heard from Kajal lately, and could make out that her precious little happiness had been nothing but a brief illusion. She recalled hearing a palpable hopelessness in Kajal's voice. Ms Ray also admitted to having felt a deep, nagging fear within herself that she might find Kajal's familiar voice go missing, or be lost forever, or that yet another train journey might bring her back at the gates of the Berhampore Mental Hospital.

Few things or incidents or people leave an indelible mark on the heart forever and Kajal, much like her name, is one such soul.

A wish for Kajal to walk towards light, towards life—

Let everything happen to you: beauty and terror
Just keep going. No feeling is final...
...Nearby is a country they call life.[125]

(With thanks to Ratnaboli Ray and Aditi Basu of Anjali—Mental Health Rights Organization.)

AN INSIGNIFICANT QUESTION

Eli Prue Marma

'Mita! Mita!' My Amma was calling me. At first, I could not recognize her voice because it was as soft as a whisper. Then her voice grew louder and clearer and gradually I could hear her. Why was she crying out loud calling my name?

'Mita, get up my dear. Can't you hear me, my darling?'

Of course I do, Amma, I reply.

Still, she continued, 'Please, get up, Mita! Oh Lord! What has happened to my child?'

I could not see her. I could not see anything. No! I saw only darkness. It was everywhere. I needed to get up. I needed to prove she was crying for no good reason. But as I tried to move, I failed. I tried again and again. Still I failed, as if I did not have a body! I got a bit scared. Had something happened to me? Was I paralyzed?

I cried out, 'What has happened to me, Amma?'

She did not reply. I ask her again, louder this time.

But she only kept crying. I could not understand why she did not respond to my call. Why wouldn't she? I could not understand why she kept crying. I had never heard her cry like that. She was a strong woman. Then I heard some other weeping voices. What are they lamenting for? I could not even figure out who most of them were. Apart from all this weeping and crying, I also heard voices shouting and speaking loudly. Did we have some programme today at our place?

Suddenly, I heard a woman's voice from the crowd, 'Poor Mita's mother lost her husband four years ago, now her only daughter too. She is virtually alone in this world. How will she live the rest of her life?'

What? What did she say! Was I dead? That's impossible. I am not dead, Amma. She was lying. If I were dead, how could I hear all these things?

Amma, stop crying. I'm not dead, I shouted as I tried to move and get up. But I failed again. I tried to gain control over my body, but I could not even feel it. I became afraid. I cried. I cried loudly. Amma, what's happening to me? Can you hear me, Amma? I'm scared...why don't you respond to me? Am I really dead, Amma?

My Amma was silent now. I could not even hear the sound of her weeping. Amma, why are you silent? Amma! Amma!

Had she also become mute like me, mute forever? A heart-attack? Oh! My dear Amma! Why was this happening to us? I was praying to God. Oh Taknaisa! I cannot tolerate this situation. Please help me. Let me see my Amma.

A few voices said, 'Bring her water. She has fainted.' I realized that these voices belonged to our neighbours.

Someone said to my mother, 'Malati, wake up. It's better to cry than to lie senseless. Cry a bit.' Why are they telling her to cry? Would crying make her feel any better? Did it work that way?

Amma, please cry then. Call my name again. Call your Mita once again. I will jump into your arms, I promise. Call your dear Mita, Amma, I screamed. Suddenly, she responded, 'My daughter is alive! My Mita is alive! Let me go to her.'

But she could not reach me. Had I become too unholy?

My Amma was silent again. Someone said, 'She is senseless again.' I knew it was my neighbour, Rumboity aunty. Oh Taknaisa! Give her strength to control herself.

She said vehemently, 'How can Malati bear this? We never imagined that we would lose Mita this way. She was young and beautiful like a blooming flower. How old was she, eighteen?

All the dreams that she had about her daughter to end this way! This is intolerable!'

'Mita was mature for her young age and looked after all the things like a son. She was intelligent too. She had been giving lessons to my two kids since last autumn. I forbade those two from coming here. How'd I let them see this? They loved her so much,' said Purba aunty.

I wished I could cry. I wished I could hug those two pupils of mine for the last time. I knew they also felt bad for me. I could hear everything that was happening around me. But I could not see, nor understand why I could not remember anything. What had happened to me? A man said, 'We should report this incident to the police. The boys who found her first—don't leave. They might have questions.'

Two voices in unison said, 'We're here. We won't go anywhere.' I recognized one voice. Poltu! I whimpered. Please come to me. Tell me, friend, what's happening?

I heard some people mention that it was getting late. 'It's almost eleven. The police will arrive in the morning,' they said. After half an hour I guess, people started to leave. My mother was sitting beside me and probably some people were guarding me—my body. Now I was inside one of our rooms.

The night was dark; but to me, it was darker. My tension and impatience have added to the night's dark pigment. Now I could hear nobody. Everybody seemed silent. Those who were sleeping would wake up and see the golden rays of the morning sun light up the village, river, and hills after the dark gloomy night rolls away. But to me, it would probably remain dark. Now darkness would be my mate. But for how long?

Will this night ever end?

* * *

I thought it was morning as I heard noises again. I knew people were congregating. But the police hadn't arrived yet. Our Tripura village was too far from the police station. I also wanted to know what had happened to me. Why was nobody talking about it? People died. I get that. I saw my father die in front of my eyes. I had cried. I still cry. I will cry forever for him even though I know he will never come back. He died of cancer. But how did I die? Was it an accident? Did I fall while climbing the hills? Bah, that is impossible!

My mother had cried a lot yesterday and gone mute. I don't think she had eaten any food at all. I could feel her still sitting beside me; I could feel her breathing. But she had turned as silent as a block of stone.

The police arrived after a while. A man said, 'Mita's mother, we have come from the police station. We want to talk to you.'

My Amma was not in a condition to tell the police anything. But she had to speak; there was no other way.

When they asked her what had happened, my Amma replied with a trembling voice, 'Mita went towards the river to take a bath in the late afternoon yesterday.'

'Can you tell me the exact time?' one of the policemen asked.

'It was around five. I saw her carrying a water jar with her. I was busy feeding the pigs and doing household chores. After finishing my work, when I called out for her, she didn't respond. I searched for her everywhere. But she didn't come,' she said. And then my mother started crying again. Some were consoling her.

She resumed, 'Two hours passed. After that, I went frantic with worry. I called Mita's friends and we went out looking for her. After another three hours of searching, some other village kids found her in the jungle's bamboo bush, lying dead.' She started howling anew at this point, 'Oh, my Mita, my poor child, oh my Mita...'

'Where are those village boys?'

'We are here, Sir.'

'You four boys, don't you know that in these types of cases you cannot touch a dead body until the police arrive?'

'No, Sir. We knew nothing. And how could we leave our friend's dead body in the jungle?' came Poltu's voice.

I heard a loud noise. Someone was shouting. The rest of the

crowd joined him. The villagers were agitated by the behaviour of the police. The situation became chaotic and violent. Locals raised their voices demanding justice. The policemen out-shouted them, requesting them to be calm.

One of the boys said, 'What are you talking about? Would we let her body lie there the whole night? Impossible! She is like our sister. She has already faced an inhuman act. Didn't you hear? Human beings did it to her! You want wild animals to eat her too?'

Another boy added, 'Plus, we knew you guys weren't coming before having your morning tea. So, all we did was to ensure the poor girl got some peace after her death.'

The police told everyone to calm down. Then they inquired about the place where they discovered my dead body. The boys said, 'We found her body in the bamboo grove under a teak tree which is kind of solitary. We found her lying dead and half-naked.'

What! I freaked out. I felt ashamed. I was trying to remember everything. But nothing popped up into my mind's eye. Mind's eye! If I were really dead, how could I even be thinking then? What was this? Was this life after death?

That boy continued, 'Poor Mita! When we found her, her eyes were partly open. There was blood and gore on her face, all over her nose and mouth. Her mouth was open too. She had multiple ligature marks on her hands and legs and her neck is probably broken. Her pants were found hanging from a nearby tree branch.'

Then it was all clear. I was raped and then murdered.

They raped me and then killed me.

Goodness! Now I could remember. I could remember everything. Those beasts with human faces.

Amma, can you hear me? I can't tolerate this anymore, Amma. I know who they are. Listen to me, Amma. Where are you? Amma, I'm telling you. They were four settlers. They were Bengali men. They jumped on me like wild animals. I couldn't even scream. They took me into the jungle. I could hardly breathe. They raped me and then tortured me until I died.

Amma, can you hear me? I want them to be punished. I want them to suffer as much as I did, Amma. Can you make it happen? I screamed only once after biting a hand, Amma. But nobody responded. And then someone punched me in the face, and everything went dark. It is still dark.

Then, suddenly, I heard the voice of an old woman. It was my achoi! She said, 'Police sir, I want to tell something about yesterday evening. As Mita's mother said, when she went to take a bath in the river, I saw four settler-men walking towards her. She probably had not seen them. It must have been them.'

'Who are you and where are you from?' asked one of the policemen.

'I'm from this village, but I live in Jumghor, a bit far away from here. I often come here walking by that road. Mita was such a lovely girl. She used to call me grandmother! I loved her too. Who wouldn't?'

The policeman said, 'Well, we'll take your statement. We will investigate and seek out the criminals. Now, we have to take the body for post-mortem.'

I felt hopeful that those rapists and murderers would be captured soon and punished. The only dream I had was to get educated and take care of my poor mother. I tried to console myself; they must be punished. How would they not, after such a horrifying deed?

The police picked up my body and put it in their jeep. They were taking me to Sadar Hospital in the Khagrachari district where the post-mortem would be done. The vehicle started gaining speed. After a few minutes, I suddenly realized that I would not be returning to the place I had always known as my home. I heard that scream again. Amma...How will you survive without me!

Now in the jeep, one of the policemen said, 'I hate these cases. Soon, her news will be all over social media. And a group of workers from an organization or two, yes, those human rights activists from these Pahari communities will raise their voice against this crime and form human chains. Then after some weeks, nobody will bother, nobody will be caught, and the case will die closed. People forget too easily. Besides, she does not have a strong male relative. Poor girl!'

'We'll do our duty, Monsur Bhai,' replied another.

'Yes, I also need to see those bastards. What if they had found my girl instead of her?'

* * *

The engine stopped. Then I heard, 'Take the body to the post-mortem section. I have to talk to the doctor. We need the report as soon as possible.' This man was probably called Monsur and I guessed he was the senior inspector.

I heard the sound of a trolley. It stopped and then started again. I knew I was on it. Then it stopped again. They left me. I could hear them leaving. Was I alone in this room? It seemed so. What should I do? What could I do except think?

Had just some moments passed or a few hours? I had lost track of time. A man said, 'We have to inform the police that Mita Tripura's report is ready.' It was the doctor. Everything went quiet again.

Note: *Rapes and murders of indigenous women in Bangladesh are a regular occurrence. In 2018, an article*[126] *published by the International Work Group for Indigenous Affairs (IWGIA), showed how indigenous women of all ages in the Chittagong Hill Tracts are targeted and raped by Bengali settlers. In most cases, they are killed after the incident. Even when criminal cases are filed, and investigations carried out, the criminals escape punishment, usually due to insufficient evidence. This piece was written after studying three such harrowing occurrences between 2018-19. In each case, a girl was found half-clothed or naked in jungles not far away from her home. The questionnaire that came from the police in these cases was callous and showed little concern for the dead. The reaction of the law enforcement agency and people beyond the indigenous community was lukewarm at best.*

The case of Lakingme,[127] *who was found dead almost a year after her abduction, is a horror story, and there are many such stories, with, in some cases, victims as young as seven. The first-person narration is employed in this piece to make the events seem more precise and believable. It is high time for Bangladesh to examine its laws and rethink its stance, which is to claim that 'Bangladesh does not have any indigenous population'. Rather than counting them as just an 'ethnic minority,' Bangladesh should adopt the United Nations Declaration on the Rights of Indigenous Peoples.*

SREEJA'S STORY

Nishi Pulugurtha

I completed thirty-five years of my marital life last year. Most people will wish me the moment I refer to it. For the past twenty-five years, I have been a patient of manic depression and schizophrenia. I was under treatment for some time, but then I stopped taking my medicines as I felt that all were conspiring against me, even the doctor. I refused any food prepared by anyone else.

Things became worse; my daughter, too, is under medication now. It is she who convinced me to see a doctor and start taking medicines again. This is my story. I think it needs to be told. People have spoken about it in my absence; my relatives talk about it too.

I was still in school, Class 12, when I met Deb. He was in Class 12 too, and studied in a nearby school. Our school timings were the same and that was how we met for the first time. I noticed him with his friends on the way to school. He walked to school. I used to travel by rickshaw.

My mother did not want me to walk that long a distance. Our lives had not been easy ever. My father had been involved with another woman. My working mother could not take that and had moved out with me. I remember noisy scenes at home. He lived with the other woman in another town, miles away from us. It had been some years since we moved back to Calcutta.

My mother, my mashi (that is, my mother's older sister) and

her children, my maternal uncle and I—we all lived together. It was not a big house but that was the only home that my mom and my recently widowed mashi knew. Mama, my maternal uncle, did not marry and he was more than happy to live with his sisters, both of whom had been in difficult situations and needed support. We did not need financial support—mother had a government job—but her sister needed all kinds of support. Being together meant I grew up with cousins and that made my childhood and adolescence a partly happy one. I was able to overlook the absence of my father. After some years, that did not trouble me. It continued to trouble my mother though. She never divorced my father and I never spoke about it.

The furtive glances that Deb and I exchanged soon gave way to brief conversations. We discovered we lived in neigbourhoods close to one another. I liked talking to him. He was not handsome and shorter than me by a couple of inches. All that did not matter to me. He read poetry, scribbled verses too, and I liked listening as he read them out. He participated every year at local cultural events and encouraged me to be a part of them. I liked poetry and had acted in school plays. Play reading was something I enjoyed. I told him that I would like to do that at one of the functions, if possible. That was how our bond grew stronger and blossomed into love.

When my mother got to know, she was furious. She tried to dissuade me, convince me that there was something about Deb she did not like. She was certain that he was not the right kind of person. She had seen much, and she wanted to make sure that I did not err in my choices. I did not pay heed to her.

I was in love with Deb and wanted to spend the rest of my life with him. My elder cousin, my aunt's daughter, Didibhai as I called her, knew about it all. She was my confidante. I trusted her above all. She had met Deb much before my mother did. She said he seemed to be genuinely in love with me. I decided to stand up to my mother.

Despite all her objections, my mother made the arrangements for my wedding and actively took part in it. She went out of her way to make the event a grand occasion. I was twenty-three when I married Deb, he was twenty-five and had been working for a year as a medical representative.

I moved into a joint family consisting of Deb's parents, elder brother, his wife and a small daughter. My new home was close to the house where I had grown up. I was used to living in a joint family. So, it was all familiar territory.

What was unfamiliar was the mentality of the people who belonged to it. My father-in-law and mother-in-law ruled the household with an iron fist. My sister-in-law ignored me most of the time. When she did pay attention, it was to taunt and belittle me. My brother-in-law and Deb had absolutely no say in the affairs of the household. The ambience was not genial, but I tried to ignore all of it.

I was in love.

After a brief honeymoon, I was slowly trying to settle into the new environment. My mother-in-law stopped cooking after my marriage. Of course, she still controlled the kitchen and the household. Mamoni (that was how I addressed my mother-in-law) took all the decisions. Didi, my sister-in-law, and I took turns to cook. Didi never smiled, never spoke as much as a word, kept to herself, did whatever was required of her and then went off into her room. She made sure to even take the napkin that she used in the kitchen with her when she walked off to her room. If I entered to do something, I had to look for another one.

A few days later, I went home to meet Ma and my uncle and aunt. Didibhai was there, too, with her husband and baby son. It was a nice family reunion. I always shared everything with Didibhai and that day was no different. When we were alone together for a while, we walked to the terrace as we always had. She started asking about my new home and family members. I told her all—there was something amiss in that family. Didibhai said that I was 'reacting too much' and that I needed to give them time. Moreover, Deb was a nice person and surely, with the passage of time, things would be different.

Deb's job as a salesman was tedious and he had to travel

a lot. He was away from home for more than half the month. When he was around, he made sure he spent time with me. We went out to the movies, visiting relatives, a walk in the park and the like. He insisted on taking me everywhere. He made sure I never went out alone. I was alright with that. It was always nice to have company.

When he was travelling, he called up to enquire about me and always made it a point to ask what I did during the day. He asked for details, minute details. Initially, it did not bother me. He would ask about things I had told him over the phone after he got back too. Casually, as if he had forgotten what I had told him. I mentioned it to him once and he smiled and shrugged it away, saying it must have escaped his mind.

It was a Sunday. I was in the kitchen making tea. I poured it and took it out into the hall to give it to Mamoni and Baba. Didi was in her room. I then went to give Deb his cup. Holding the cup in his hand, he walked into the hall and settled on a chair. He took a sip and spat it out shouting, 'Don't you even know how to make a cup of tea?' The expression on his face frightened me. I was about to say something when he stood up and emptied the contents of the cup onto my face. The others in the hall looked in the direction of the noise, turned away and walked off.

I did not know how to react. I was stunned, deeply hurt and pained by it all. How could Deb do this? How could the others ignore it?

Greatly disturbed, I called up Didibhai, my anchor and friend, and broke down. She told me such things happen in marriages and that I should ignore it. 'I don't think he will do it again,' she told me. 'Something must have been troubling him.' I was surprised at her reaction, but believed it after a while.

Deb tried to make amends. The rest of the family did not seem at all bothered. I was upset for a few days and then things went back to the way they had been.

I decided to ignore it and that was the biggest mistake I made.

I kept on ignoring all that Deb went on doing and violence

became a part of our relationship. Two children and many years later, I am still in the relationship. I don't have the urge to do anything new. There is no way I could do anything.

My mother got to know of my troubled marriage when Deb kicked me hard and pushed me down the stairs—that was the first time my bruises and injuries became visible. She came home and spoke to my in-laws who preferred to look the other way. She spoke to Deb, too. She asked me how long all this had been going on. She was angry that I never told her about it. She was angry that Didibhai, who had known all along, had never spoken to her about it. She asked me what I wanted. She wanted me to leave, she was sure the violence would continue and increase. I just cried in her arms.

During Durga Puja, my friends had made elaborate plans and Deb was part of it. We made plans for Ashtami; we would all enjoy the day together. Just the evening before, a phone call from Deb's cousin created a huge issue for me. Deb was insistent that we change our plans and stall going out with my friends. I tried convincing him, as his cousin would not arrive till late at night. We would be back home by then. Deb created a ruckus. He refused to see the logic. It did not affect anyone else in the house.

He suddenly stood up and started banging his head against the wall. It took me a few seconds to realize what he was doing. I tried to stop him, he pushed me away, real hard. He kept banging his head against the wall and asking me—*will you go, will you go*. This scared me—he was hurting himself. I shouted out that I would not go. That made him stop. That became his way of dealing with what he disapproved of. I would give in, always be forced to give in.

My first pregnancy took me by surprise and was functional in deciding my course of action. I decided to continue with my troubled marriage and not leave. A few years later, my second daughter was born.

The violence that had now become a habit that never ceased.

There were times when angry for a trivial reason he pulled me by my hair in front of the children and pushed me onto the bed, throttling me. My screams, as usual, went unheard. I started working once the kids were able to manage on their own. Deb would accompany me to the interview; it had to be a girls' school and one with only women teachers. If I spoke with or interacted with men on social occasions, at events, he would observe me carefully from the corner of his eye. After we got home, he would accuse me of paying too much attention to other men. Maybe, he would say, I was having an affair with one of them.

The emotional and verbal abuse also led to physical assaults; he would fling his shoes at me, hold me by my hair and shake me hard. It just went on. I was never able to hold onto any job for long.

On one occasion, he took an overdose of sleeping pills. He wanted to stop me from going on a holiday with my mother. I panicked and called for the doctor. It was not a big cause for worry, the doctor said. Later, Deb told Didibhai and me: 'I am a medical representative. I have been working in this area for a long time. I know exactly the kind of dose that would be needed to scare your sister and not cause my end.'

We did not know how to react.

My mother died fifteen years ago. She tried to intervene a number of times. She tried her level best to make me see reason. She was terribly upset with the state of things. Didibhai, however, kept on telling me things would get better—after the children are born, after I get a job, and so on—they never did. I only wish I had listened to my mother and not depended on Didibhai so much. Now, I no longer have the energy or the desire to do anything. I just let it be. I did the things I was supposed to do mechanically. I do not like social events and occasions. Deb is under medication too. Yes, I am still living with him in that same house. It is no longer a joint family scenario, but things are just the same as they had been before. The whole world is against me, I know. Even Didibhai—yes, she did help us at times, with money whenever we needed it.

What still keeps me going are the dreams of my younger one, I need to see her fly high. I hope and pray she does.

Note: *This story is based on the account of Sreeja, as narrated to the author by Sreeja's Didibhai, whom she knew. The name Sreeja and certain details have been assumed to protect privacy and confidentiality.*

I DON'T WALK ON
YOUR CARPET ANYMORE

Ankita Banerjee

I don't remember when it started.

If my body was a window, it was overwhelmed by waterspouts before I reached puberty. I hated looking in the mirror. The bulges growing on my chest were the reason I invited trouble, I was convinced. I stopped wearing chemises by the time I was ten and insisted I needed a bra. I thought it would flatten my bulges. The straps sunk their teeth into my skin, so I hooked it even tighter—to the point where the pain made me slouch. When my lips turned dry, I scraped off the skin and rubbed salt on them. I squeezed the summer boils on my face until I bled. They left marks, unlike the bruises on my confidence. I wasn't old enough to understand if I were enjoying the pain, but I was convinced I needed to punish myself.

I don't remember the nightmares, but they made me wet the bed until I was fourteen. My lack of bladder control was my fault, I was told.

I was an ugly-looking, attention-seeking dolt who invited only bad luck on my parents. It was me who made my saint-like cousins play perverts. I asked for it and they just didn't know where to stop.

They were the sons of my mother's elder sister, my maasi. My mother adored them, and they loved my elder sister. In my childhood, we used to visit their home frequently. Our families were very close. My male cousins liked to take turns to play 'tell-me-where-my-hands-will-go-next' with me when our mothers took afternoon naps in the next room. Whenever our parents weren't around, they would tickle me in the places I understood as a child they weren't supposed to.

In the beginning, I felt annoyed. I wanted to be left alone. Every girl innately knows what bad touch is, but not everyone can stand up to a sexual predator.

It was a day or two before Saraswati Puja. I was twelve. My mother and aunt were rolling out coconut laddoos sitting on the floor and I was sleeping on my aunt's charpai in her living room. They were chatting about this and that, barely two feet away from me. I was trying to hear what the adults were saying, until I dozed off.

It was probably around then that he came and lay down beside me. He was one of my two male cousins. He was twenty. I was sleeping under a blanket. He, too, had pulled one over himself.

At first, his fingers on my thigh felt like part of a dream I was dreaming. Or was I really dreaming? I can't say now. When you spend all of your twenties trying to bury a bad memory, the details fade with time.

But some stings sting no matter how hard you try to pluck them out.

He slid his hand into my underpants.

My mother and aunt were still on the floor, chatting and rolling laddoos.

Shocked, I opened my eyes wide and looked at him. He was lying straight on his back. With his eyes closed, he pretended to sleep as his right hand reached for the part of my body under my blanket that I definitely knew it shouldn't. My senses went numb, like they still do, years later, every time the memory of that day flashes in my mind.

I don't remember how long it took my cousin to shove his finger into my vagina.

When I jumped off the charpai, his posture remained

unchanged. His eyes were still closed. He was still pretending to be asleep. My mother was there in the room, totally unaware of what had just happened under the blankets.

A year or two later, during one of those unworldly painful menstrual cramps, when I rolled from one side of the bed to other in agony, I cursed all the gods and my mother for not doing anything to stop the sons of her sister from doing what they did to me. All these years later, I couldn't tell her everything; I couldn't tell any of my boyfriends everything; I couldn't tell my husband everything. I still don't know how to select the right words for the shame I felt.

I started losing impulse control when I was fourteen. Whenever my mother asked me to visit my maasi's place, I used to bolt. I used to scream and ask her how she could be so oblivious. She didn't understand what I was saying. She never tried to understand why I said the things I said.

We were middle class. Our problems were more pressing than my cousins violating my body. More than anything else, it was inappropriate for a girl to even insinuate such a thing about her cousins. We belonged to decent families. Things like this don't happen in decent families and even if they did happen, decent girls shoved it under the carpet. It's like if you are walking on the road and fall over a pile of dirt, you don't tell the whole world about it—you take a shower and forget it ever happened.

It's as simple as that.

* * *

During one of those days when I was alone in the house, I burnt the letters of my first boyfriend. Breathing in the smoke, reliving his slap at Elliot Park and his threat—'You will see how I destroy your whole life in a month'—I had my first panic attack. I thought it would have been better if I was raped or had acid thrown at my face. I had no scar to show as medical evidence. The thought was so sickening that I puked yellow water over the ashes of my old love letters.

My elder sister—the blue-eyed girl of the family—was going through her first heartbreak. Her issues were more painful than those of her younger sister hating her existence. During my meltdowns, she made it clear with sharp-edged words that I was making things up for attention, that I was in a hurry to grow up. She never faced any problems with the brothers, so, how could I? She was prettier than me, she was smarter than me, she spoke fluently while I fumbled to say even one sentence clearly, she went to the best schools while I soiled my pants because I was afraid to ask the teacher if I could use the toilet. Of course it was a game I played to blackmail my family. Just like my polycystic ovary syndrome pains were a ploy to get more attention.

It made me angry at that time, but now I think she was right. Perhaps I did crave attention. I wanted attention and reassurance from my mother. I wanted lots of hugs, kisses, and maybe dozens of ice creams. I wanted her to tell me it wasn't my fault.

But that never happened.

* * *

When I was fifteen, I tried to kill myself for the first time. I locked myself in the bathroom with a rusty blade and held it close to the green vein on my wrist. My head was fogged with the horrid visuals of that crowded culvert where a man had brushed past my eleven-year-old self and groped my breast. I was with my mother, clutching her hand tight so that I wouldn't get lost in the crowd. The man came back—this time I saw his face—and groped me again. This time so tight that even my legs pained.

Later, I was told he did that because the fabric of my top defined my breasts in a wrong way. My sister said that I wanted people to look at me, so they looked. I made up the other stuff to build a sob story.

I touched the rusty blade to my vein and watched the blood coming out. I banged the back of my head to the bathroom wall until the blade fell from my hand. I was never brave enough to end it all with one smooth gash or stand up to the cousins, my ex, that stranger on the culvert and many others who rubbed their libido into my body without consent.

Every predator I faced crawled on my skin like leeches, just like my own lack of defiance.

When I developed appendicitis pain, my mother took me to a local vaidh or herbalist. To detect the source of the problem, he put his hand into my frock from the top and reached my belly to inspect. My mother sat there, worried about my stomachache, but oblivious to his unacceptable diagnosis procedure. I was seventeen then. Later, when I asked her if I had inherited my stupidity from her, she cried and said she had faith in the vaidh, and I was overreacting, as usual. I was a bad child who couldn't fathom the amount of anxiety I gave her for skipping meals every time I had a meltdown.

A few weeks later when they brought me out of the operation theatre after taking the appendix out, half-awake, I realized I had lived all my life in the same daze—without the anesthesia. Life happened the way it had to but I remained at where I began—frozen.

I was still the same person my grandparents refused to visit after birth because I was a girl. My paternal aunts taunted my mother for my dark skin and masculine features, while my elder sister had the face of the goddess Lakshmi. I saw my mother break down every time they left. It was *her* misfortune I couldn't please my relatives as a child.

But I couldn't become a different person because of how life happened to me.

Mine is not a story of inspiration. I'm in my thirties and I still have recurring nightmares where the people I love stand around doing nothing as they watch me getting violated. Mine is not a story of fighting back. My body still carries the imprints of bad touch.

But I no longer care if anyone thinks I'm making things up. I have pulled up the carpet, and my truth is out there. Turn your face, shove it under a new carpet if the truth makes you uncomfortable, but I don't allow you to tell me I invited it. Not anymore.

WOMEN ARE CHARPAI

Selma Tufail

Salama's words of wisdom for any woman with marital problems are always, 'Bibi, women are charpai.' She always says this with a slight shrug of her shoulders and a defeated look in her eyes. I wonder why she compares women to a traditional string cot commonly used all over Pakistan.

For almost two decades, Salama has been the cook in a friend's house. Her husband is an unemployed drug addict. The only son of his parents, he expects his wife and children to care for him the way his mother did. He, on the other hand, is an abusive husband and father. Thanks to Salama's job, the whole family lives in a small quarter in the housing usually reserved for factory workers in this major industrial city of Punjab.

'Peace', that is what her name means, but it is a far cry from the reality of her existence.

***

The European Institute for Gender Equality defines gender-based violence as:

'...violence directed against a person because of their gender. Both women and men experience gender-based violence but the majority of victims are women and girls. Gender-based violence and violence against women are often used interchangeably as it has been widely acknowledged that most gender-based violence is inflicted on women and girls, by men.'[128]

Gender-based violence remains a major issue for women and girls in South Asia. Despite the tireless efforts of social workers and numerous NGOs, the situation on the ground remains much the same. With issues ranging from the identification, apprehension, and castigation of perpetrators to the healing of traumatized victims and their reintegration into society as healthy individuals, the challenges are enormous.

Women and girls in rural areas bear the brunt of this imbalance of human rights. While access to opportunities for self-empowerment, such as education, public transport, and a wider range of employment options makes life a little easier for women and girls living in urban areas, their lives are still far from perfect. Salama and her family are city-dwellers. The Department of International Development, United Kingdom, has found that in Pakistan:

> 'Most of the violence against women, particularly in the domestic sphere, goes unreported. Approximately 70-90 per cent of Pakistani women in rural areas are subjected to domestic violence.'[129]

The subjugation of women over centuries has allowed abusive behavior to infiltrate every aspect of life. And because of this deep-rooted, unchallenged acceptance of abuse, there is no simple way to surgically remove it from our society. Reversing this systemic subjugation in an intrinsically patriarchal environment will prove to be a Herculean effort, mainly because each action on its own may not necessarily be considered abuse but, put together, it has a major effect on an individual's sense of self-worth. For any affirmative action to be effective, every aspect of violence—from the cause and perpetuation by the abuser to the protection and empowerment of the victim—must be addressed in parallel. The goal must be to create an environment with a balanced, equitable distribution of power between genders.

***

As mentioned earlier, the comparison of a woman to a charpai is a little confusing at first. These string cots are an integral part of every household and also of a woman's dowry. The groom's charpai is always larger than that of the bride. The legs are traditionally painted a garish red much like a traditional bride herself—a red bridal dress, red bedsheets, red henna. Everything is red. I try to find the connection as I listen to Salama's story. Below is a narrative based on what she told me a few years ago.

Salama had been married for over twenty-five years. Six years into her marriage and two baby girls later, she finally gave birth to a baby boy, Aslam. Zakia, the second daughter, was just ten months old when Aslam was born. She still slept in the cradle hammock tied to the side of Salama's charpai. There was a tray of sand placed directly under the makeshift cradle to catch the baby's urine during the night—a simple cost-effective alternative to nappies or diapers used by many young mothers in low-income communities.

Laddoos were sent around the workers' colony to celebrate the arrival of the first son. The births of Misbah, the eldest, and then Zakia, had been celebrated with sticky orange jalebis because laddoos were special and only distributed on the birth of boys. This is how it begins, with seemingly insignificant acts of discrimination.

Caring for three young children alongside a full-time job at my friend's house was too much for Salama, so Zakia was unceremoniously plucked from the security of her mother's charpai and sent to her maternal grandparents' house. The rationale being that she was too young to understand that her mother and the charpai were now needed for the baby boy. This was Zakia's first lesson in placing her brother's needs over her own. There would be many more to follow.

Salama's mother brought Zakia over every so often. The little girl would play 'house' in the triangular space made by the charpai leaning against the courtyard wall. That's where she ate her meals and played with her doll, choosing not to interact with her siblings. She now had two more: a second brother and a baby sister. When she tired of playing house, she would climb up the slope of the string cot, plugging her little toes in the gaps of the weave. Once at the top, she'd climb onto the wall and peep into the neighbours' courtyard. Then, she'd walk along the top of the wall and climb onto the roof of the house. Salama tried to stop her but Zakia never paid heed. She had a mind of her own. Zakia stayed with her grandparents for almost twelve years. Then, not wanting to take on the responsibility of a menstruating girl, they sent her back at the onset of puberty.

After school, Zakia used to join Salama at my friend's house. She helped her mother cook and clean, then went indoors, found a quiet corner, and did her schoolwork. She attended a different school from her siblings—apparently a better one that her grandmother had enrolled her in. She was always asking questions, always wanting to know more. She also studied English with a lot more enthusiasm than her siblings. With a more disciplined approach to life, Zakia was definitely a better student.

My friend—an educator by profession—promised to fund Zakia's university education when she got through high school. She had made the same promise to all of Salama's children. The other two girls dropped out of middle school, one got married and the other works as a maid in another house. Both the boys joined the factory—one at the age of thirteen, the other a couple of years later. They were clearly not suited to academic pursuits.

Zakia was different. She went on to get teaching credentials and my friend found her a teaching position in a local school. My friend is a firm believer in education being the solution to all problems, big and small.

* * *

The government invests resources for the welfare of the national population in general, but its efforts tend to favour men. A report published by Human Rights Watch titled 'Shall I Feed my Daughter or Educate Her?' states:

'Pakistan was described as "among the world's worst performing countries in education" at the 2015 Oslo Summit on Education and Development. The new government, elected in July 2018, stated in their manifesto that nearly 22.5 million children are out of school. Girls are particularly affected. Thirty-two percent of primary school age girls are out of school in Pakistan, compared to 21 per cent of boys…Only 13 per cent of girls are still in school by ninth grade. Both boys and girls are missing out on education in unacceptable numbers, but girls are worst affected.'

Non-governmental organizations like the Malala Fund support education for girls both within Pakistan and in other developing countries but it is not enough. According to the same Human Rights Watch report:

'Pakistan spends far less on education than is recommended by the United Nations Educational, Scientific and Cultural Organization (UNESCO) in its guidance on education.'

Changes in government policies and budget allocations to support the empowerment of women must be a substantial part of the solution.

Having acknowledged that education is an extremely useful resource to help establish financial independence in general, there are, in my opinion, many other impediments that restrict the self-empowerment of women in the country. Lack of basic healthcare, mobility, and access to public spaces in general confines women to low-paying jobs and traps them either into a life of financial dependence on men, or poverty. These are just some of the areas that need to be addressed by city planners and local and provincial governments.

* * *

Now that Zakia was a teacher, she dressed smartly. She enjoyed teaching the nursery classes and her confidence grew. There were a number of mothers in her community who were eyeing her as a potential daughter-in-law. Salama and her husband made the best choice they could from the pool of suiters and within a year, Zakia was a married woman. She was also working as a full-time teacher.

Zakia was well aware of her worth at the time of her marriage. She had worked very hard to achieve that success. It was a challenge catering to the whims of every member of the joint family of which she had now become a member. In a culture where women are expected to be the gatekeepers of peace for the greater good, Zakia struggled to fit into the submissive role of a non-person, as expected of her in the early years of her marriage. Her financial independence was a double-edged sword. The more her self-confidence grew, the less likely she was to submit to the demands of her in-laws and her husband's extended family. In the end, it was her ovaries that let her down.

Married life, for most young women in her part of the world, revolved around the ability to produce babies. Zakia was having a hard time conceiving. Her in-laws believed it was because of the stress from her job. They pressurized her to stop working. She resigned. It took a good eighteen months and numerous visits to doctors and shrines before she finally became pregnant. There was also the taweez which her mother brought from a holy man. She sewed the folded piece of paper into her pillow. The cryptic numbers and symbols written on the taweez would help her conceive—or so they believed.

Pregnant at last, Zakia enjoyed some months of peace. Then, when she gave birth to a baby girl, the situation took a turn for the worse. She had not provided them with a male child, so her value as a wife dropped considerably. Nasty comments intensified as she and her daughter now became a burden on her poor husband. They were nothing more than parasites. Despite the perception of her worthlessness, she was not allowed to return to work. They would not let her former self-confident attitude return.

'I told her to do what they expected of her—to not talk back—to not let her frustration show on her face even,' Salama tells me. 'I told her a woman is nothing more than a charpai. She has to understand that. There is no point in trying to change her fate. This is how life is. They criticize Zakia for everything: her appearance, her speech, her daughter—everything.' She smiles wearily and repeats an age-old saying, '*Why does she rock forwards and backwards as she kneads the dough?* In their eyes, whatever Zakia does and however she does it is wrong. It will continue to be like this until she produces a son.'

At some point, Zakia decided to start tutoring children at home. The meagre income it generated made her feel less of a burden and the work took her mind off the day-to-day squabbles at home. This little bit of control she regained over her life gave her strength. There was a bedsheet separating a little corner of her room from the sleeping area. Zakia had hung it over a wire connected to two nails on adjacent walls. Her students usually came in the evening when the school day was over. The curtain gave her husband privacy as he relaxed on his charpai on the other side.

One day, as Zakia was teaching her neighbour's daughter she noticed that the bedsheet had not been fully pulled across the wire. She got up and fixed it. This happened again the following week and, thinking she had not pulled it properly, she fixed it again. This happened a few more times. Zakia then realized that something was not right because this only happened when her neighbour's adolescent daughter came for tutoring.

The next week, she waited for her young student to arrive, having made sure the curtain was fully drawn. She seated herself on the stool facing the curtain and waited. A few minutes later, she saw her husband's hand slowly sliding the bedsheet to one side. When he saw her facing him, he was momentarily taken aback. Zakia got up, glared at him, and forcefully closed the curtain.

Now that he had been caught, and (wordlessly) reprimanded, Zakia's husband lost control. His fragile ego couldn't handle the embarrassment, especially in front of the girl he had been ogling for weeks. He pulled his wife through the curtain and started hitting her. The young student quickly picked up her books and fled. Zakia, who was also angry, shouted and confronted him through her tears. He grabbed her by her arm and threw her into the courtyard. The other family members came out to see what was going on. By this time, Zakia was being beaten with the wooden paddle used for washing clothes. No one intervened.

Zakia dragged herself out into the street without shoes on her feet or a chador to cover her head. Blood was streaming down her face and one of her eyes was swollen. Her neighbour helped her into her home and called Salama. That day, Zakia moved back to her parents' house—without her daughter.

A few days later, when Zakia had recovered enough to speak, she asked for her daughter. Salama explained that her in-laws would never allow her daughter to join her. They may not have wanted the girl, but she was their blood. She was their property. If Zakia wanted to be with her daughter, she would have to go home. Where else could she go? But Zakia didn't want to go back. So Salama took Zakia's case to the local jirga.

* * *

The local community has a major role to play in the protection of women and girls. In traditional Pakistani communities, there is usually an elder, or a group of elders who take the responsibility for resolving domestic disputes. This all-male committee is called a jirga. In my opinion, expecting a group of men to protect the rights of female victims of gender violence is nothing short of allowing the fox to guard the hen house. This set-up is more likely to prevent the victim from receiving justice—more of a hindrance than the much-needed help she is looking for. This committee usually serves only to reinforce a woman's inferior status in society. They propagate the requisite subservience of a female taught through selective religious texts and instructions.

* * *

A few days later, Salama and her son-in-law were called to state their respective accounts of the case to the jirga. When both sides had been heard, the head of the jirga offered a few words of wisdom. He said women should be respected because that is what their religion taught them. According to him, women in the West were not treated with the same respect as they were in Eastern cultures. However, he added, it was just as important for women to make themselves worthy of that respect. They should be obedient and submissive because their husband was their majazi khuda—a term based on a hadith (narration of sayings) that if a sajda (prostration) was permitted for anyone other than Allah, it would be for a husband by his wife. Like Allah, a husband has every right over his wife, and a wife should always try and please her husband.

Then the head of the committee turned to Salama and told her that her son-in-law was at fault. He said that she could beat him as much as she felt was necessary to feel her daughter had received justice.

Salama sat on the low stool staring at her feet. Tears streamed down her cheeks. She wanted to beat him senseless the way he had beaten Zakia, but what would that achieve? Any action she took today would backfire later, and her daughter would bear the brunt of those actions. She thought back to the efforts of her own mother, my friend's encouragement and financial support for Zakia's education, and Zakia's own hard work. How did any of that protect Zakia from her fate with this man? Despite everything, Zakia's fate wasn't much better than Salama's.

Putting a maternal hand on her son-in-law's head, Salama forgave him publicly. The next day, Salama took Zakia back to her husband, hoping that this time, things would be different—better.

When she was ready to leave and return to her own abusive husband, Salama hugged her daughter and whispered, 'Remember child, women are charpai—we stay where we are put. We don't decide our fate.'

* * *

Protection offered by the immediate family is perhaps the most important of all. The extent of family support offered to the victim when gender violence is reported is crucial—especially if the perpetrator is a family member. Questions we must ask ourselves include: is the abuser being protected in a shroud of silence by the rest of the family? What are the repercussions for the victim of the abuse? Is she blamed and shamed? Are the women and girls of the family expected to walk on eggshells to ensure their personal safety around this particular family member? How much control do the women and girls have over their own bodies? How does one protect vulnerable women and girls in the private spaces of their lives—their own homes? This is perhaps the biggest hurdle we will need to cross.

* * *

Zakia is still living under the same roof as her husband—her abuser. Has she learned the survival skills her mother has tried to teach her? How many times will she be beaten in her own home? Will she ever produce a son? Will she make a space for herself as an individual in her own home? Or has she finally transformed herself into a charpai?

The end of her story could be any, or all of the above. How did she get there? Her life started off on a path which was believed to be the best way forward—the way to self-empowerment and financial independence. Who, then, is to blame for the situation in which she finds herself? The government, for failing to provide the necessary infrastructure for the self-empowerment of women? Salama, for pulling her daughter down to her own level of helplessness? My friend, for giving Zakia unfounded hope for a better life? Zakia's grandmother, for enrolling her in a good school and setting her up for disappointment? Her abusive husband? Her in-laws and the extended family? Her neighbours? The all-male jirga? Who?

My younger self might have said everyone in Zakia's life who participated in her abuse, actively or passively, has to assume responsibility for her suffering. But now, with many more decades of experience, I believe that the situation is a lot more complex than that. We need to focus on the ideology that leads to the subjugation of women in our society and every single source that promotes it. In addition to all the characters mentioned above, we need to examine the role of our national media. What messages are being expounded by the 'talking heads' on our screens? Which organizations support these ideas that the 'scholars' and 'experts' disseminate? Who stands to benefit from them? Because it is certainly not our women and girls.

The actions and the inaction of all the characters in Zakia's life (and the lives of all the other abused women and girls in our society) are only the symptoms of the disease. The disease is the ideology that supports the degradation of the basic human rights of women and girls. That is where we need to focus the bulk of our attention. It is this ideology that needs to change if we really want to empower the whole population of the nation.

PART TWO
Imagined Realities

THE WITCH

Aruna Chakravarti

Malda, 1956

Eidun was twelve when her father fell in love with her. Her body had just started putting out tender sprigs with tiny buds rippling at the tips. Her mind was a sea of rain-washed leaves. Tremulous and teary. Brimming over. Perhaps that was why her father fell in love with her. He liked to see women weep.

On the nights that he drew the sack curtain against the others, Eidun rose from her kantha at first light and stepping across the crumbling wall of the mosque, came and stood in the graveyard. 'Ai Eidun,' her dead grandmother beckoned to her with skeletal fingers, and the dying moon and stars nodded their heads at the girl. Eidun sank on her haunches by the aush vine that had pushed a pale green shoot through the brown earth of Zaitoon Bibi's grave six months ago and now ran lush and wanton all over it.

'*O lo! O Eidun!*' The dead woman's voice called in a cracked whisper. 'Why do you weep?'

'Nani *go!*' Eidun let her tears fall on the spiky leaves and paddy gold flowers of the aush. 'Why don't you take me in your arms and let me lie beside you? To sleep under the moon and stars?'

'Hush child!' the ancient voice rumbled from a phlegm-filled throat. 'Why should *you* lie beside me? There's bhaat in your father's house. Eat your fill and wait for the prince who is coming for you.'

'Prince!' Eidun's voice was resentful. 'There is no prince.'

'There is. There must be. You were born for some other world. Some other destiny. You will live your life with someone kind and beautiful. You will know love such as you've never known before. I knew that the moment you were born. Be patient...wait...wait.'

The voice wavered like a dying flame and was snuffed out as an enormous crimson sun tilted its head precariously from the edge of Pannajhuri Lake. 'Don't go Nani. Don't go!' Eidun flung herself on the grave, the rough leaves and fronds of the aush chafing her tender breasts. 'Take me with you!'

But the grandmother was gone and so were the moon and stars with her. And now the sun rose, a great flaming orb against which a cloud of bats wheeled, their crooked wings moving in languorous silence. Eidun trembled and balls of sweat, large and heavy as raindrops, broke out all over her body. The night of dread was over but another day and another night awaited her...

'*Bh-a-a-at...*' Zaitoon Bibi's voice came to her ears in a long-drawn-out croak, '*Bh-a-a-a-t...*' Eidun's lips twisted in a bitter smile. In the last days of her life, Nani had thought and spoken of nothing but rice. And the obsession had followed her to the grave...

Zaitoon Bibi had lived at the far edge of Hasanpur in a tiny hovel with nothing in it except a mud pot and a tattered kantha. The few square yards of land around it were parched stony earth. Nothing grew on it except a tamarind tree whose branches swept the roof of the hut. The tree was as old and gnarled, as starved and barren as its mistress. They had both yielded fruit, year after year, in their breeding years, but now there was nothing left in their wombs but a raging hunger that burned day and night, feeding on them like a canker...nibbling, gnawing, hollowing their bodies from within.

Zaitoon Bibi rose at dawn each day and, rubbing the catarrh from her eyes with the edge of the rag she wore, came and squatted under the tree, her form dark and shadowy against the hoary trunk. She sat in infinite patience, her body immobile, till she saw her son-in-law, Moin-ud-din, approach, his daughter Eidun trailing behind him. 'O Baba Moin!' she called out ingratiatingly, 'Up and about so early! Where are you taking the goats? To the east bank?'

Moin-ud-din drove his herd past her hut but did not deign to reply. 'What a good hardworking boy!' she tried again, 'May Moulah's blessings fall on your head, my son! May my years be added to yours.'

Moin-ud-din stopped but did not look back at her. Lifting his lungi, he scratched at a patch of ringworm on his thigh. '*Hatt! Hatt!*' he prodded his goats with the babla branch he carried in his hand and sauntered on—chest puffed out in self-importance.

'Eidun *re!*' In her desperation to be heard the old woman called out to her granddaughter, 'Are they all well at home?'

'All well, Nani,' the girl answered quickly and hastened after her father.

'Why do you waste your time talking to that old crone?' Moin-ud-din barked at her. 'Have you nothing better to do?'

'I only answered her question.'

'There's no need to. Ignore her. She has the evil eye, and every child who comes near her shrivels up and dies. She has killed off all her own and now she is after mine. Have I not told you that, time and again?'

'She has never harmed us, Abba.'

'Why do you think your three brothers died in a row? Why so many of my children were stillborn? The old hag sucks the marrow from their bones while still in the womb and leaves them dead and dry as jute stalks. And that worthless woman, your mother, lets her.'

'But Ojju Bubu is alive and Meroo Bubu and I and Jeeni.'

'Hah!' Moin-ud-din's yellow teeth flashed in a bitter laugh. 'She takes my sons and spares the girls who are of no use to me. Who eat my rice and talk back...'

'I didn't talk back, Abba. I only...'

'Quiet. Disobey me once more and I will punish you. No ordinary punishment.' He turned a baleful eye on her. 'Something so terrible you'll wish you were dead.'

'I wish I were dead already,' Eidun muttered, taking care not to let her words reach her father's ears.

Zaitoon Bibi sat where she was for a long time. Then, after the two figures had disappeared beyond the grove of mango trees that separated the villages of Hasanpur and Peerpur, she straightened her back, her hump throbbing as though red-hot needles were being jabbed into it and rose to her feet. Reaching for the length of bamboo that served her as a walking stick, she started off on her long, slow, daily hobble to the other end of the village where the terracotta palaces of the ancient kingdom of Goud were crumbling to dust. Where her daughter Ruksana lived.

Part of her way lay through the Hindu palli. As she walked past the pond, stopping from time to time to pick a few greens and herbs that grew at the edge, she saw someone approaching her from the opposite direction. It was a young woman dressed in a coarse but crackling new sari with rows of plastic bangles on her arms. Her brow and parting were bright red with sindoor, and a tiny gold stud winked wickedly from one nostril. She walked with an attitude, her body swaying this way and that, the brass pot at her hip swinging lasciviously.

'*Tui ke lo*? Who are you, girl? Are you from Peerpur?' Zaitoon Bibi put up a hand to shield her eyes from the sun's glare and peered into the face before her. Her mouth opened in a grin. '*Aa maran!*' she exclaimed, 'These old eyes are no good to me these days. Of course, I know who you are. You are Madhusudan's new bride, aren't you?' The girl simpered and looked demure but did not answer. 'Your mother-in-law has put you to work already, I see.' Zaitoon Bibi frowned in annoyance. 'What can she be thinking of? A bride of yesterday being sent out to fetch water! *Chhi! Chhi! Chhi!* I must have a word with her.'

Still, the girl didn't speak. She didn't go away either. 'But Madhu is kinder to you, is he not?' Zaitoon Bibi grinned and stroked the downy cheek with her claw-like fingers, 'Tell me, Naat Bou,' she inched close. 'What does he do with you at night? Does he kiss this pretty face *mchoo mchoo* like this?' Her toothless mouth puckered up and she made kissing sounds in the air.

'Jah!' the girl gave her a push but didn't look displeased, 'You're a nosy old woman.' Tossing her head, she flounced away. 'I won't tell you a thing.'

'*O lo!*' Zaitoon Bibi called after her. 'I may be a nosy old woman today, but I was young once. And loved by my husband just as you are.'

The old woman hobbled on. She felt tired already though she hadn't walked even half the way. Passing Nitai Pal's cowshed, she peeped in. A fat black woman squatted on the ground, squeezing the udders of a bony, white cow that looked as sick and dispirited as its mistress was vigorous and healthy.

Really! Zaitoon Bibi thought indignantly. *These people know nothing about rearing cows.* She had kept a cow while living in Peerpur. Her beloved Begum jaan. What a glossy black coat she had! What clear shining eyes! She had taken Begum every day at dawn to the east bank of the lake where the tenderest grass grew. She had saved all the fruit and vegetable peelings of the household and fed them to her with her own hands. She had even stolen bhaat from her mother-in-law's kitchen and dumped it surreptitiously in Begum's trough. She had washed her and dried her coat. She had talked and sung to her.

She remembered Begum's last day in Peerpur. Begum had sensed that she was being forced out of the house. That she was leaving, never to return. She had nuzzled Zaitoon Bibi's neck and breast and looked at her with pleading eyes. Zaitoon Bibi could swear that she had seen tears running down Begum's cheeks. Poor Begum! Who knows what became of her? *Cows are like human beings*, she thought wistfully, *they need to be loved and nurtured.*

She sighed and fixed her glance on the white cow. It looked as though it was ready to drop down dead any moment. Its head hung listlessly to one side and it seemed too tired to even lift its tail and wave away the flies that buzzed around its emaciated rump. Zaitoon Bibi opened her mouth to impart some wisdom in the woman's ears but thought better of it. There were more important matters at hand.

'*O lo!* O Shona Bou!' Zaitoon Bibi called.

'*Ke?* Oh, it's you!' The woman rose to her feet. She held a small pot of milk in one hand. A naked baby hung precariously from one hip.

'How is Nitai today? Has the fever gone?'

'Yes. The fever and vomiting have both gone. He ate jhol bhaat for the first time yesterday. He wants go back to work in a day or two.'

'Allah be praised! But work can wait. He must get back his strength first.'

'That's what I tell him. But will he listen?'

Zaitoon Bibi was very tired by now. Her legs were shaking and she was hungry and thirsty. She wished Shona Bou would invite her into the house for a rest and offer her a pot of water and a lump of gur. But just at this point the baby created a diversion. It set up a piercing wail and began kicking and screaming, banging his little fists against his mother's breast.

'Hai Allah!' Zaitoon Bibi cried out, startled. 'What ails the boy?'

'He has the shitting sickness. His belly's been running like rain since yesterday.'

'Ah...the poor little mite!' Zaitoon Bibi fished into the pile of greens she had collected in a corner of her sari and came up with a handful. 'Here, take these gandal leaves. I picked them for Rukku. She birthed a boy day before yesterday and she too has the shitting sickness, as new mothers do. Boil them for half an hour then cool and strain with a clean cloth and feed to the baby three or four times today. And only the thinnest rice gruel. No milk.'

Shona Bou nodded and hurried into the house with the bawling baby. Zaitoon Bibi sighed and started walking again. She passed a number of homesteads but there was no one outside and she was hesitant to walk in without permission. Then, after what seemed an inordinately long time, she came across old Harihar Kundu sitting in a canvas chair on the veranda of his house smoking a hookah. Zaitoon Bibi dragged her feet over the last few steps and dropped down on the floor beside him. He looked at her out of the corner of his eye but said nothing.

'*Ki go*, Hari Dada!' Zaitoon Bibi said as soon as she had recovered her breath, 'Why are you sitting all alone puffing phuruth phuruth at your hookah? Where are all your cronies?'

Harihar Kundu frowned. 'At my age,' he answered, his jowls shaking with self-pity, 'cronies are either dead or dying. What else can I do but sit alone and wait to join them?'

'Allah forbid!' Zaitoon Bibi touched her ears and bit her tongue, 'You are in fine condition. Don't tempt Providence by uttering such unholy words.'

'Hmph!' the old man grunted and turned a baleful glance on her.

'And you...you're no chicken either. What are *you* doing walking this distance every day at your age? All for a meal. What's wrong with Moin? He passes your hut every morning on his way to the lake. Why can't he carry some food for you?'

'He leaves the house at dawn. The cooking is done much later.'

'He can bring you some dry provisions, can't he?'

'He has offered to...many times,' she lied glibly, 'but the truth is, Hari Dada, my cooking days are over. I don't have the energy anymore.'

'Strange! You have the energy to walk two miles and back in sun, wind and rain every day! But you can't find the energy to light a couple of faggots and set a pot to boil!'

Zaitoon Bibi was trapped. She waited a few seconds them mumbled softly, 'I...I...could I have some water Hari Dada?'

'Yes, yes. Why not? *Ore ke acchish re*!' He turned his head to the door and roared in a voice that belied his eighty-three years. 'Zaitoon is here. She wants some water.'

Zaitoon Bibi understood why he had made a point of mentioning her name. Special vessels were kept in Hindu households for Muslims. But the knowledge brought no bitterness. *Different people behave in different ways*, she thought in easy acceptance. *Allah tells us to live and let live.*

In a while, one of Harihar's granddaughters came in with an earthen pot of water and a large coconut ball wrapped in a piece of banana leaf. 'Here, Nani,' she held her hands out with a smile. She watched as the old woman drained the pot in one swallow and said, her eyes round with surprise, 'You were *really* thirsty! Do you want some more?'

'In a while. After I've eaten.' Zaitoon Bibi ate the sweet sticky confection greedily, rolling it over and over between her toothless gums, then drank some more water and sighed in satisfaction.

'Thank you, child,' she said wiping her mouth with the end of her sari. 'May Allah shower his blessings on you.' She sat comfortably, her back resting against a pillar, chatting with her host, picking up the thread of the conversation they were having before it had become embarrassing.

'Where is Gopal Babu?' she asked, 'He's neither dead nor dying. I saw him only yesterday.'

'Gopal has gone to Malda town for a bride-viewing.'

'For whom?'

'His grandson Lalit.'

'Lalu!' Zaitoon Bibi exclaimed. 'Is he old enough to get married?'

'Gopal seems to think so. He's bent on seeing another generation of his line before his death.'

Zaitoon Bibi sighed. *Little Lalu,* she thought, *it seems only the other day that he was born. I helped with the birthing. It was a difficult delivery.* Mouthing a few stock phrases about how swiftly time passes, Zaitoon Bibi rose to her feet.

An hour later, Zaitoon Bibi stood outside the broken archway that led to the cluster of tenements that housed the poorest Muslims of Malda. Her breath came and went as though her lungs were a pair of bellows. Her legs tottered under her feather light torso and runnels of sweat streamed down her face and got lodged in the hot, brown creases. She looked around furtively. There was no one nearby.

'Rukku,' she called softly, 'Rukku!' But just as she took a step forward, her eldest granddaughter turned a corner and walked towards her. The end of the girl's sari was damp and sagging under a pile of kolmi greens. Some of the stems had escaped the confines of the coarse brown cloth and hung out, waving fat green leaves and tendrils bursting with sap. Zaitoon Bibi swallowed painfully. Ojju, whom she loved so much, was her sworn enemy. She was her father's daughter entirely and hated her as much as he did. Her tongue spat venom more viciously than a snake's. A wave of panic rose in the old woman's breast. Conquering it with difficulty she smiled, revealing grey puckered gums. 'Ah! Look who's here! Arjumand Banu! My beauty! My angel!' The words rolled off her tongue unctuously though she knew very well that her granddaughter was neither beautiful nor angelic. Peering into the bundle at the girl's waist she sucked her cheeks greedily. 'You picked kolmi? What will you make with it? Jhol or chenchki?'

'What are you doing here?' Ojju fixed a stern eye on her grandmother. 'Hasn't Abba told you to keep away from us?'

'I came to see your mother. I brought some kalmegh. Jeeni said she had a bellyache.' Ignoring Ojju's scornful snort, she went on with a sort of desperation. 'Kalmegh is very good for newly nursing mothers. It relieves after-birth pangs.'

'You're not here to give us anything. You're here to fill your maw. To snatch the little rice we have from our mouths. You do it every day, you shameless...'

'*Tobah! Tobah*! How you talk! Your father is a king. There's enough bhaat in his house to fill twenty stomachs...'

'You not only stuff that bottomless pit of your stomach from our share, you even cast your evil eye on us. You're a witch. Everyone knows...'

'*Moulah! Moulah*!' The old woman raised her hands to the sky.

'Abba has complained about you to the elders of the village. They met yesterday and took a decision. They are going to make a public proclamation on Tuesday at the weekly haat.'

'What proclamation?'

'That you're a witch. What else? You'd better not walk the village paths again. You'll be stoned to death.'

'But I...I've never,' Zaitoon Bibi's long, thin face shook like a bamboo leaf in a storm. 'I've never harmed anyone. I don't even know how...'

'Witch! Witch! Witch!' Ojju shrieked shrilly. 'Haven't you stuffed your stomach already with all the blood it can hold? You want more? Get out of our tenement before I pick up my broomstick and lash the life out of you!' Pushing the old woman aside with a sharp thrust of her elbow she went in.

'Ojju *re*!' A feeble voice came from within. 'How can you be so cruel? Your Nani is old and cannot fend for herself. Give her a handful of bhaat from the cooking pot. No one will miss it.'

'You shut your mouth. What do *you* do all day except lie on your kantha and order me about? I must cook, scrub the vessels, wash your babies' bums and also listen to your lectures. What do you take me for?'

'Wait till you get married.' The voice turned into a whimper. 'Wait till you bear a child every year only to see it die before your eyes. Wait till all your flesh and blood is consumed and only the bones are left...'

'Who kills your children? Don't you know? Yet you let the blood-sucking witch come and eat from our share. Shame on you! Abba should have kicked you out long ago and brought another woman.'

'*Hai re*!' The mother broke into loud sobs. 'My own daughter wants me out of the house! You'll get a stepmother soon enough, never fear. You won't have to wait for long.'

Ojju's mouth tightened cruelly around her buck teeth. 'And you...' she turned on her grandmother who had tottered to a heap on the ground. 'Get up this minute and go back to your hellhole if you value your daughter's life. Abba said he would come home early today. You know what he'll do to your precious Rukku if he finds you here.' Picking up the broom that rested in one corner, she waved it in the old woman's face...

Zaitoon Bibi sat outside her hovel under the tamarind tree, her bony back fitting neatly into the hollow of its trunk. It was the hour of twilight. The shadows of tree and woman had moved away and merged with the dark. The old woman clutched her stomach. How empty it felt! No, not empty. It was swollen with cold, bleak wind that moved upwards clawing for space, sending spasms of pain shrieking through her ribs. Her mouth quivered and pouted like a child's. *Amma re-e-e*! she wept for her mother, dead and buried these fifty years. *Khete de*! *Khidei mori*...(Give me food. I am dying of hunger.)

She peered into the night, ears cocked, as though she really expected her mother to come to her with a bowl of rice in her hands. Then, when all she could see was the deepening dusk and all she could hear was the rushing of bats' wings in the branches above her head, she opened the knot in her sari in which the kalmegh leaves she had gathered that morning lay dark and wilting. She took a few and crammed them into her mouth. At the first hit of the bitter black juice, her empty stomach revolted, and she vomited noisily on the bare earth. Her head reeled and sank on her breast. *Miyan go-o-o*! she groaned, calling out to the husband who had left the earth so long ago that she had lost count of the years. *Tu kotha...?* (Where are you?)

With this cry, the present receded and the past was with her. She was sitting on a mat on the floor of her husband's house in Peerpur, his head in her lap. She was stroking his hair and he was looking into her face with tiny, twinkling eyes. It was a pretty face. Heart-shaped with a hint of a cleft in the chin, surprisingly light eyes and a glittering black mole on a smooth brown cheek. She had been the belle of the village then, and many eyes turned to look at her as she walked to the pond, long neck held high, hips swaying, a smile on her lips. Ruksana had inherited her looks and passed them on to Eidun. The dregs had been shared by Meroo and Jeeni. Only poor Ojju had been forgotten.

The thought of Ojju brought Zaitoon Bibi to the present with a jerk. Ojju was the image of her father. Tall and brawny with a great slab of a face. She was twenty-one and unwed. Her second sister, Meroo, had been married these five years to Shamsul, the barber in Malda town, and was the mother of two already with a third one moving in her belly. Offers came for Eidun; even ten-year-old Jeeni, but none for Ojju. Even sixty-year-old Saifullah Sheikh had refused to take her for a third wife. No wonder her heart burned with spite and envy...

Zaitoon Bibi remembered the threatening broom. *Poor Ojju!* she thought sadly. *She hates everybody. She thinks no one loves her. Not her father, though she obeys every command of his. Not her mother, though she does all the work of the house. Not me, although it was I who first took her in my arms, showered her with blessings, and gave her the name of a queen. Arjumand Banu, I called her. She suffers, the little one, but none of us sense her suffering. We only see her hate and anger. A husband and a few children and all her troubles will be over! Allah go!* She prayed raising her hands in the air. *Send her a man. Rich or poor, it does not matter. Only...only let him be a good man. All she needs is a little tenderness.*

Even as she sat bemoaning Ojju's fate she heard footsteps and a hum of voices in the distance. Peering into the dark, she saw a small knot of men walking towards her. Her heart leaped with hope. She would ask them for some food. Surely, they wouldn't grudge her a handful of rice if she told them she had starved all day. They would go home and one of them would bring her some. She saw it before her eyes. A neat mound stacked on a banana leaf with a tiny heap of salt and two green chillies. She sucked in her cheeks and swallowed.

They were close enough now for her to make out their forms. Saifullah Sheikh, the village headman, walked in front—his burly, rough-tongued son Shahid by his side. Behind them came Rasool the grocer, Aslam the fishmonger, Nayeem the blacksmith and Ekram the caretaker of the mosque. There were some Hindus among them too. She could see the lanky form of Nitai Pal's brother Niranjan, the dark good-looking Madhusudan Das and two of Biswajeet Saha's sons. There were some others she could not recognize. Moin-ud-din stood right at the back—a little apart from the others.

'Baba Moin,' her voice trembled as she addressed her son-in-law. 'I die of hunger. Not a grain has passed through my lips all day. I went to see Rukku this morning. I hoped for...' But her plea was cut short.

'Zaitoon Khala,' Shahid Sheikh's harsh voice broke into her

ears. 'We cannot let you stay in our village anymore. You must leave at once.'

'Leave?' Zaitoon Bibi turned her eyes on the faces before her, one by one. 'Leave the village? Where shall I go?'

'Go back to Peerpur. From where you came.'

'But I have no one in Peerpur.'

'Your husband's family is there. His brothers and their sons.'

'But they threw me out.' She looked hopefully at Saifullah Sheikh, appealing to him as the oldest and wisest of the group. 'They threw me out the day I was widowed. My mother-in-law took away my gold nose stud and silver bangles as soon as I returned from the burial. "Get out," she said, "and don't show your face here again." I begged and pleaded. I told her what she knew already. That I had no one in the world. But she wouldn't relent. "Get out, you cat-eyed witch," she screamed and told her sons to push me out of the door. I took Rukku in my arms, she was only two then, and walked all the way to Hasanpur. What else could I do?'

Saifullah Sheikh gave an embarrassed cough and said solemnly, 'We know all that, Zaitoon Bibi. That is why we have let you live amongst us all these years. But we can't allow it any longer. Your presence is not safe for us.'

'Why? What have I done?'

'You came to our cowshed this morning,' Niranjan Pal's shrill treble rose in the air, 'and as soon as you left, our Dhabali sank down on a stack of hay. She hasn't risen since then or eaten anything. She's dying.' There was a clamour of shocked exclamations then Shahid's voice hissed in her ears like that of an angry snake. 'And Moin's newborn son died an hour after you left his house. You still ask what you have done? You're a witch. A blood-sucking witch. You're dangerous!'

And now two sharp flames flickered in Zaitoon Bibi's dim old eyes. The foul, bitter taste of the kalmegh rose from her stomach and filled her mouth. She spat on the ground and cried out in a trembling voice, 'Nitai's cow was half dead when I saw her this morning. I thought of warning Shona Bou but she, poor thing, was so distraught with Nitai and the baby both ill that I didn't want to add to her worries. As for Moin's son, he died because Moin has a secret disease in his loins. My daughter gives birth year after year. But the tiny mites are either still born or die after a few days. What do I have to do with it?'

'You are making a false accusation, Zaitoon Khala.' Aslam, Moin-ud-din's partner in his frequent trips to Bilkees Banu's brothel in Malda town, spoke in his defence. 'You may say what you like. We cannot stop you. But can you deny that all your own sons died? That only your daughter survived? Did your husband have a secret disease too? Did your mother-in-law call you a cat-eyed witch for nothing?'

'But...but...'

'Poor woman! You killed her son and grandsons! What else could she do but throw you out? And now you've done the same thing all over again. Moin's daughters you spared but what use are daughters? A man needs sons. He wants you out of the village and so do we all.'

'But I have nowhere to go.' The flames in Zaitoon Bibi's eyes turned to ash. 'I'm old and feeble. I don't have the strength...'

'We give you three days. Then we'll do what we must.'

'What will you do?'

'You'll see.'

Zaitoon Bibi sat where she was, her back resting against the tamarind trunk. The men had left hours ago but she wasn't thinking of them or their threats. Her head was filled with thoughts of a distant past and she was reliving every minute of it. The long walk from Peerpur with Rukku in her arms, crossing the mango grove, then sinking her aching legs under the shade of this tree. It had been young then. Strong and sturdy. The branches above her head had hung heavy with fruit. Great swelling bunches of pods filled with tart-sweet flesh. She had built a hut beside it with her own hands using sticks, stones, straw and whatever else she could find. The tree had helped. It had spread its rich fronds over it to form a natural roof. It had showered its fruit on the ground which she had gathered, cut, scraped and dried and sold at the haat week after week. Hers was the best, the richest, pulpiest tamarind and people bought readily from her. The tree had protected her and given her a livelihood...

Rukku had grown under its shade from a scrawny infant to a maid so lissome and lovely that old Zulfikar Quddus had been ready to pay two hundred rupees for her. For Zaitoon Bibi, who had never seen two rupees together, two hundred was a king's ransom. But she had no intention of selling her daughter. She preferred the penniless but strong, hardworking goatherd, Moin-ud-din Mirdha. Rukku had been happy in the beginning. She had borne four healthy daughters and then...then the curse had come upon her. The old woman's heart swelled with pity. Poor Rukku! Broken in body and spirit. The little girls, too! How much they suffered! Anyone who carried a drop of Zaitoon Bibi's blood in her veins suffered. Ojju! Unwanted and unloved. Vicious and violent with the injustice of fate. Meroo, living her mother's life all over again, with an abusive husband and a child every year. And Eidun...dear sweet Eidun...whom her father loved in a sick, unnatural way. Rukku knew but was powerless to protect her. *It is my fault*, Zaitoon Bibi thought, her heart twisting...*I have passed on the curse to my progeny.*

She sighed. The men had given her three days in which to leave the village. But three or thirty, they meant nothing to her. She had neither the strength nor the will to move...

On the fourth night, a few hours before dawn, a fire broke out engulfing hovel and tree in a mass of dancing flames. No one heard the old woman's screams or the frightened swishing of the tamarind branches. No one came near them. The village slept in peace.

Next morning on her way to the lake, Eidun was overcome by a strange sensation. It grew stronger as she approached her grandmother's hut. Above her head an ugly black cloud hung in the middle of a brilliant blue sky. The air felt warmer and smelled different. Eidun was frightened. 'Stop, Abba!' she called, 'Something is wrong. Terribly wrong.' But her father did not hear her. Swishing his babla branch, he urged the goats forward and walked on with rapid strides. 'Nani! Nani *go!*' Eidun ran screaming, her eyes burning from the pungent haze, her body streaming with sweat from the heat.

And then she saw them. Woman and tree...two charred old bodies...locked in an embrace.

THE PHONE CALL

Radhia Rameez

Today is the day.

He wakes up in a bad mood. She thinks it is because he has a headache, though she isn't sure. But he has that air about him, an ugliness in his face, a twisting of the lips, that watchful quietness that comes alive and fills the whole house, slithering into every corner like some swollen, noxious serpent. That's what frightens her the most, she thinks, the quietness. It would have been better if he was loud and drunk and stoned. At least then there would be something to blame, an explanation, a reason for the madness. But there is no madness, no loss of control, no heat-of-the-moment flare-ups, only cold, calculating knowledge. And the quietness, which is so loud, it is deafening. It swallows her voice. It creeps under her skin. It watches.

Even her six-year-old exists under a blanket of silence, walking around on tenterhooks, with those wide eyes far older than her years. Farha. Her baby. Her love. The reason she was still alive. How ironic that the name means joy and laughter. Because she never laughed, her daughter. She just watched, silent, like a deer trapped in a tiger pit.

She is glad Farha is at school today.

She pours the morning tea quickly, measuring out the sugar with meticulous care before dropping it into his cup; 'too much sugar,' is one of his favourite excuses for a good bash-up. While he takes a bath, she packs his lunch and irons his clothes. There's not a single wrinkle by the time the job is done, and the trouser crease is perfect. Six years of being either coldly castigated or flung across the room for something as trivial as a crooked pants crease has taught her to master perfection. She still slips up now and then, but not today. She cannot afford to give him an excuse to stay back from work. A prayer repeats in her mind, a voiceless mantra: *leave, please leave, please leave, please leave. You must leave. Leave. Leave. Leaveleaveleaveleaveleave.* Repeat a word long enough, and it either changes or ceases to have any meaning at all—she notices that the word 'leave' melds together to sound like 'live'. Or perhaps 'love'. She can't tell.

But he finally does leave. She watches him get into the car, sunglasses flashing in the morning glare, watch gleaming on his wrist. No goodbye. No acknowledgment of the breakfast, or the ironed clothes. Not even a glimpse in her direction; she might as well have been a piece of furniture. How handsome he looks today. The crisp white shirt against the brownness of his skin. The stethoscope around his neck. The shiny shoes she spends ten minutes polishing each day. She can see how people are taken in. He wears his mask well, this man.

She waits until he drives off, watching until the car disappears around the curve of the lane. Then, shutting the large iron gates, she goes back into the house, grabs the clock off the counter and sits down in his reading chair, clutching it in both hands. She counts the minutes.

Eight five a.m. He has passed the first junction.

Eight thirty a.m. He is now in Colombo.

Eight forty-five a.m. He has reached the hospital and just clocked in.

Nine a.m. The board meeting would be starting. His phone would be switched off. There would be no chance of a surprise call or visit for the next two hours.

Now.

Her heart is beating so hard that she presses her hands to her chest, trying to keep it from exploding out of her ribs. Slowly, she turns her head. Her gaze falls on the nondescript white phone, then follows the thin connecting wire to the small black device with a digital screen. The caller line identification. Caller ID box, he calls it. How innocent it looks, just sitting there, boringly flashing the time and date; but it records every incoming and outgoing call. This device was the reason he felt comfortable buying a landline for the house. This device was a part of her well-camouflaged prison.

But she has been fiddling around with it for a few weeks now. She knows how to delete information from it. There are benefits to being thought of as stupid.

Her fingers curl around the cool surface of the receiver. She lifts it, puts it to her ear. The dial tone is loud and shrill, like an endless, spiralling scream. It bores into her head. It grates on her nerves. She keeps it pressed against her skull for a minute, punishing herself. Then she reaches out her other hand, extends a forefinger, and presses down on the smooth, oblong number two button.

Beep.

The dial tone stops, abruptly. Her finger finds the number seven button.

Beep.

For a moment, there's a mad scramble of panic in her brain; has she forgotten? She had memorized it so that there was no chance of him finding it written down. Then it comes to her.

Beep. Beep. Beep. Beep. Beep. She hits the numbers in quick succession.

A pause. Then a ringing tone.

She pushes her fist into her mouth, biting down on the knuckles. Her heart has not slowed. It feels like her ribs have splintered under the blows of a battering ram. The thud-thud-thud fills her ears. Over it, she hears the steady ringing, as if from a great distance. Perhaps no one will pick up. Perhaps they're closed. For a second, she feels a wild sense of relief—time to end this madness—then there's a *clack*, and someone picks up the phone.

'*Assalamu alaikum.*' Peace be upon you. 'Colombo Grand Mosque.'

She removes her hand from her mouth. There are half-moons on her knuckles from where her teeth had sunk into them.

'Hello?'

Her voice is barely a whisper. 'Hello.'

'I'm sorry?' the man says. He speaks in Tamil. Again, the panic—what if he doesn't know English or Sinhala? She swallows.

'*Walaikum salam. T-Tamil theriya.*' I don't know Tamil. 'English? Sinhala?'

There is a pause. 'I speak English,' the man says. He has a kind, cultured voice. 'I am Moulavi Thasleem. What is your name, sister?'

'Zafira,' she replies, and immediately wants to slap herself. She gave him her real name! What if he finds out? What if they tell? What if they track her down? 'Mariam. I mean Mariam.'

'Okay.' There is a brief silence, as if he was waiting for her to go on. When she says nothing, he asks, 'How can we help you, sister…Mariam?'

She tells him then, but her thudding heart has filled her ears, and her tongue trips over itself so that all the syllables run together. The words crowd at the back of her throat and fall out of her mouth in a senseless jumble.

'I'm sorry, sister, I didn't understand. Could you repeat that?'

Stupid, stupid, stupid. Pull yourself together, you stupid woman. She slaps herself across the face sharply, once, twice. The pain clears her head. The thudding lessens slightly.

'I want to leave my husband.'

It is the first time she has said the words out loud. She wonders if the walls and the furniture will hear it, absorb it, and whisper it to him when he gets back home.

'Ah.' The Moulavi sounds a little startled. 'I see. You want to get a divorce?'

'I want to get away. He hurts us.'

'Allah has allowed divorce in Islam. Allah also does not like men who hurt their wives,' the Moulavi says. 'Tell me about yourself. Do you have children? For how long have you been married? What does your husband do?'

'I have one child. A daughter. My husband and I have been married for seven years. He's…a doctor. At Nawaloka Hospital.

He's in a meeting right now. He hurts me all the time. Even my daughter, though not as much. But it's only a matter of time before he turns on her. I need to...keep her safe. With me. I don't know what to do.'

'I am very sorry you are going through this, sister Mariam,' he says. 'What does he...hurt you about?'

'About...nothing. Everything. It can be because lunch is late. Or because the tea is cold. Or...just because. It's so strange. He takes care of me, buys me clothes, food. Sometimes, things are good. But when things get bad...' She trails off.

'Do you work, sister?'

'No.'

'Any qualifications?'

'No.'

'Any assets?'

'None.'

'If you were to get a divorce, and take the child, where would you live?'

'I—I don't know. Maybe I could stay with my family. My mother.'

'Do you know which mosque your family is affiliated with?'

She swallows. 'They're not Muslims. I was Buddhist. My family is Buddhist. I converted after I got married.'

'I see.' There is a pause, then the Moulavi clears his throat. 'How important is it to you that you get full custody of the child?'

'I would die if I lost her.'

She hears a sigh.

'Sister, do you want me to be completely honest with you?'

'Yes.'

'If you do ask for a divorce, there is a very poor chance that you will be allowed sole custody of the child.'

Time slows and stops and speeds up. She pushes her fist against her mouth again. The fingers of her other hand tighten around the receiver so hard that she thinks it might snap.

'Sister Mariam, usually, it is the mothers who get custody of young children. But your husband sounds like he has influence.

A doctor. He must have lots of connections. And rich ones at that. You don't work. You have no qualifications. Then there's the fact that your family is Buddhist. He can easily argue that keeping the child in that environment can corrupt her or lead her to leave the faith. And whether it makes sense or not, the Qazi courts are most likely to favour him.'

'But he hurts us,' she cries shrilly. 'I thought—I thought the mosque would help. Aren't you a man of faith? Do you think God would want me here, suffering?'

'Sister Mariam,' he says gently, and she thinks she hears sorrow in his voice. 'If I could go around saving all the women and children in this country, I would. In an ideal world, you would get your child, child support, and never have to see your husband again. But this is not an ideal world, and our system is corrupt. Of course, there is a chance that you could get what you want. There is a chance. But there's a much bigger chance that you will lose custody of your child to him. And once you start this chain of events, you can't go back. These are the facts.'

For a few seconds, neither of them speaks. She can hear him breathing on the other end of the line, and she wonders what he looks like, this man of God with the kind voice. She wonders if he has a wife, or a mother, or a daughter. She wonders if he beats them up, if his kindness is a mask.

'I can help you start divorce proceedings, if you'd like,' the Moulavi says. 'Can I give you my phone number?'

'No.'

'Just take it down. In case...you need it in the future.'

'I won't need it,' she whispers.

'Please. Just take it—'

'I won't need it.'

'I will pray for you,' he says. 'May Allah ease your burden. *Assalamu alaikum.*'

She replaces the receiver. The click is loud in the silence, as though she had slammed a door. Tilting the caller ID box towards her, she deletes the last outgoing number. She carefully checks it multiple times to make sure the number is gone. Then she sinks into the chair and stares into nothingness.

OVER AND OVER AGAIN

Tisa Muhaddes

Despair reigned. Anju's frail body lay cocooned in a sheath of soft cotton. Perched on the bed, I surveyed the room like an eagle scouting the lay of the land. I wanted to cry, but my voice lay smothered in the embers of unspoken thoughts. I was mute but alert.

The caravan of women—the older ones shrouded in white—floated through the rooms, commiserating in hushed tones. 'What a tragedy,' they whispered. 'How could life be so cruel to such a young girl…?'

'It wasn't accidental—they say she was pushed!' exclaimed others. 'She was so beautiful…How could she have fallen from the roof like that—and when there were other people around, too,' they continued.

'What misfortune! Look at her catatonic father curled up in a corner in the bedroom. Look at her mother pleading desperately for the return of her child,' the women said. 'What a dreadful tragedy!'

I was six when he started. It was never in a dark room. Shards of memory are my only proof. They rear their heads from the depths of an abysmal darkness, pricking and piercing me mercilessly with their truth. I see and comprehend with a clarity that shields my shame. Random scenes unfold like parts of a film that I cannot piece together, yet am forced to replay over and over again in my mind.

I remember my pigtails bobbing, my plaid dress brushing against my body as I hurried to catch the events that were causing such a commotion. 'Oh, oh, oh,' I thought. 'I must see why the children are shouting outside.' His bedroom opened out into the biggest and longest balcony overlooking our courtyard. One could stand there and glimpse the outer boundaries of our neighbourhood.

The neighbourhood then was bordered by lush, vivid foliage that shimmered and shimmied under the adoring gaze of the sun. Block-shaped white buildings rose from the earth to complement nature's greenery. Our house was the oldest in the area, our property the largest, our family the first settlers on this once-fallow land.

I exploded through the doors, oblivious to his presence in the bedroom, and made a beeline for the balcony door. It was locked and I crashed headlong into it. He laughed as he saw me rub my forehead, wincing and befuddled. He materialized from the bathroom, adjusting his pajamas, and with one swift movement, scooped me up to his chest.

I wriggled and squirmed as he admonished me to be careful. 'Open the door! Oh, open the door!' I pleaded. Laughing, he gently planted me on the floor, and unhinged the locks. Once my feet touched solid ground, I plunged forward onto the balcony, fearing that the commotion had dissipated just as I arrived. But it hadn't.

Someone had dropped a brick from our rooftop, and it had landed on the brand-new car that Sajid Bhaiya, the local heartthrob, had bought just the day before. It was prominently parked in our courtyard, basking shamelessly in the sunlight which gilded its lustrous silver body. Now the windshield was broken, a huge gash ran along its body, hundreds of little cracks branching out from the scar like small crooked fangs.

The brick lay on top—shattered, exposed, and shamed. The culprit had absconded. Sajid Bhaiya stood silently next to his car, disbelief and outrage emanating from his every pore. His mother stood slightly apart, screaming at the crowd that had gathered.

She was shouting obscenities and cursing over and over again.

I leaned against the wall of the balcony, teetering on my tiptoes, brimming with unbridled excitement. What would happen next? Who was responsible? Would Sheila Aunty beat someone? Would Sajid Bhaiya speak?

I heard my name, softly whispered behind me. I turned back, expecting him to conspiratorially wink at me, relishing another's misfortune. But he didn't wink. He was staring at me. Oddly. A sudden coldness seized my body. I took a step back, unconsciously creating distance between us. He abruptly walked back into his bedroom. I returned to the commotion outside...

He had me pinned against the bed. I looked at him, but his face was a blur. I could smell his warm sticky breath as he whispered my name, nuzzling my ears. His free hand was roaming, meandering its insistent way over my sullied skin. He gently lowered his body on top of mine...I looked at the locked door...He placed a hand gently over my mouth and whispered, '*Eita shudhu ador*...this is only affection,' over, and over again.

I heard my ayah calling my name outside his door, the panic swelling in her voice. He emerged from the bathroom and yelled to give him a minute. He walked over to where I was lying naked, trying not to stare at the small puddle of milky liquid gathered in the folds of the bedsheet. Speaking in a soothing voice, he put my clothes on me one at a time, gently repeating '...*eita shudhu ador*...this is only affection...'

When he opened the door, my ayah almost tripped in her hurry to pick me up in her arms. She immediately started chastizing me for disappearing. Then she apologized for disturbing Choto Sahib. She demanded I say sorry to Choto Chacha for ruining his afternoon nap. She assured him she wouldn't lose sight of me again. She noticed the crumpled bed, the milky puddle, and my frozen state. She didn't say a word.

I cannot remember other episodes, or even if there were any more. But his stench, his kisses on my shoulders, on my chest, on my arms, on my legs, in my secret crevices—those I cannot clean away.

As I sat quietly in a corner of that room, its aura pregnant with misfortune, I sighed with a relief that seemed twenty years too late. I spied Choto Chacha in his daughter's adjoining room, clutching a framed picture of Anju on her ninth birthday, attempting to fathom the injustice of his loss.

All it took was a simple push to make the world all right again. Curling and uncurling my aching fingers, I remained still in the corner, staring at Anju's body, whispering silently, 'It wasn't my fault, it wasn't my fault,' over and over again.

BIRTH OF A DAUGHTER

Sangita Swechcha

Sujata was waiting impatiently for a bus with her two daughters. The vivacity I knew in her seemed to have shriveled with her cheeks. I had ridden on my motorbike in the crowd, slowly by her side. She did not look at me. Perhaps, she could not identify me in my helmet. Or was she pretending not to have noticed me?

Sujata and I used to play and go to school together. Then she got married. She visited her maternal home infrequently after her marriage. I could not visit her home as I was buried under my own responsibilities. I was also afraid of my wife— too apprehensive to invite an old female friend home during her infrequent visits to her parents' home. My mother had warned me that my wife did not like the idea of Sujata visiting us. I did not want to hurt my wife and thus maintained a distance with Sujata intentionally.

Sujata would pass by my house on her way to her parent's home. I would grin from the balcony. She smiled back. But that was it. We never visited each other. Sometimes, I would think of going to her home to find out how she was doing. But I was scared of offending her husband. I never wanted Sujata to be unhappy because of me.

So, our friendship had been limited to our pre-nuptial interactions. It was not enough to have an empathetic mind and a clean heart. It is strange that a human has to be vary of other human beings in this society. A few times, I asked after her welfare from her brother, Deepak. I was delighted to learn everything was going well with her. Then I heard rumours that her husband's family was unhappy because she had again borne them a daughter.

As I watched her closely, Sujata's face seemed to have lost its supple softness—now she was only skin and bones. Lines of anxiety were scattered all across her face. I wanted to talk to her. She was carrying her elder daughter and leading her younger daughter. I could not pause since she had crossed the road to the bus stop on the other side and I was in a hurry to reach my office.

Time rode on a winged chariot. My wife had had a daughter like a doll just before our first anniversary. I went to Sujata to invite her on my daughter's Pasni—a solid food-feeding ceremony for a child held when they are five or six months old. The doors were locked. I left the invitation card at her maternal home. She did not turn up at the party.

I was surprised to find that my daughter's face bore a resemblance to Sujata's younger daughter. I decided to visit Sujata with my daughter when she dropped into her parents' home again. The idea even embedded itself into my dreams at night. I was thinking, perhaps God bestowed daughters on both of us so that their friendship would transcend the constraints imposed on Sujata and me by societal norms.

It was Saturday. I was planning to watch a movie at home. I was drawn out by the sounds of weeping. I went to the veranda. It was Sujata's mother. She was running out of her home, crying and howling. I chased her and called out, 'Mother! Mother!'

Sujata's mother ran fast, pushing aside my hands. I could not understand. Deepak, too, ran with a sad face.

'What's the matter, Deepak?' I asked.

'Sujata committed suicide.'

'But why?' This question misted my mind.

I woke up so happy today to be met by this terrible news!

There was a crowd in Sujata's maternal home. People around were anxious and shocked. I entered. I saw two police officers taking notes.

Sujata hanged herself. Her body was lying covered with a white cloth. I felt as though she would suddenly come alive again and talk to me, but that was not a possibility. She was gone forever.

No suicide note was found. I just wished I had talked to her before. Maybe I could have prevented this tragedy. It was too late now in any case. The pain of losing a dear friend is unbearable.

Sujata killed herself on the face of it but, to me, it was a murder. One of her neighbours said that the ruthless words of her mother-in-law had forced her to commit suicide. A woman murdered a woman with cruel words for the birth of a daughter! What a misfortune! Her only fault in this ruthless society was not to bear a son.

I just don't understand how people can disrespect a woman while they, too, are born from the womb of a woman. Where does this convention take us? I was shocked.

Sujata had had a love marriage. She was happy the first year. But she bore three daughters one after another. An alcoholic husband and the torture of a mother-in-law was too much for her to bear. This society swiped away Sujata's existence.

Only cowards are said to commit suicide. But I was witness to an episode where a modern and independent woman like Sujata too had to resort to suicide. I saw Sujata at the bus station in front of my house for the last time. Now I see but a corpse—Sujata's corpse.

The day I saw her the last time, she had come to seek shelter with her mother and brother. However, her mother and brother had persuaded her to return to her abusive husband and his family, saying that it was not in good form for a married woman to stay in her parents' home. She would have to endure her husband and in-laws, whatever the circumstances.

To endure? To what extent? It was limitless. The mother had returned a daughter, teaching her a lesson in fidelity towards her husband. Sujata stayed a couple of days with her husband and mother-in-law after she was sent back by her own family. She returned the night before to her mother's house—this time only to leave three young girls with them. Later, when her family went out, she hanged herself from the ceiling.

Women have to endure injustices in a society reigned by patriarchy. I think of what educated women in Nepal have to endure in the light of Sujata's story. She had been a post-graduate and a working woman. To snatch away the freedom of women is a violation of human rights. A question hovers in my mind. Am I the only person who advocates in favour of a woman, seeks the freedom of women despite being a man?

I was startled by the sound of Pranita's voice just as I was delighting in my upright and idealistic thinking. 'Are you in a reverie? Your daughter is crying without a stop.'

I rushed to pick up my daughter. Some neighbours have nicknamed our home as a 'hen-crowing home' (a matriarchal home) as I help Pranita with the household chores. Neither do I regret, nor repent that. I care more for the happiness of my wife and daughter. So, who cares about what society says!

This is my heaven—the only thing I care for. I feel that I am a change-maker; and if all men and women change their thought processes, society would inevitably transform. I am, therefore, not bothered. Let society say what it wants for now!

(Translated into English by Hem Bishwakarma)

THE SOCIAL WORKER

Aysha Baqir

Zarina Saleem fastened her choker. The creamy South Sea pearls, a gift from her husband, were flawless. Her fingers fluttered, tucking a few strands of loose hair into the perfect chignon. She straightened her silk kaftan. Azra was late again. That lazy wretch invented one excuse after another—her daughter had exams, her drunken husband hadn't gone to work, or the bus was late. How hard was it to show up on time? Actions had consequences and Azra was going to find out.

Zarina awoke before their neighbour's rooster exploded with his maddening crows. She devoted the first two hours to Mr Saleem. After he left for office, she hurried to pluck the list of chores printed on the fine stationary paper pinned to the study door. There was no time for breakfast. She dusted the porcelain, polished the silver, stocked the groceries, sorted the mail, bills, and receipts, and tended to her mother-in-law's prized bonsai trees. Her mother-in-law inspected them every day. Today, Zarina had nibbled on a cold roast for lunch while the cook complained about the salt. He finally left muttering under this breath. And now, through no fault of hers, she was going to be late. She had to wait until Azra showed up to sweep the house. An unexpected rush of tears pinched Zarina's eyes.

It was dangerous to walk in late when Mrs Shaukat Hafeezullah, the president of The Social Welfare Trust, chaired the committee meetings. Zarina had crawled and clawed to entrench her position on this board. She was not going risk it at any cost. *Damn*, she had to stop. The lines would mar her face for lifetime. Already, she could see the beginning of a furrow. *Stop*. She puffed her cheeks and raised her brows until they hurt and soothed her forehead with her fingertips.

Breath in. Hold. Breathe out. Think positive. Repeat.

She was a member of the oldest and most prestigious charity in the city. As per the mission statement, The Social Welfare Trust provided living, educational, and health facilities to homeless and needy girls to enable them to improve their lives. The committee took important decisions, and she was part of this force. Yesterday, popular journalist Sana Mizri had called her about a possible interview in the monthly magazine, *All About Town*. Zarina wasn't going to let one late attendance ruin years of hard work. No. But she *was* late and there was too much at stake.

At the last meeting, Mrs Waseemullah, the committee secretary, had turned to her with a wide smile. *And does Mrs Saleem, our youngest member, have anything to contribute to this year's plan?* Cautioned by a patron that she was going to be called upon, Zarina proposed a dowry fund. Shock and disbelief flashed on the faces. *Dowry?* It was outdated, disempowering, and so politically incorrect.

No. Zarina had spoken up. It was debatable whether girls or women needed dowry, but not debatable whether a marriage needed it. They lived in a poor country. Education was important, but dowry was necessary. It was fuel for a good marriage. Seeing the faces darken and frown, she had lightened her voice and softened her gaze. There were over fifty unmarried girls at the shelter. Didn't the committee members want them to get married and move out? Didn't they need space for other girls? *Numbers mattered. Donors looked at numbers, and to date, their numbers didn't say much.* She had paused to make a point and then added softly that if the dowry was 'outdated', they could always call it something else, and repackage it into a *social support fund?* She had let the half-question float in the air and glanced around again. Many of the women nodded their support. Zarina decided it was a good time to stop.

She had been startled when Ms Tehseen Bano, the distinguished principal of Firdaus College, the leading women's college in the city, requested to address the committee. Ms Bano with her dykeish cap of silver hair and crumpled handloom kurtas had never spoken in any of the meetings during the time Zarina had been on the committee. To date, Zarina had never exchanged a single word with her. What did she have to say now?

Ms Bano did not dispute the social support fund, but she opposed any cuts to the education fund. Cutting into the already paltry education fund was detrimental to the future of the girls and women and endorsing one fund at the cost of the other was foolish. Education was an invaluable gift that girls and women could cash in whenever they wanted. Education gave girls and women an opportunity to earn, be independent, and support themselves and their families. If the Trust invested in education, the demand for dowry would end.

Zarina cringed and nodded along with the other committee members. Let them believe what they wanted. Feeling the pointed looks of the women around her, she erased all emotion from her face. They wanted her to react. These so-called do-gooders, what did they know? She held an MBA degree. She had been voted the most likely to succeed. After a long, heated discussion, during which she remained silent, the committee members decided to postpone the vote to the next meeting.

Zarina took out her phone and debated whether to send a message. The vote was today. If she walked in late, the committee members would think that she was afraid of losing. But what if they voted without her? The news would spread like a wildfire. Her position and status were at risk.

The kitchen door creaked. Zarina called out, but there was no response. It had to be Azra. Grabbing her patent bag, Zarina hurried into the hallway and caught Azra slinking towards the back. Was that wretch going to pretend not to have heard her? And she was wearing the smelly rags again—the stench lingered on for hours after she left! Just last week, she had given one of her old outfits to Azra. What had she done with it? And how did she get inside the house? She told the guard to ring the bell before letting anyone inside. Actions had consequences. A deduction from his salary would teach him a lesson. 'Azra,' she snapped. She had to take control.

Azra spun around. 'Zarina Bibi, forgive me, I had to go with my daughter,' she began and shivered, unsure if it was because of the icy air conditioning or the bite in her Zarina's eyes. She had no choice. Her crazy ambitious daughter, Sara, was determined to become a doctor. Azra had gone to her daughter's college to plead for more time for payment of the next term's fees. Sara had topped the exams. How could they refuse? But the administrator had refused. It was against their policy. They would hold Sara's place if they received the money in time. Azra was desperate. Surely, Zarina Bibi remembered her daughter. She had brought Sara along to meet Zarina Bibi last month.

Zarina stepped out in her crystal pumps and stopped to recover her balance. The wretch had a nerve to ask for an advance. What did she think Zarina was, a bank? She drew in a deep breath.

'Zarina Bibi?' called Anwar. He dropped his clippers and hobbled over to the porch. He had been loitering in the front garden, pretending to trim the hedges while waiting for the front door to open and Zarina Bibi to appear. The chowkidar had demanded Rs 100 for allowing him to wait there. Anwar had agreed. He didn't have a choice. His wife had said not to come back without help.

He clasped his hands and bowed. He knew Zarina Bibi was in a hurry, but he was helpless. Stammering and stumbling over his words, he pleaded. He had married his eldest daughter, Gurya, to the son of the local grocery shop owner last year. Did Zarina Bibi remember? He was indebted to Zarina Bibi and Saab for their generous contribution. And hated to bother them but he had no one else to turn to. Last night, his cousin had arrived with the news that Gurya's in-laws were planning to douse her with gasoline and set her on fire. They were angry with his daughter. She had not conceived as yet, and then had the nerve to tell them that that her doctor wanted to run some tests on her husband. Which man went to the doctor for this matter? Anwar shook his head. Yes, she was a foolish girl, but they didn't have to take her life. She was his only daughter. His daughter's life was in Zarina Bibi's hands and only she had the influence to save his daughter.

Zarina stared at Anwar's balding head. He had been working at the house before she had been brought into it as young bride. But what right did he have to harass her with this problem? Was she the local police? And now she was definitely late. She stepped back and shook her head. She was sorry, but she had an important meeting. But she was going to help him and give him paid leave so that he could go to the police station and file a report. The police would help him. She nodded at the driver, and he leapt to open the door. Stepping past Anwar's slumped frame, Zarina slid into the back seat of the Mercedes. How dare he upset her. How dare he make her feel bad? She would never reach on time. Was the whole world against her trying to do some good?

* * *

Five hours later, Zarina turned the key in the front door and let herself inside. She breathed out seeing the dim light spill under the study door. Good. He wasn't back. And she had done valuable work today. Her proposal had passed with two votes, but on the condition that Zarina would lead the fund-raising campaign. The social support fund would be set up within the next month. Zarina was sure that Sana Mizri would be thrilled to feature this in her magazine.

After the result was announced, many of the ladies had turned to congratulate her and Zarina had promptly dipped her hand into her bag and pulled out a crisp Rs 5,000 note to endorse the fund. Taking her cue, the other committee members followed. Ms Tehseen Bano had walked out of the room.

Zarina wasn't worried about the Rs 5,000 contribution. She had told the guard about the Rs 100 deduction from his salary. She was sure there would be other penalties. The month was just beginning. Her win at the committee meeting eased her guilt for not helping Azra. Who knew if the woman was even telling the truth about her daughter's fees? It was better for Azra to save for her daughter's dowry. She had told her that.

* * *

But there had been more drama at the meeting that had delayed her. Mrs Shaukat Hafeezullah had brought an urgent matter to the committee's attention. The office manager reported to her that Sabina Liaqat, the new young supervisor in the girl's dormitory, rushed into The Social Welfare Trust office this morning with bloodshot eyes and torn clothes. Trembling and crying, Sabina confided to the office manager that Nazir, the shelter's guard, had assaulted her in the women's bathroom this morning when the girls had left for school. She had stopped him from entering the girl's dorm last night and he had sworn revenge. There were no witnesses, but Sabina demanded justice and threatened to go to the press if the committee didn't register a case against Nazir. The committee had to take a decision. After Mrs Shaukat Hafeezullah stopped talking, a deep silence filled the room and the committee members watched Mrs Shaukat Hafeezullah and Mrs Waseemullah, the two titans, exchange long, cold stares. Everyone knew that Nazir had been retained on the recommendation of Mrs Waseemullah's driver and Sabina had been working in Mrs Shaukat Hafeezullah's daughter's house as a maid. The committee members had voted to hire Sabina as the dorm guardian on Mrs Shaukat Hafeezullah's daughter's recommendation after the last supervisor had left without any explanations or notice.

Zarina had clasped her hands under the table. This was a battle to watch. She had to think carefully and bet on the winner. That poor girl, Sabina. She would get no justice. Rape was just not about rape anymore.

Now, catching her own reflection in the hallway mirror, Zarina puffed her cheeks and soothed her brows. She walked into the lounge. Yes, it had been a good day. She had done something important. She had taken a stance and won. Hearing the muezzin's call to prayer, she sighed. She had some time. She felt strong and there were opportunities in the air. Even Mrs Shaukat Hafeezullah had congratulated her on the fund approval. Hearing the doorknob turn, she froze.

The door opened and Mr Saleem walked in. His right hand clenched. He tilted his head towards the study.

'Why?' whispered Zarina. She shivered. Her fingernails dug into her palms.

'The salt. I had to hear it from the cook. And is this the time to come home? When will you learn? When?'

Looking away, Zarina walked into the study and crossed the Persian carpet until she faced the Chesterfield. Without a word, she dropped her bag, pulled her kaftan over her head, and undid her pants until they heaped around her feet. She shivered feeling a draft against her bare legs and chest. She bent over and clasped her arms around the back of her knees. Cold pearls fell into her open mouth, and she pushed them out. Her hair loosened and swept the rug. She pressed her lips together. She had stopped screaming. She knew her mother-in-law listened.

Five years. Every week he waited. One mistake. Any mistake. It had begun with the paltry dowry her parents had given her. Then it was about anything and everything. Salt. Sugar. Spice. Zarina had stopped counting.

Hearing the lock click, Zarina stiffened. The web of scars on her back and legs prickled. She opened her eyes. Through the gap between her knees, she saw the ends of the whip surge forward like a rattlesnake.

ESCAPING THE MIRROR

Farah Ghuznavi

Dia was having a good day. Her tea party had been a great success, and her carefully prepared food had been consumed to the last crumb. Even the guests had behaved well, despite her earlier concerns about whether they would all get along.

Mixing guests was always a risk. She was well aware that her Barbie Doll was jealous of her teddy bear, for example. But teddies were special, as everyone knew. Besides, he had been with her the longest, a gift from her parents when she was a baby. So, Dia had no hesitation in justifying her preferential treatment of him. On this occasion, her Barbie had behaved gracefully, mingling with her other guests, and even at one point chatting to her teddy.

Now, as she packed away all the tea items, and threw away her leftover ingredients of leaves, flowers and twigs, Dia hummed happily to herself. Suddenly, she felt a slight prickling along the nape of her neck. She stopped singing and looked around. Minhas was standing at the entrance to the L-shaped veranda, watching her.

Dia's mood changed immediately. Why was he standing there? She hated Minhas! He was always sneaking around, always watching her while she played or was busy with her various activities. Dia did not know why that bothered her so much, but it did.

Minhas was their driver. He was young and smart, and a

great favourite with her parents. He was treated differently from all the other staff and was often heard to say boastfully that he was like a member of the family. Dia did not think so and she wondered why he said it. But nobody cared what *she* thought; after all, she was only seven years old.

It had not always been this way. When Minhas first came to work for them, the previous year, Dia had liked him. He was fun. He told her stories and made her laugh—he didn't treat her like a little child. Sometimes, he even brought her presents: a bar of Mimi chocolate or an ice lolly after school.

Best of all were the forbidden goodies he bought her from the itinerant vendors clustered outside the school gates, enticing students to their bamboo baskets full of savoury snacks— jhalmuri that made Dia's mouth burn even as she savoured the delicious snack of puffed rice mingling in a symphony of flavours with chillies, onion, mustard oil and crispy fried lentil-noodle fragments; or peeled amra, the tart green fruit sculpted into a flower shape with 'petals' to be snapped off and dipped into a chilli and salt mixture.

Her parents did not approve of her eating these things. In fact, all the adults had terrible stories about how children got sick from eating street food, but Dia rarely had an upset stomach. Besides, the occasional bout of diarrhoea was a small price to pay for these delights.

So, these forbidden treats remained a secret between Dia and Minhas; one that he made much of. 'Your parents would be very angry if they knew that I was buying you this,' Minhas often said to her.

'But who will tell them?' Dia would reply, determined not to be deprived of the treats she so craved.

'Well, if you're ever mean to me, perhaps *I* will tell them!' was Minhas' teasing response.

'But why would I ever be mean to you?' a puzzled Dia would ask, unable to comprehend a scenario in which this could ever happen.

Dia did not know when her feelings started to change.

Perhaps it was after Minhas insisted that she sit in the front seat with him when they were travelling alone. Dia's parents had two cars, but her favourite was the big blue American car, the Dodge Dart, which Minhas drove.

The Dodge had black leather seats with a retractable divider that served as an armrest in the back. When Dia was really little, she had liked sitting on top of the divider, because it made her feel taller and gave her a better view of the road. Even when she grew a little older, the Dodge remained her favourite car—although she was soon too big to sit on the divider anymore.

The drivers who worked for Dia's family had designated cars and duties. Minhas was Dia's father's driver; he was much friendlier than the one who usually accompanied her mother to work—grouchy old Abbas. In any case, it was Dia's father who usually dropped her off at school before heading to work, so she invariably saw more of Minhas.

In Dia's first few years at school, her father used to come home for lunch, and would pick her up on the way. But when her father started staying at office throughout the day, Minhas came by himself to pick up Dia. It was sometime after that change in routine that Minhas suggested that Dia sit in the front seat with him.

Initially, Dia demurred. It wasn't that she minded sitting in front, but she was used to sitting in the back, and it seemed more natural to her. Besides, she liked using the divider in the back as an armrest. The front seat didn't have one; it was a long, sofa-style seat.

But eventually, it became difficult to refuse. Minhas would say, 'It's because I'm just a driver, isn't it? You think you're too good to sit in front with me...'

Dia hated it. She felt funny when he said that.

Her parents had taken pains to make her understand that while some people were born into rich families and others were poor, that was simply a question of luck; all of them were human beings, and it was wrong (and rude) to treat anyone with disrespect. She understood that somehow Minhas was trying to say that she was that kind of person, a bad person. Even though she knew it wasn't true, Dia felt compelled to move to the front, just to prove him wrong.

In the beginning, it was fine. But then Minhas started insisting that she sit closer to him. He said that if she sat on his lap, he could teach her how to drive. Dia told him that she wasn't old enough to drive yet, but Minhas insisted that driving was a lot of fun. It certainly *was* fun when he made the car zigzag wildly, as he sometimes did, sending her rolling from one end of the seat to the other. So, Dia tried to watch him and learn, even though it looked rather complicated to her.

Minhas had a very good memory. He had learnt large sections of Koranic verse and could recite it at will. Dia found this quite fascinating. She understood no Arabic (neither did Minhas, who had only learned to read the script), but the sounds were intriguing. So, sometimes, she would ask Minhas to recite for her. He was always very happy when she asked him to do this, saying that she was a good girl, a pure girl.

But Dia had another reason for asking him to do the recitation. She knew that when Minhas began speaking in Arabic, his concentration was focused on the verses he chanted, alongside driving. At such times, he did not talk to her about other things, stranger things. He was mentioning those things more and more often. And Dia had begun to find this increasingly disturbing.

Like the time that Minhas had dropped her off at her grandmother's house, one Saturday.

Dia's grandmother, Nanima, had been a widow for many years, and lived with her eldest son. It was a spacious house and they had a spaniel called Mishti. Dia, who loved dogs, enjoyed playing with her. There was a lot to do there, and she was never bored, but sometimes, she did manage to get into trouble...

One time, Nanima's living room was being re-painted. As soon as Dia arrived at the house, she was warned sternly by her grandmother not to go there. But at some point, during the day, a combination of boredom and the irresistible lure of the forbidden drew her towards the room.

As she slipped inside the door, she saw two workmen. One was mixing the paint, and Dia watched with fascination as he expertly blended the contents of two containers together in a bucket. The other man was standing on top of a step ladder, dipping his paintbrush into the pot balanced precariously near his feet, and applying even brush strokes to the upper part of the wall. As Dia watched the men working, she began to lean, unnoticed, against a freshly painted section of the room.

By the time she went to join Nanima for lunch, she had a thick uneven white stripe of paint running along the left side of her body. She even had some of the sticky white stuff tangled into her thick, black hair.

Nanima was not amused. Keeping up a running commentary on Dia's disobedient nature and the faulty gene pool on her father's side that Nanima held responsible whenever she was displeased with her granddaughter, she was unnecessarily vigorous in applying turpentine to take off the paint. But despite her watery eyes at the end of the session, Dia remained unrepentant.

Nanima got her revenge a few days later. When they played their regular game of Ludo—which Dia, not competitive by nature, as usual lost—Nanima took a particularly vicious pleasure in 'killing' her tokens and returning them to the starting point, time after time. At the end, a tearful Dia surveyed the devastation Nanima had wrought on her blue tokens—three of which were still languishing at the starting point, while all four of Nanima's red tokens had romped to victory. Cackling with laughter, her grandmother said, 'You are too soft! You will have to learn to be tougher. You'll never win *this* way!'

Dia thought long and hard about what her grandmother had said. She wondered if it was true. Maybe that was why Minhas had been behaving so strangely with her lately. After all, he seemed to be acting just the same with everyone else.

That morning when Minhas dropped her at Nanima's house, Dia was preparing to get out of the car when he suddenly said, 'Aren't you going to give me a kiss before you go?'

Dia looked at him in surprise. 'Why should I kiss you?' she asked.

'Don't you love me?' he countered.

She didn't know what to say. Minhas was her friend, but she didn't want to kiss him! Why was he asking her to? Minhas waited for her answer, but when she didn't reply, he continued, 'If you don't love me, I'd be sad.' When Dia remained silent, he repeated insistently, 'If you love me, you can prove it by giving me a kiss. Come on...'

Suddenly, Dia just wanted to get out of the car. But as she reached for the handle, Minhas's long arm shot out and pushed down the lock of the door. He did not remove his arm after locking the door; it stayed where it was, pinning her against the back of the leather sofa-seat. 'Let me go!' cried a frightened Dia.

'Only after you kiss me!' said Minhas, with a teasing smile.

'Let me *go*!' This time Dia screamed as loud as she could, pushing against him with all her strength. Abruptly, Minhas removed his arm, leaving her to fall forward against the dashboard, as the pressure holding her back disappeared without warning. He had a thunderous scowl on his face.

Dia scrambled out of the car and rushed into the house without looking back. She was so scared, she couldn't breathe. Badly shaken, she locked herself into the bathroom next to the library. Several minutes passed before she felt calm enough to enter Nanima's room.

Dia told no one about what had happened that day. She didn't know how to explain it, because she couldn't understand herself why she had been so frightened. After all, Minhas had just asked her for a kiss. He hadn't even really hurt her. And it wasn't as if she was *going* to kiss him.

But the incident changed something in their relationship. Dia could not forget how trapped she had felt, pinned against the car seat. Minhas was so much stronger than her. She knew she couldn't stop him if he really wanted to do something. But he would never hurt her—would he?

After that, Dia avoided being alone in the car with Minhas. Although he pretended that nothing had changed, she knew that he sensed the difference, despite her attempts at normality. In any case, it was hard for her to really avoid him; he was still the driver who delivered her to and from school.

And now, Dia never sat in the front with him. Even though Minhas made fun of her for sitting in the back by herself, she remained firm. She was well aware that he didn't like it, though.

Something else was different. Minhas had started using the rear-view mirror to watch her, as she sat in the back. Dia would move from one end of the backseat to the other, but to no avail. Wherever she sat, he would simply adjust the mirror to ensure that she couldn't escape his eyes.

And each time she allowed herself to look into the mirror, she would see him watching her. He made no attempt to hide the fact that he was staring. Even when she refused to look up, she could feel the intensity of his gaze boring, laser-like, into her stubbornly lowered head.

She grew to hate the car that she had once loved so much, and to dread each time she had to ride in it. Years later, Dia would think to herself ironically that the car was well-named; but no amount of dodging or darting in the backseat made her feel less afraid of that mesmerizing gaze in the rear-view mirror.

Gradually, her behaviour began to change. The child who had been famous within her family for chatting to total strangers—to the extent that her parents were constantly worried she would be an easy target for kidnappers—became increasingly reluctant to meet new people. She was more reserved with others around her as well, only ever relaxing in the company of her parents or close friends. The changes were so incremental that nobody noticed; the warning signs were missed by the adults around her.

Dia had a large bed in her room, but she usually slept on the left side. Now, she began sleeping in the centre of the bed, as far as possible from the three open sides.

Each night, before she went to bed, she carefully, almost religiously, carried out a detailed ritual. Four of her stuffed toys— the same ones every night—were placed around the bed to guard in all directions. Her teddy sat on the right, her stuffed dog to the left, respectively facing the door and windows in her room.

At her feet sat the monkey that her grandmother had given her. And propped up against the headboard was the weakest of the four, the baby kangaroo.

Any deviation from this routine caused her severe anxiety. The occasional washing of the toys often meant an agonizing wait to see if they would dry before bedtime.

Dia also altered her patterns of play. She never went to the garden by herself anymore, because Minhas could usually be found hanging around near the car, which was parked in the garage close by. She also stopped going to the roof alone, although that had been one of her favourite haunts in the past—a wide-open space where her vivid imagination could run riot, dreaming of space travel and pirate ships, costume balls and desert islands.

While she was less likely to see him there, there was only one staircase leading up to the roof. So, if Minhas *did* follow her, Dia knew she would have no way of escaping. Consequently, she only went to these places if there was another member of staff or one of her friends accompanying her. But once again, no one noticed these changes in her behaviour.

Minhas was beginning to get angry with Dia now, and it showed in the increasingly aggressive comments he would make to her during those endless, excruciating car rides. Sometimes he said things like, 'If I took you somewhere and kept you locked up there, no one would ever know. I could just say that I left you at school, and you weren't there when I came to pick you up. They would never find you!'

Her threats to tell her parents about his menacing comments carried little weight. 'Do you think that they'll believe you? Of course, they won't! When I tell them what a bad girl you are, they'll believe me, not you. And they'll be *very* angry with you!'

'If you aren't kind to me, I will tell them that you've used bad language with me. Who'll be in trouble then?' he would say threateningly. And despite Dia's increasingly desperate denials, she couldn't help believing him. It was true that her parents liked him, and it was also true that they became very angry if she ever used abusive language, especially with the household staff.

Despite worrying obsessively over her parents' reaction, Dia *did* try to tell the adults around her what was happening. But she didn't have the words to explain her fears about his behaviour, and Minhas had already begun spreading his poison. Dia's parents were worried that she didn't like him because he was a servant. They had done their best to bring her up to be polite to all adults, and they couldn't understand why she was behaving like this.

Her father tried to reason with her. 'Sweetheart, you used to like him. Now, he says that you are very rude to him. Why don't you like him anymore?' he asked. The more Dia tried to explain, the less she was able to make herself understood.

In the end, she settled on the one phrase that she kept repeating, to no avail. 'He *looks* at me! I don't like the way that he looks at me!' she would cry.

'But we *all* look at people, baby. Why shouldn't he look at you?' asked her puzzled parents. Dia had no answer for them; at least, none that they could understand.

Slowly, Dia began to believe what Minhas had been saying to her. She *was* a bad girl, and this was all her fault. Why else would this be happening to her? She sensed, somehow, that nothing similar had ever happened to any of her friends. So, she couldn't bring herself to raise the subject with one of them either.

No one believed her, Dia thought despairingly, just as Minhas had warned that they wouldn't. Perhaps, if her parents really found out the truth about the kind of girl that she was, they wouldn't love her anymore. After all, they already thought she was a naughty girl to be so mean to Minhas.

One night, lying in bed, with her mother sitting next to her and stroking her hair, Dia asked, 'Ma, you know how the Prophet—peace be upon him—was the messenger of God?'

'Yes, of course,' replied her mother.

'Well then, do you think that I am the messenger of the devil?' asked Dia hesitantly.

'Of course not! Why would you say such a thing?' asked her horrified mother.

'I just wondered,' said Dia, longing to make her understand.

Her mother soon forgot about the conversation. Perhaps she was even a little disturbed by it and wanted to forget. But Dia did not.

The years passed, and Dia gave up trying to talk to anyone about the problem. As far as possible, she tried not to think about it. But that was difficult to do with Minhas' malevolent gaze constantly following her around. She became an expert at ensuring that she was never alone. But even the most carefully laid plans can sometimes spiral into chaos.

In the large, open drawing room of Dia's house, a curving staircase led the way to a corridor on the second floor, which opened onto three adjacent bedrooms. These were occupied by Dia, her parents, and any guest who was visiting. Under the staircase, there was a small, sheltered corner, hidden from view by a number of potted plants. It was one of Dia's favourite play-spots, and a relatively safe one, because the drawing room was very near the kitchen, where one of the household staff could usually be found.

One night, Dia decided to go down to the kitchen to get a drink. She made her way down the staircase and was passing through the darkened drawing room when suddenly somebody grabbed her from behind. She realized that it was Minhas. He had been standing underneath the staircase where he couldn't be seen. Perhaps, he had heard her voice as she told her parents she was going down and slipped into the space to lie in wait.

Held tightly against him, Dia could feel the heat emanating from his body. The smell of the cheap cigarettes he smoked was unmistakable, and as she struggled to get loose, he pressed her against himself even harder. In panic, instinctively, Dia bit him hard on the shoulder. More in surprise than pain, he let go of her, and she ran to the kitchen.

The housekeeper was surprised to see her, and even more surprised by the child's demand that she accompanies her back to the stairs. 'I'm scared of the dark,' said Dia, who was not just scared at that moment but terrified. And perhaps something of her fear communicated itself to the woman, because she walked her back to the staircase without further comment.

Minhas continued to look for opportunities to carry out his peculiar form of psychological warfare. As if the way that he stalked her and the regular episodes in the car were not frightening enough, he continued with his threats to discredit her in front of her parents. And yet, although Dia believed what he said, she couldn't bring herself to consent to the alternative and give him what he wanted.

On another occasion, things almost went too far. She was walking past the garage entrance, trying not to look in that direction, when the Dodge Dart came to life with a sudden roar of its powerful engine. Before she knew what was happening, she found herself being pinned against the wall by the front bumper of the car. She looked through the windscreen to see Minhas grinning evilly at her.

By the time one of the guards came running in response to her cry, Minhas had reversed the car back into the garage. Dia knew that he had done it to frighten her. And he'd succeeded. Her legs were shaking so badly she could barely stand, but there was no physical evidence of what had taken place, and the guard witnessed nothing.

In subsequent years, Dia's state of preparedness for possible sneak attacks by Minhas became almost second nature. As she grew and matured into a teenager, she also learned better how to hide her fear, cultivating an attitude of cold indifference.

Whether Minhas realized that she would not give in, or whether he had simply grown bored with the game, his focus shifted elsewhere. The one element of his behaviour that remained unchanged though, was his use of that rear-view mirror. And so, the thing that continued to bother Dia through most of her teenage years—in spite of her newfound composure—was the familiar, sickening sensation of being watched whenever she was in the car with him.

It was more than a decade after it all started that Dia was able to put a name to what had happened. By that time, Minhas had long disappeared from their lives; fired, of all things, for stealing petrol.

Unexpectedly, she came across a magazine article about the sexual abuse of children. The article included information about the nature and frequency of such abuse, providing a compassionate insight into its consequences for child survivors. Unsurprisingly, Dia found that the piece had considerable resonance for her. Perhaps the greatest relief though, was in knowing that she was *not* the only one to have been through such an experience.

Even then, it might have all ended there—what was the point, after all, in reliving that misery—if it had not been for a chance remark by her father. 'These Westerners are crazy,' he said, 'See, things like that never happen in *this* country!'

Dia felt as though her head would explode from the sudden, overwhelming rage that swept through her. 'What do you mean, Abba? How can you say that it never happens in your country? It happened *in your own house*, and you didn't even see it!'

It took her a moment for her to recognize her own voice as the one speaking. Her father had gone pale as he looked at her in horror, 'What do you mean, Dia? What are you saying?'

She couldn't stop herself from continuing, though; it was as though a dam had finally broken—the spider-web of cracks on its facade that she had not even been aware of simultaneously giving way. 'You *know* what I mean, Abba! Think about it! I'm talking about Minhas...'

Her father seemed to age before her eyes as he said, 'Minhas? You mean, Minhas...' He couldn't finish his sentence; his voice broke. 'Why didn't you tell us?' he said, in anguish.

Dia was calm now. This reckoning had been a long time coming. 'I did,' she said sadly, 'I told you in the only way I knew how to.'

'But all you said was that...' Dia waited for him to finish completing his sentence, watching the realization dawn on him, even as he said, '...that he looked at you...'

'But I didn't understand what you *meant*, Dia! You should have told me...' her father continued, brokenly.

'I was seven years old, Abba. I didn't understand what was happening. I just knew that I didn't like the way that he looked at me! What else could I say? And even then, no one listened—you all thought that I was some spoilt, horrible child being mean to the driver!'

And finally, with a tremendous sense of relief, the tears came—the tears that had been held back for so long; blurring her vision as Dia looked at her father, holding his head in his hands, sitting there in the unbearable realization of his failure.

SHADOW PLAY

Radhia Rameez

You tiptoe through the dark.

The night is huge and filled with shadows. They are alive—you are sure of it; you can see them follow you out of the corner of your eye, claws and spikes and teeth and talons, fleeing into corners each time you turn your head. When you look away, they are out again, swooping and swirling around your pyjama-clad legs, reaching for your small bare feet. They tug at the furry teddy clutched in a sweaty-palmed grip. They pool in your eyes, and you wonder if you are blind, if the darkness has filled you and swallowed you from the inside so that when the Monster Behind the Curtain realizes that you are out of bed Past Bedtime, it can take you easily. But it is not shadows in your eyes, only tears, and you wipe them away in case they fall and make a sound.

Because he must not hear you.

You can hear him, though. Over the sounds of the night—crickets chirping, pipes gurgling, the distant caterwauling of the neighbourhood cats—you hear the Fight Sounds. Bumps and bangs and muffled cries. Hands slapping, teeth gritting, chairs toppling, heart bleeding. You're not sure if hearts actually bleed, but you can picture hers, silently guttering in a pool of stagnant blood. Quietly now, quietly. Is that your heart, thudding like hammerheads in your ear? Still it. Don't sneeze, don't slip, don't cough, don't trip. In fact, better not breathe at all. You reach the top of the staircase and hold Teddy under your armpit so you can clutch at the rail with both hands.

One step.

Two steps.

Then you crouch and watch the nightly shadow play through the bannisters.

It looks exactly like the shadow puppet play you saw on TV last year; cardboard-cut silhouettes walking and pirouetting behind a screen, their casters hidden from view. There was a horse in that one, you remember, as well as a prince and a princess. You can't recall the story, but it was gentle and tranquil with a happy ending. This one is different, of course.

Because it is not happy.

And it never ends.

The shadows roll and turn, morphing, merging, madly lurching, thrown across the wall by the dim table lamp downstairs. Big shadow, small shadow. Father shadow, mother shadow. Father shadow looms, a story-book ogre come to life, one hand wrenching her hair, or clutching her throat, or gripping her arm— it's hard to tell with shadows—and the other swinging. You hear sounds like a pestle pounding a slab of raw meat. Mother's quiet cries (so as not to wake you) fill your ears, and Bad Words hit you in the face like thrown stones.

Keep still. Hold back. Don't run to her like you are dying to or he will only get angrier. You are by far too little to help. Just watch, for now. Don't turn away, don't block the sounds. Bite down on your lip until your teeth draw blood. Swallow your screams, your fears, your angst, your tears, and feel them settle against your crashing heart.

Leave them there to go septic.

There it will stay until you grow up and out of this helplessness, and perhaps then you can bleed clean. But till then, all you can do is crouch, night after night, and watch the shadow play.

The lights go off.

The Fight Sounds stop, though the sounds of the night continue.

The play is over.

You grip the banister to pull yourself to your feet and quietly climb the stairs.

One step.

Two steps.

Then you walk back to your room.

The shadows still follow you, sinuous and stealthy, reaching with tentacled arms, but you realize, as you do each night on the trip back, that there are things far scarier than shadows. You slip under the covers, wave goodnight to the Monster Behind the Curtain, and pray that you will grow up fast.

THE LOST SLIPPER

Supriya Rakesh

In the magical land of Mumbai, there stands a grand, white castle right by the sea. On the fourth floor of Sea Castle apartments, lives a girl named Sundari.

It is a hot summer afternoon and Sundari is lying down, trying to take a nap.

She rests on a ragged carpet in her chambers—the storeroom at the back of the kitchen. It is small, but enough. She finds a shelf for her belongings, a tiny window to hear the humdrum of the street, and a humming table fan that cannot stay the heavy humidity of May.

Next to her carpet-bed, right by the old pillow, is her stack of books. Most of them are in Hindi, from two years ago when she still used to go to evening school. But her prized possession is an old wooden chest full of her mother's sarees and sundry objects that she carried from her village.

Afternoons are usually quiet, like this one. There is not much work to be done. She can catch her breath, maybe even a wink. But it's difficult to fall asleep with the sweat gathering around her neck, her back, her kurta. She fans herself with her cotton dupatta and wills herself to rest.

'Sundari!' A scream resounds from the other end of the house. 'Where the hell is my dress?'

Oh yes, it is time to try out the dresses.

* * *

Sundari is up, splashing off her slumber at the kitchen sink. Today is the big party and she has to help her sisters get ready.

Yes, they are indeed her sisters. The fair, spoilt, English-speaking twins who live in the large bedroom facing the sea. At least, that is how they were introduced to her when came into this house, seven or eight years ago.

'Nita, Aliya, this is your older sister, Sundari.' Kaka, who she had only heard of until then, as the distant uncle from the city, prodded them in his kind voice.

The twins had so many questions.

What, we have a sister? Why have we never seen her before? Why is she wearing these frumpy clothes? Why is she called Sundari—she is so dark!

Over time, and especially with Kaka passing away, the questions had turned into orders. Where were you? I need you to iron this top. No way, zip me up first. How does this shade look? No, get me the other one. Can you make some coffee? I need a pick-me-up.

But Sundari did not have any complaints.

Here, in this house, she has grown very quickly from a young girl into a helper, a caretaker, a servant. She does not mind the work; she has seen women in her village toil far harder in the fields and their homes. She knows that gratefully accepting the kindness of this family is her best option. She is blessed with daily meals, a roof over her head, her books, and most importantly, the sea.

Sundari loves the sea.

On her way to the market, or on her way home, she lingers by the seafront. She sits by the promenade; the great equalizer of this kingdom, accessed by nobles and commoners alike. She likes to breathe in the open air, feel the salty breeze on her face. Here, lost in the sea of humanity, she is one amongst many, and yet one of a kind.

It was on one such day on the promenade that she came face to face with the Prince.

'So, is everyone invited to this party? Everyone from the building?' Alia wonders, slipping into her little black dress.

'Yes!' Nita confirms, brushing furious strokes of pink up her narrow cheeks. 'Not everyone. I mean, not the plebeians.'

She vaguely nods in Sundari's direction, but the eye roll does not go unnoticed.

'Actually, you should come too, didi,' Alia is quick to add. 'Hussain Aunty wants some help in delivering her samosas. Her arthritis is acting up again.'

Sundari's brows rise at the suggestion, but only slightly.

'But please, not in these rags. If you can't find something decent to wear, just take the side entrance,' Nita commands and the girls exit the room.

Sundari sits down slowly before the large mirror.

* * *

Things were not the same at Sea Castle apartments ever since the Prince moved in a week ago.

The rumours had started much before his arrival, confirmed by 'Page 3' reports and the paparazzi clicks. After a break-up with his longtime girlfriend, Bollywood heir Raj Kumar, a.k.a. Prince, had moved out of their shared condo, and into his new penthouse on the tenth floor.

Now, spotting a movie star is a common occurrence in this part of the kingdom. Yet, it is quite different to have one living right in your midst. The women in the neighbourhood, maidens and dowagers alike, have not stopped fawning. Even Nita and Alia are huge fans of the Prince; his dreamy smile, his puppy-dog eyes and perfectly sculpted body.

So, imagine the excitement when the entire apartment complex gets invited for a house-warming party. Tabloids speculate that this is only the first of many parties that the Prince is so famous for hosting and an attempt to placate his new neighbours right at the start. But who knows the real truth?

Preparations for the party have started early, and Sundari can hear the sound system being tested, food and drinks being delivered, staff bustling in and out, running errands. The whole castle seems to be at the Prince's beck and call; everyone hoping to catch at least a glimpse of Bollywood royalty on this gala day.

But not Sundari. She has already had her glimpse, or rather, a moment.

* * *

Last evening, she was sitting with her bag of vegetables at her usual spot by the sea. She knew she could take her time today. Kaaki was out for a work trip, and the twins had their boyfriends over. She watched the passersby, as she often liked to do, noticing their quirks, how they talked to each other, their strange clothes and stranger dogs.

Suddenly, one of them paused and looked right back at her.

She strained her eyes to bring the face into focus. Wait, was it him?

Wearing what she had come to understand were 'running clothes', he looked exposed and chiselled, covered in sweat and water. He appeared slightly older than in the posters or the screen, with crinkles around his dreamy eyes.

She continued to stare, flushed, rooted to her spot. He gave her a wide, indulgent smile. When she wouldn't respond, he laughed, running past her.

Sundari felt a strange warmth in her belly.

* * *

The music in the penthouse starts at half past seven.

Everyone has left for the party. The house is empty and dark. Sundari sits by the window, her gaze sad and fixed on the people and cars heading in through the front gate.

It is not like her to feel morose, as she does this evening.

She is used to the twin's pettiness and snide remarks. They are, after all, younger and she has learnt to ignore them. When she first came into this house, Kaaki used to give her the twins' old clothes. But she soon grew out of them; they never felt or fit right.

In fact, clothes never felt important, especially for someone like her. What was the point, who would really see her?

But today, something is different. Their words pierce her skin, forming wounds. Her face and her fortune are at odds and yet aligned to a singular reality. She is a lesser person. She has to be.

She wraps her arms around the thick window curtains and cries softly. Thank God, there is no one at home.

After a really long time, she misses her mother. If only she was here, in the flesh. She longs for her village as a flood of childhood memories consume her mind.

'Please be watching over me, Ma,' she sniffles.

The last time she prayed like this, she had just found out her Ma was no more. She had passed on to heaven, in the midst of giving her a younger brother. When Ma was around, she used to tell her stories and sing her songs. She called her Rani, my darling, my dear queen. No one had called her that since that day.

Suddenly, and very jarringly, the doorbell rings.

'Is no one at home?' sings the friendly voice of Mrs Hussain on the other side of the door.

* * *

Half-an-hour later, Sundari stands awkwardly in Hussain Aunty's home, watching her pull out clothes, jewellery and other knick-knacks excitedly from her large closet.

Mrs Hussain is the large, friendly woman who lives next door. With henna-dyed hair and gold-rimmed glasses, she is one person who has always been nice to Sundari.

You remind me of my daughter Maya—she always tells her.

It is years since Maya got married and moved to a different country. But Aunty still holds a candle and a shrine in her name; a room full of treasures, not unlike Sundari's old chest.

'This is too much, Aunty,' she murmurs.

'That's rubbish. Try out this blue anarkali. You'll look so beautiful in it!'

Beautiful. Sundari is unsure if she should be taking this

favour, borrowing Mrs Hussain's daughter's nice, expensive-looking things. But, beautiful?

She doesn't resist.

She wears the dazzling blue anarkali and applies kohl to her eyes. She lets Mrs Hussain do her hair and lets loose her braids. Then, a dash of rose-scented perfume.

'And what about this dupatta?' All silk and shimmer.

'Oh! Some jewellery now. Wear these chaand-balis. They curve so nicely against your chin! And this kangan, an old favourite of mine.'

'Surely, not the necklace, Aunty. It looks real gold, and the stones sparkle really bright.'

'Don't fret, beta! Just look at yourself in the mirror now.'

She can barely recognize herself. She looks like a leading lady from one of the Prince's films. Or a queen from her Ma's stories. Rani.

'I won't stay there for too long, Auntie. I will be back to return your things.'

'No worries, dear. I sleep off by midnight, you can stay until then.

'Off you go now. Here, this is the tray of my best, freshest samosas. I will call you the resident lift. Make sure you enter by the main door.

'Wait, what about your feet? Here, these are the mirror work mojdis I just ordered from Jaipur.

'Now, you are perfect.'

***

Sundari exits the elevator and climbs the seven steps up to the penthouse landing.

As she walks, the pleats of her kurta sway and rustle, her ornaments tinkle, and a rich commotion follows her everywhere.

On the way, she runs into some familiar faces. People from the apartment complex. They do not recognize her, it appears. They smile and say hello, their glances curious.

She walks with her head held high, her shoulders straight. Just like Hussain Aunty has instructed.

The sounds from the apartment beckon her. Loud music and lazy chatter. Clanging of glasses. The scent of smoke and perfume.

She reaches the main door, then as she's about to shed her footwear, she hesitates for a moment. Is this really her place?

She glances down at her beautiful slippers. Yes, today it is.

Just as Sundari walks in through the doors, the music stops. The blast of the air-conditioner ruffles her hair. The conversation comes to a standstill and all eyes fall on her. What an entrance!

Some say, this was the result of a momentary glitch in the sound system. But who knows the real truth?

Sundari keeps walking, looking straight ahead, making her way to the host's kitchen. It is exactly fifteen steps from the main door to the kitchen. Sundari knows, because she is counting them as she walks, holding her breath, balancing her tray of snacks.

Even so, she is very aware of her surroundings. The layout of this flat is quite similar to the ones below, only larger, grander. It is, after all, the top of the castle.

She is also aware of the looks she is getting.

Yes, it is the twins sitting on the beanbags, staring at her in disbelief. A few other neighbours are whispering to each other furiously.

Further, towards the right, the spacious drawing room opens into what appears to be a terrace garden. Here, she recognizes some faces she has only seen on the screen. Film moguls huddled together, engrossed in their conversations and drinks.

As she takes her last few steps, her heart is beating just a little bit faster. She is aware of another pair of eyes following her.

When she turns, it is the same indulgent smile, the same crinkle at the eyes.

* * *

It is almost midnight now.

The guests are slowly trickling away, saying their goodbyes, amidst hugs and drunken laughter. The lights have been dimmed and the music softened, keeping in line with the law of the land.

Sundari has stayed behind, to help the staff serve food and drinks; especially the samosas from Mrs Hussain's kitchen. It is a special request from the host, she was told. So how could she say no?

The party is almost over. But not for Sundari.

She is cleaning up after the guests, picking up odd plates with half-eaten snacks, glasses lying carelessly about. But her moment is not over yet. Till she is in this beautiful dress, she is and will be a princess.

She walks over to the terrace. She has never seen anything this majestic.

The roaring expanse of water, slow-dancing palm trees, the soft breeze running through her hair. Is this how the royals look down upon the rest of the world?

The night is dark and the moon casts playful shadows on the patterned mosaic. She takes in a full, deep breath.

'Hi there!'

She turns slowly.

It is the Prince himself, at the other end of the terrace, gathering used bottles into a large garbage bag. The rest of his entourage, his large staff of servants, is not to be seen.

'Oh! Let me help you with that.'

Helping comes naturally to Sundari. Her dress is heavy and gets in the way when there is real work to be done.

'Thank you. What is your name?'

'Sundari,' she can barely whisper. Even the courage to answer is failing her. Why is he trying to talk to her? She is not that brave.

But the Prince doesn't know that. Who would not feel blessed to be graced by his presence?

He walks over to her side. Soft music still plays in the background.

Sundari does not raise her eyes, kneeling to clean the floor. But she can feel him moving closer. Her eyes instinctively dart towards the drawing room. All the guests seem to have left.

She is alone with the Prince.

'Do you live in this building?' This time the question is in Hindi.

It is darker now and the shadows on the mosaic are starting to look ominous. He is sitting really close and when he speaks again, she can smell alcohol on his breath.

He reaches out and places his hand on hers.

She doesn't know why but she feels a growing panic in her bones. The kind that turns you to stone and does not let you move.

He caresses her face, placing a stray wisp of hair behind her ear. That is a signature Prince move, replayed oh so many times, on screen and off it.

His fingers are gentle, but her heart thuds really hard. She remains flushed, rooted to the spot.

Suddenly, at that very moment, the large clock in the drawing room strikes once. It is midnight, time to leave.

The trance is broken. She lets go of his hand and picks herself up in a hurry. The Prince smiles at her sudden coyness and extends his arm to pull her back toward him. She is quick to step away.

The clock continues to toll, a slow twelve times, as Sundari rushes toward the door. Her feet tremble and flail as she tries to slip into the mojdis lying by the entrance.

Suddenly, she feels a cold palm on her back.

* * *

After that evening, Sundari is nowhere to be seen.

'Carter Road maid runs away with neighbour's gold,' local tabloids claim.

Word in the castle is that she made off with Mrs Hussain's jewellery, taking advantage of her generous and trusting nature. Whispers in the servants' quarters say she has left for her village. But who knows the real truth?

The old lady is heartbroken and refuses to speak to anyone.

Her employers, Kaaki and the twins, are shocked. 'She was like family to us! We will fully cooperate in finding the truth.'

The police may investigate her belongings for further clues. In particular, a large wooden box in her living quarters.

Some neighbours recall she was last seen at the Bollywood star's party. When contacted, the Prince declined comment.

The only reliable witness is a lone slipper, fallen astray on the penthouse landing.

FIRE

Sucharita Dutta-Asane

I saw her the first time one winter morning, fresh from her bath, swaying, or so I felt at the time, beside a man I dearly loved. The sun's fresh warmth was on her back and bare neck. She turned around for an instant and spat red and green on a tuft of yellow grass, wiped her mouth with the back of her hand only to smile and accept the handkerchief her companion offered. Her smile held no shame; his gesture no rebuke.

When he saw me, he laughed aloud, 'O ho! Sharat! Come, come. Welcome to our village.' He enveloped me in a hug whose warmth I carry with me.

Her smile was warm, too, young and carefree, lips moist and dark with the juice of betel leaves.

* * *

When I meet her again, her youth has slid off her once-narrow shoulders and the parting in her hair is ashen.

I meet her on the other side of a raging fire, its flames crackling with discontent. The villagers stare at the fire, the flames etched on their foreheads, their fields within those flames, the crops roasting before the plucking.

I am back in the village, tracking, once again, the story of land. *Who has done this to them? Have they accepted niyati, fate? Will they fight back for what is theirs? How will they fight?*

A figure disengages itself from the group, tall and gaunt. It swings a long braid away from itself...two hands come up to wind it around the head...the figure moves away with a familiar swing of the hips.

Savitri, Dileep's wife, enters a hut. Shadows dance on its walls, of kitchen flames, of human beings.

Should I ask questions of the shadows first? *Who burnt their crops?* If shadows can laugh, they will at me; ask some other question, they will say.

Savitri stokes the fire and puts a heavy vessel on the mud-baked oven.

I am meeting her for the first time after Dileep's death. My questions dry up in my throat, but she must have sensed my presence; she turns to look at me standing in the dark outside.

'What do you want here, Sharat Babu?'

I hesitate at the threshold.

'Come inside. Why do you stand there, in the darkness?'

I enter and stand quietly.

'What do you need?' She raises a thick, shapely eyebrow, a dancer's eyebrow.

'Uh, actually, I wanted to talk. With you.'

'Then stand to my right, my left ear is not much use.'

I know about it. The iron rod had just about spared her left eye, or that, too, would have become useless. 'You had a narrow escape.'

She smiles and I see a trace of that first smile.

Her words are hushed, as is the dance of the kitchen flames.

I sit beside her on the cool mud floor, draw up my knees and wrap my arms around them.

'A war has casualties.'

'Yes. More than human casualties. Much more.' She gives me a cursory glance and turns to the woman kneeling at her elbow with a banana leaf plate. Savitri doles out rice and lentils on the leaf. 'They come for our minds. When we hold those back, they kill our bodies.'

The rich aroma of hot rice and dal spread out on fresh banana leaves fills the thatched room and reminds me of my own hunger. The men eat hurriedly and leave. They have work to do, vigil to keep. These are no ordinary nights; these are nights of terror and of vigil. I have seen terror stalk the village in the initial days and heard the youthful discontent of that time: *the land is no good if we have to die for it.*

'Our young understand money, Sharat Babu.'

'Do they support you now?'

'My husband spent sleepless nights convincing them.'

'And?'

'You ask so much.'

'Are you people united now?'

She turns sharply towards me. 'And why do you want to know?'

'Do you suspect me? I am only doing my work. You know that. Do you want me to leave?'

'Aren't you here now, whether we want or not?'

Her ebony skin glows in the light from the kitchen fire; her eyes search mine. Between us stands the ghost of her husband, Dileep, the one who trusted me.

There's a hint of a smile in her dark eyes. 'You ask whether we are united. We say, yes, we are; outside this village, they will say it's a story, that everybody wants the money except a foolish handful.

'You ask whether we are united. We say no, we are not; they will say, so let's divide them further; money, food, drugs, women.

'Go away, Sharat Babu, watch, write what you will, don't ask anything. But first, eat.'

She pushes a leaf plate of dal and rice towards me. As a concession for my status as guest, a blob of boiled and mashed potato with a dark green chilly thrust into it.

The dal is good, fresh and salty; its aroma and taste mingle with that of the steaming rice, the potato pulp and the warm leaf.

When I return to the hut after washing my hands, Savitri and a handful of men and women are huddled around a rickety table in the middle of the room, away from the door. Savitri looks up at me, her eyes two pinpoints of ember.

'Go, Sharat Babu. We have work.'

Nobody disobeys that tone.

In the fields, the flames lunge one last time for the moon.

As I walk into the darkness, my thoughts slowly wind back to Dileep, idealistic, driven, dead.

Reports of the initial stage point to dissonance of thought and action—the young wanted money in lieu of land; for the old, the land was all they had known since birth. Dileep and Savitri had been among the handful of men and women who had opposed the 'land-grab'.

'The dalal came on his phatphati,' Dileep's voice rings in my ears. 'We heard before we saw; what we saw was a cloud of dust, and then he emerged from it, white clothes layered with brown dust, sitting astride a black and red motorcycle.

'You should have seen his drama, Sharat. He got off his vehicle taking more time than necessary, as if he were performing a scene: he extended a hand for his companion's handkerchief, wiped grime from his forehead and face, then turned around and spat dust, took off his spectacles and wiped them. Finally, wiping betel juice from his mouth, he looked around like a lord. Lord of all he surveyed.

'We were standing at a distance, a little confused. What did this man want? I must have stared the hardest.' Dileep had laughed, tickled by the memory. 'Anyway, he noticed me staring at him and shouted out with a dismissive wave of his hand. "*Aiee!*"'

Dileep's mouth had turned at the corners.

'When he told us of his demands, I refused, along with Gopi, Bhanu and some others; those who crowded behind us carried the odour of fear in their sweat.'

'What did he have to say?'

Dileep had turned around and pointed to the hill behind us. As far as I could see, there were sal and mahua trees, interspersed with flaming palash. On top of the hill, coconut trees swayed in a gentle arc around a newly painted temple. The river shimmered between where we stood amidst the crops and the trees. This is the picture I would draw in my sketchbooks as a child—the sun yellow, the river a straight line in blue, a couple of triangular boats bobbing on the water.

'See all this? Mineral rich. This land is sona, Sharat. Gold.' He spread his arms, palms turned outwards, indicating the spread of hill, land, river, crops, in one sweeping gesture. 'Why should we enjoy all this alone? That's what he came to ask.'

His lips curled. 'We are sleeping on a treasure trove, Sharat, that's what he said, as if we needed the information. And we? We, illiterate, uncultured dregs don't understand its worth. He wanted to educate us.'

We were walking along the river. In the monsoon months, it would swell and sometimes wash over the land next to it.

'Uffh! The dreams he tried to sell.' Dileep chuckled. 'Money, city clothes, air-conditioned cinema, hotels, motorcycles...'

He suddenly stood still, wrenched imaginary sticks from the breeze around us and thrust his clenched fists downwards. 'We are exhausted, but we haven't given up. One day, you might find I am no more, my bullet-ridden body lying in some...'

I had interrupted him that day, pushed away the image to the sidelines of vagrant thought.

The sole motorcycle had made way for much more. Bulldozers, excavators, trucks, shovels, drills, and workers began to assemble outside the village. Tin-shed hutments and armed guards grew in number and billboards went up announcing the future factory and township site.

Villagers who were against the intrusion mounted their resistance, at first silently, then with increasing and louder momentum. A worker setting up the makeshift office was gagged and beaten. Work came to a standstill. The villagers celebrated.

Then the village came under siege.

Inside the village, the police roamed free, searching, arresting, questioning.

Some of the villagers said they were beaten up.

On my trips to the village, I didn't notice any such incident, but women would supposedly disappear to return raped and tortured; children had dropped out of school.

Within a fortnight, the village began to look storm-ravaged, uprooted trees and deep ditches lined its periphery; there were whispers of mass revolt everywhere. Dileep said the village came together to fight the day Bhola's pregnant wife returned home bruised, eyes swollen with shame and pain, her stomach deseeded.

I wrote what I saw, surmised what I didn't. One morning, as I was returning from a meeting with the policemen who'd set up camp in what used to be a primary healthcare centre, I met Dileep.

'You should be away from women when they are angry,' he said.

'Don't tell me you have time for domestic squabbles now.' I laughed aloud.

'Domestic squabbles? Yes, of course, why not? *Vasudhaiva kutumbakam.* The whole world is one family, isn't it?' He smiled and dipped his toes in the river water. 'She thinks I am lying to our people.'

'She does?'

'You see, Sharat, I told them banks rob people in the cities.'

'What!'

He thumped me on the back. 'No, no. I didn't quite say that. It's what they want to believe.'

'But...'

'Have you seen the sky during monsoons? We wait for the clouds to appear, celebrate their arrival...we are full of faith. The clouds are not darkness but the promise of a better time, but they are clouds, whisked away by the next gust of wind. Do those clouds lie?'

'Why is she angry?'

'Timir, Kailash, Aarto...most of the younger men want money for land. How long will that last, Sharat? You tell me. How long? What will they do afterwards? Pull rickshaws? Wash other people's vessels? Live ten to a room in dirty hovels? Money vanishes from banks, not from land.'

Dileep died the next day, or perhaps that night; his body was found the next afternoon, spread-eagled at the river's edge, one foot in the water.

In the evening, the village congregated at his house, offering sympathy to Savitri, talking of fate, of power and pelf, of the need for submission.

Savitri sat by her husband's corpse, dry-eyed, the parting in her hair still vermilion-bright.

By the time we were ready to leave, she had ruled out submission.

* * *

Sunrise is hours away. What is happening in the lamplit room?

In this village, among the jungles and hills, power supply is erratic, water exists only in its rivers and ponds, and the villagers have cut off the roads, or whatever's left of them. I can move around at will, but am suspect on either side of the divide. Damned either way. What am I doing chasing this story? I don't know, except that other stories reverberate in my mind, my father's stories, tales of losing land, of losing identity, of regretting that loss, the eternal pining away of souls. My father never reconciled himself to that loss.

A slight sound. A whip's crack in the heavy night. I swivel around from my uncomfortable post where I must have dozed off at some point. Figures move about quietly, flitting through the moon's light and shadows.

The village seems active. Leaves and tender branches tremble in the breeze. All around me, I sense urgency. I stand up and take two slow, quiet steps, careful not to make any noise. A hand clamps over my mouth, a disembodied voice whispers in my ear. 'Go back to your room at dawn, no snooping around today.'

My tape recorder and digital camera are in the room. I count the hours, knowing well enough that the first movement from my place could be my last. I was commanded to be quiet and have no desire at this haunting moment to interrupt whatever is going on in the village.

When the sky comes alive, I head for my hut. All around me, numbness pervades the air, a silence that brooks no intrusion; the leaves beneath my feet seem too noisy.

There's a sudden movement above me. I look up into the eyes of a child. A slingshot across his bare chest, arms akimbo, bare feet placed apart on two adjacent branches, head shrouded with leaves, he looks down at me with eyes that freeze my soul.

...I never forget them, day or night:
They beat on my head for memory of them;
They pound on my heart and I cry back to them...

Sandburg out of the blue, out of hazy memories of coffee smoke and nicotine stains, out of nowhere in particular.

I am in a hurry to get my recorder and camera. Another row of huts and then mine. Where are the babies and the old?

Aah!

Something seems to hit my head, over my right ear. I turn to my side and fall, slowly, as in a story, into the soft beds of paddy that frame the mud tracks, not knowing for long seconds what's happened to me. Another ear-splitting crack and my senses return. Bullets. But who? Where? These are bullets whizzing past. The villagers don't have guns.

Do you have guns in the village?
Crazy, are you? Guns? Who will buy them for us, Sharat
Babu?
The police think you do.
The police think many things.

Something slices the air right before my eyes, and then a stifled scream. I get up, crouch, and run for cover to the nearest hut.

The men who camp along the outer periphery, in the panchayat office, in the school building, the market shed, don't believe me.

'How are they fighting us without arms and ammo, sir? Who are you with?'

'You forget, I am only reporting.'

'Your paper has blanked out all the noise. So, for whom do you report?'

'Freelancing.'

'What?'

'Nothing.'

A constable looks from me to his senior. 'We have to protect the villagers, sir.'

'You shut up. Want a transfer to a non-family posting, do you? Or do you want these people to sit beside your wife and sister and issue their orders? *Protect*, he says! Just do your work.'

The village lies low. Provisions and supplies must be running out.

The women chop vegetables deftly, steel in their hands, experts at their work. I sit close to them at the door to the hut, listening to their conversation, writing.

'Sharat Babu, why are you still here? Don't you have enough fodder for your paper?'

As I turn to look at her, Savitri looks at her companions, then back at me. 'We want to know...are you with us?'

I nod vaguely; she jerks her head at me in an unexpectedly awkward gesture, her neck taut. 'Come with me.'

'Where?'

'I'll trust you, Sharat Babu, for your friend's sake, in his memory. Stay near me, not too close, but don't give yourself away. Batuk will accompany me.'

'Then why do you need me around?'

'If something happens, somebody should know. You go everywhere, nobody will suspect you.'

Delicious irony.

'What are you up to, Savitri? There may be search operations again. What will you do?'

'You're thinking of your work, Sharat Babu. You can go, we'll manage.'

'No! Wait, Savitri! I didn't mean it that way. I'll be there. Tell me the time and place.'

'Tomorrow night. Batuk and I will go to town.'

'Why you?'

She turns away.

* * *

The tamarind tree seems to grow out of the well beside which it stands. The water in the well is sweet and cool. In our childhood, we would listen to countless stories about ghosts living in tamarind trees. In this silence and dull moonshine, I wait like a spectre under the tree and recollect those stories.

What is expected of me?

Leaves rustle in the light breeze. After a while, two familiar shadows appear on the red path between the burnt paddy fields.

Savitri knows myriad ways around this village where she first came as a young bride, perhaps knows it better than anybody else; she should, for Dileep and she had crawled through its depths chalking out a course for their fight, setting traps for their enemies, identifying alternative trails. Perhaps, this is the reason she was making this trip, and not the men, perhaps the only reason, but where would she go?

There is much I will never know.

'What will you do if they take away what is ours, Savitri?' Dileep had once asked his wife. We were sitting by the river where he would one day die.

'What will you do?' she had asked.

'Fight to the end.'

'Then why ask me?'

'You are weak before their double might, power and brute strength...when I'm not there...'

'I'll wrest it back from them. Live up to my name, like in the story.'

Dileep had scoffed at her reference to mythical aspiration. 'Name! In this day and age! Even you can be foolish, Savitri.'

Their weapons, the ones I had seen, were relics, a throwback to medieval times; arrows, poison vats, spears, hatchets and axes, hammers and clubs, and mashaals, flaming torches. Yet, I had heard bullets whiz past, felt their aftershock.

At first, there was the flurry of daily newspaper reports. Then the media suddenly deserted them, moved on to other stories. It confused them but it also helped them in a way, I think; it helped them fight in a more cohesive manner, the unity of feeling deserted by the world.

The shadows move on; I follow almost involuntarily, three ghosts flitting through the scalded memories of crops.

All of a sudden, I stop short, almost stagger into Batuk's back; he has suddenly halted, right behind Savitri who extends restraining arms towards us.

A solitary point of light shines in the dark among the trees, moving surreally from one point to another. I can barely discern Savitri push back at Batuk, step back and crouch, one palm over her mouth.

Slowly, she turns around and places her forefinger and middle finger in a V at her mouth.

Cigarette.

The pinprick of light is being passed around from one mouth

to another, one set of fingers to another. As the two glide away from the spot, I stumble along behind them at a distance.

It's a long walk towards the riverbank. Under the cover of darkness, a boatman waits, a trusted fellow no doubt, but why this mode of transport?

Then I remember, the roads are cut off; what remains is under the command and surveillance of opponents who do not fight with antiquated weapons.

I often feel convinced that the village has its own cache of arms, gifted by the people who had initially supported them. When they withdrew support, did they take away their gifts, too? Unlikely.

We whisper for a while, instructions for their return, instructions in case of no return, and then Savitri and Batuk disappear down the slope towards the river, the gentle splashing of oars the only sound that trails their existence through the darkness. They will return tomorrow at the same time, under this cover of darkness. I should cover their tracks.

Will I find my way back alone?

Slowly, I retrace my steps, the soft swish of the oars, barely audible, sounds loud to my ears as I look for the signs I'd left behind, subtle indicators only I would notice—a half-chewed bit of gum, a piece of paper stuck in the bend of a tree, a trail of stones.

I am bone tired when I reach my hut, with no desire to venture out till it's time for their return.

* * *

The boatman's oars must have been a little too loud, the trail Sharat left behind a little too obvious, the men at the village edge a little too practiced when they jump him the next evening.

The blackness of the afterhours is all he could remember when confronted about the incident.

Savitri is on her way back. Her heart jumps a beat at not finding Sharat by the Mahua tree near the rocks. The river had given her anonymity, she is on land again; she shouldn't have allowed Batuk to stay back in town, but it is too late to rue the decision.

In the distance, the panchayat office looks like a dull white smudge; she has to keep low, stay close to the broken wall that circles the party office. She carries only one bag, but it is heavy, it slows her down. Fifty metres away from the panchayat office, she stumbles on a lump, steadies herself and moves on.

She walks ahead and stops, then retraces her steps as if in a trance until she reaches the object over which she had stumbled. She stoops low and touches it. Soft. The smell of human blood. Her fingers warm and wet from contact, she kneels beside the body.

Is it somebody from the village? Only she knows of this path, and anyway, nobody had reason to venture out, not until she and Batuk returned with the provisions, not till Sharat conveyed the all-well message.

She doesn't get the time to think or to draw back the sackcloth that covers the victim's face.

* * *

A thousand moons wax and wane before Savitri can wrap her torn garment around her trembling body and draw herself up to her feet. She staggers out of the low-roofed building that was once the village school where her husband used to teach, the only cement and brick house in the vicinity, now in the hands of the land mafia and their political bosses.

Distress gnaws at her body and mind, a numbing rawness envelops her being, but she stands straight and stiff under a moon that shines listlessly around her on the fields, disappears in the bushes, and emerges on the other side in the water that glistens.

'Tell your women. We'll come for them!'

One of them kicks her in the stomach, lightly, playfully; their toy for the night, their open challenge to the village.

Their laughter spills out behind her.

She could have slashed out with the sickle she hid under the folds of her garment, but that had fallen off in the scuffle somewhere near the body.

Her mind claws its way forward, inch by painful inch, trying to grasp all that had happened in the past few hours...how many? She loses count. The rawness and the blood coagulated in patches on her body remind her that humiliation is not countable.

Their laughter and their threat follow her through the black-green jungle and fields. Sweltering, throbbing, she walks. She thinks of the women and girls of her village, of the sickle she has lost, and feels its curved sharpness against her heart.

Standing in the open fields, she inhales long and deep and reorganizes the shreds of her garment. In her mind, she hears the clamour of other rebellions, those of the past, the present, and those yet to come.

She stands surrounded by the burnt remains of their labour and ululates.

In the village, the people hear it and come out of their houses.

In the school building behind her, the men hear it and stand still for a few moments before looking at one another, their eyes white in the dark.

In the makeshift police station where Sharat is held captive, he hears and looks up at the torn piece of sky through a slit in the wall.

Savitri stands alone in the middle of a vast openness with the stars and a cloudy moon above her. Tired, she shuts her eyes and thinks of the men who raped her. She remembers shutting her eyes in agony, then opening them again to look at their faces in the flickering bulb-light. She'd watched the expressions flit across their faces—the faces change, replace one another—seen them concentrate on her body, not on her; seen their triumph after nights of subjugation.

She inhales long and deep, her mind already far away from what they had done to her body, focused on what needs to be done.

TOUCH ME NOT

S. Bari

Ma made him buy boots before he left. 'They're very expensive over there.' They keep his feet warm and dry, these ankle-high lace-up boots, but he dreads putting them on, even as his second cold winter glides into town. He fights his feet in, wiggling until the heels drop into place, and feels he has tied weights around his ankles. He spent his childhood and adolescence in rubber flip-flops and canvas 'keds' and the occasional black loafer. He hurries to class, dragging these boots through the carpet of dry snow.

When he first arrived, he relished the chill autumn, the sharp crack of dry leaves, and the colours along the treetops—yellow, mustard, gold, saffron, vermilion, fawn—stretched out like saris drying in the sun. He signed up at student housing and picked out his classes, chatted with anyone he wished, and ate whatever he craved. But now, as the days darken and the trees bare their branches, the spaciousness of solitude gives way to the claustrophobia of loneliness.

He is a small-town boy, and he has come to study for a graduate degree in another small town, through the looking glass and across the world. For his first Thanksgiving, a local family invites him home. He diligently swallows the bland turkey meat and helps with the washing up. He calls his parents regularly, using pre-paid discount cards bought at the corner store.

'Tonight, I'm going to a political event. The town is going to elect a mayor, and my friends have asked me to help fold letters.'

He knows nothing about the candidates and isn't interested, but he wants to see how these things work here. The room is in the back of the library, with very bright lights and a long vinyl-topped table covered with sheets of paper. Music is blaring from the loudspeakers, and volunteers are shouting to each other. He feels at home in the organized raucousness. Someone hands him a letter and shows him the required fold. He follows suit, folding once, then twice, till every letter is perfectly folded in three. When the folding is done, he is handed a large brown box and a cutter.

'Posters of the candidate. Give everyone fifty each to put up around town.'

Slicing into the masking tape and folding back the cardboard, he sees her picture. 'Deborah Smith for Mayor.' Her black hair cut short now. Her chin is rounder and her jaw at once fuller and sharper. She is looking at the camera straight on, wearing something red. There are little gold earrings in her ears. Her hesitant smile is just the same.

He was ten when she came to his small town. She had signed up for Volunteer Away right after college, and when they assigned her a country, she ran home and looked for 'her' country in the atlas. There it was, wedged like a plug between India and Burma, spreading into the brown waters of the Bay of Bengal. 'More like fingers of land than an entire solid country,' she told him.

The whole family went to receive her at the train station. She was the only white person who got off the train. His parents had made him wear his best pair of trousers and a scratchy shirt with a collar. He expected a woman with blonde hair, wearing short clothes and showing the tops of her breasts like the white women in the posters his cousin hid under the mattress. But she came out wearing a salwar kameez that someone had bought her in the capital, and her hair was long and black like his mother's. As she came towards them, he saw her eyes were blue.

Ma hugged her and told her she was welcome in their town and in their home. Baba held out his hand for her suitcase. And then she looked down at the ten-year-old boy.

'Who's this?'

'My name is Aleem.'

He was speaking English to a native-born English speaker for the first time in his life. She knew not to say more—he couldn't answer more. She walked with him to the car that Baba had borrowed from Uncle for this trip.

He wondered how she knew what to do, how to eat with the fingers of her right hand, and how to cover her head with her veil at the right times. Who had told her these things? Ma said she was respectful and kind.

In the morning, he walked with her to the girls' school, where she stopped at the gate and turned to say goodbye, while he walked on to the boys' school. Her salwar was short on her, and her ankles showed. She walked like a boy. She taught English to the big girls.

'What's in here? She turned over the little packet of twisted clear plastic wrap stuffed with dark-brown paste. They stood at the candy-man's cart in front of the girls' school. Fluorescent tubes of chewing gum and chocolate in bright red wrappers lay stacked next to crackling bags of roasted chickpeas. He bit a corner of the packet and squeezed the paste out, grimacing as the sour shock of it hit his tongue.

'Tetul.'

What was it in English? They decided to stop by the market and ask the man who sold old paper for re-use and recycling. He was known to understand several languages.

'Tamarind,' he told them definitively, frowning at the two of them. 'Why do you want to know?'

She held up the plastic sleeve of tamarind paste and giggled, and he frowned again.

'You will get sick on that stuff,' his voice came after them.

He sits back on his heels, squatting the way they can't here. He holds the poster and looks carefully again. It *is* her, and she seems well.

The posters are put up in the right neighbourhoods. He becomes a campaign regular. He googles Deborah Smith, reads about her in the free paper in town. She talks about making the town a place that young people want to stay on and work in, even after they graduate. About setting up research facilities and creating jobs, about the need to be welcoming to immigrants because they create ideas and wealth, and about caring for the less fortunate. Her opponent calls her a communist and hints at lesbianism.

He goes to a political rally and sees her standing on a platform that is level with his chin. She has no security, at least none that he can see. She is muffled in a scarf, but the front of her coat is open, so she must be a little warm from the exertion of the speech. He does not remember her words later, but her voice is familiar. The high, light voice of sixteen years ago has not matured or deepened. Instead, from the elegant, coated figure in the scarf and low heels comes the voice of the twenty-three-year-old, fresh-out-of-college girl on her first Volunteer Away assignment.

He and Baba sat together at dinner time, their enamelled plates steaming with rice. Ma stood by Baba's side, serving the vegetables first—crunchy okra or slimy eggplant, tender potatoes, or his favourite, red spinach that came only in the winter. Then the fish, sometimes prickly with bones, which gradually collected at the side of the plate. Debi watched Baba delicately pick out the bones and tried to do the same, but she eventually gave up and just chewed determinedly until they were reduced to a lumpy mass. Ma laughed at her and showed her again and again how to pick out each slender filament from the flesh, without success.

Aleem's oldest cousin, who was twenty, asked if he ever saw her breasts. Aleem had not even seen the tops of her breasts, because she never wore saris, only kameez, which went up to her neck. But his cousin and he could look at the bras she wore, hanging on the laundry line, even though Ma hung them on the line behind the water tank on the roof. They were of a cloth so fine that it seemed transparent to him, and one of them had tiny blue flowers on the bowls where her breasts went.

She helped Aleem with homework, and he helped her learn

Bangla. Within a month, she knew how to buy things at the market, to take the laundry to the ironing man and count the pieces of clothing, to be stern with the older boys in the market who followed her, and to name most of the plants in the garden. The whole family went to the village for Eid, and she joined Ma for a bath in the river. He knew because they left with several other women, carrying cakes of soap and extra saris. When she came back, Ma had wrapped her in a sari, and Aleem saw her shoulders were pink with a small white stripe.

The only desk in the house, apart from his father's, was in the room that they had given their guest. In the evenings, she sat on her bed, reading and writing letters home, while he studied at the desk. 'What is the English for *ilish machh*?'

Her grubby dictionary told them it was hilsa. 'Although that's not really an English word, I think,' she would say, rubbing her chin.

They debated why there was no real word for 'thank you', except for the excessively formal 'dhonnobad'.

'Everyone knows you're a foreigner when you say that.'

'Everyone knows I'm a foreigner anyway,' she said, and they giggled. It was what the boys in the market called after her, singing about women from faraway lands that they loved. When Ma walked with her, they did not dare, but with only Aleem around, they were bolder. Sometimes they followed her down the narrow mud-carpeted lanes, wagging their hips and saying words that Aleem knew he could not translate even if he wanted. Then the stall-keepers would swear at them or cuff one of them on the head.

The campaign group is informal and unfunded. When it comes time to hold fancy fundraising events, the most they can do is wangle a banquet hall from a local restaurateur. But the food must be served, and Aleem and others are brought in, tucked into black suits and bow ties, and handed platters lined with little slices of bread cradling cucumbers, shrimps or asparagus. Trays bristle with tall glasses of sparkling wine. He is nervous with the drinks trays, an incipient wobble always threatening his elbow. Tired velvet curtains sag by the French windows under the slightly bluish lights. Across a small field of white-clothed tables, he sees her walk in.

She is smaller than he remembers. Several organizers gather by her side in a deferential gaggle, keeping a slight but constant distance. 'Here, shall we have a photo op right under the entrance?'

'Can we check out the podium?' Their voices form a bubble around her, moving with her as she glides through the crowd. She shakes hands, smiles, nods or frowns, touches elbows, and looks concerned. He, too, nods and smiles as guests graze snacks off his tray and denude his forest of drinks. He hands out tiny napkins and swings into the kitchen for refills. She is sometimes far from him and sometimes near enough for him to start worrying. What if she recognizes him—and remembers what no one would want to remember? What if she doesn't recognize him?

He is being guided by a woman about his own age towards the centre of the room. 'Can we get Ms Smith some refreshments?'

She smiles the big smile that American women own, inclusive and apparently indiscriminate. She moves him in the direction she wants without touching him. He has to follow.

He holds out the tray and Debi reaches for a drink. 'Thank you.' And looks at him with a smile.

She has not recognized him.

His father's small house was matched by a small garden. While Ma tended her dahlias and gardenias, he preferred the hidden huddles of weeds and the tiny pond where he could catch frogs. He showed Debi where the water lilies sheltered chubby splotched frogs, and she told him that people in France ate the legs of frogs. They knelt by the pond and pretended to eat frogs' legs, passing each other an imaginary jar of pickled tamarind to liven up the slimy feast, until Ma called them in before the mosquitoes set upon them.

Debi told him about her little brother who lived in a state called Minnesota and had never seen a mango or a tamarind pod. She told him how the snow piled up outside her house, and how on some days they couldn't go to school. Instead, they built tunnels and forts in the snow and fought battles with snow that they patted in their hands and made into little cannonballs. They had a bully in their neighbourhood—like the big boys in the market here who sat at the soft-drinks stall all day—but he was rather slow. So, they dared him to lick the railing near the railway tracks and his tongue got stuck to the metal because of the cold. Aleem had to ask his science teacher to explain the cleverness of this prank.

Aleem showed Debi a delicate fern, whose entire frond was smaller than his ten-year-old hand. Looking up at her expectantly, he touched it. As if a shiver had run down its spine, the frond closed. Debi drew a sharp breath. 'That's amazing. What is that?'

'A lajjabati. A shy girl.'

They checked the dictionary, but its knowledge did not stretch to obscure reaches of botany. They went to the school library, which was also proved incapable.

It was just a few weeks later that he came home from school and found Ma sitting on Debi's bed, folding her salwar kameez. On Debi's desk was a tiffin box, packed with food that was still hot, the lids unbuckled to let out the steam. Debi was on a corner of the bed, wrapping her pair of everyday sandals in a jute wrapper. Neither of them looked at Aleem. Debi's backpack, which had been emptied and hoisted on top of the clothes cupboard the day she arrived, lay open-mouthed on the floor.

'Where are you going?'

'Go wash your hands and feet. I'll get some snacks for you,' Ma intervened.

Debi did not look up. Aleem stood at the door until Ma got up and steered him to the bathroom. When he came to the dining table, she laid out his food silently and poured him cold water. He asked if Debi was leaving, and Ma told him she needed to see her family and they would have to say goodbye to her. He loitered around her door later, but Debi did not look up or even shift from her position. She held the sandals in their jute wrapping on her lap and looked at them. Baba came home and sent Aleem to his friend's house, despite it being a school day. When Aleem came back for dinner, Debi stayed in her room. Ma said, 'Poor, innocent girl.' Baba did not answer.

* * *

The speeches are made, and dinner is served. He is assigned to another table, but after dessert and another speech when everyone clinks their glasses together, she gets up and moves from table to table. She touches someone's back and leans in to laugh. After all the tables, she approaches the band of waiters near the kitchen doors. One by one, they shake her hand, and when she sees him, she pauses, holding his hand. 'Where are you from?'

He tells her. She brings her eyebrows together for just a moment, then a smile slowly rises to her lips. 'I know it a little bit. Which part are you from?'

He tells her. 'I'm much older now, but I am Aleem. I was only ten then. I'm at the university here now, doing a PhD. I just came last year. I didn't know you lived here. I'm sorry you had to see me.' He tried to stop after each thought but could not.

She still held his hand in hers. 'Little Aleem, little brother, bhai.'

'We didn't know where you had gone.'

She let out a long breath.

What happened to Debi? Why did she go without even talking to me? Did she not like our house? Were you too strict with her? For weeks, Aleem badgered his parents. She had to go back, they explained. They were more patient with him than he had ever known them to be. He heard them between themselves, with their relatives, talk about her honour. Her shame. But these were words that, to him, had no physical form, no literal meaning. He did not know to match them to the big boys with the untranslatable words in the market who had followed Debi around.

It was a few years before Aleem understood that their words had ripened into plans for an afternoon when Debi would be walking home alone through the market—the place creaking under the weight of jackfruit and red chilis and bright plastic houseware, and reeking of dried fish—past the old abandoned machinery depot with its rusting mid-century hardware, at the same time that the boys would be inside, high on *ganja*.

She asks about Ma and Baba, about the town, and about how he got from school to college and now here. She asks him to visit her at her law offices and hands him her card. He shakes her hand as if she were someone he had just met and watches her walk away.

Three days later, he puts on his only shirt with a collar, prompting his roommate to look questioningly at him. He catches the bus downtown and looks alternately at the street signs and her card till he finds the low-rise corporate building. An assistant in very high heels shows him in, and she is sitting behind a dark grey desk with a matte metallic shine. She comes around and hugs him, and he says without intention, 'You look well, you look so well.'

She pulls back and holds him by his shoulders. 'I am well. It took me years, but I am well.'

She has never made her case public, and Volunteer Away is grateful. 'I didn't want to think about it or talk about it for the longest time.'

Aleem turns away. He doesn't want to hear about it. He is ashamed, for those boys, for his town. She says it could have happened anywhere, to any young woman. She wants him to hear about meeting other rape survivors and how that helped her.

'When I was better, I didn't want to remember my assignment for only that.' She wants to remember it for Aleem, his parents, the school children, and the teachers. And the recycled-paper man.

Her parents think that the media may find a connection between her and Aleem and try to buy his story. But if she knows Aleem, her little brother, he would not contemplate such a thing.

He says seriously, 'I have no story. I didn't even know what had happened until I was older.'

Before he leaves, she says, 'I want to show you something. As soon as I had access to an encyclopedia, I looked it up.'

They go to her computer screen, and she types in 'lajjabati'.

'Touch-me-not,' shine the black letters on the glowing screen.

PART THREE

Verse of Resilience

CLAIM

Arundhathi Subramaniam

Day dawns without debts, without doubts
                                —Pablo Neruda

Before doubt octobers
the mind into a clammy stupor,
before the tongue furs
into clichés, before opinions
turn gouty,
grant us the innocence
of birdcall, unburdened
by a heritage of birds who have called
before, and better.

Let there be heat on this page,
and bile, and let us be part
of the magic, oh god,
don't leave us out.

Doubt again
and again doubt,
and I think of how many days
we have let slip
because others' voices
were louder than our own.

No, we don't serve up
neat styrofoamed verse.
We sprawl, we lumber, we stain.
We love like everyone else,
with the thick odour of pathology.

We are ink and syrup
and virulent acid.
We are the midgets
who turn in three strides
into lords of the universe.
We are here to restore order,
to put the voices—of books, lovers,
teachers, customs officials—
in their places.

We are the upstarts,
ready finally to take up space,
demand time,
settle down on the page.

BIRANGONA

Sadaf Saaz

Heroic one.
The name bequeathed you
But you would have to
Be much more than that
In the years to come.

The wrong we did by you
We all knew
What you went through
Never black and white
Fighting through the greys
The multiple ways
You had to.

That official line
Our mothers and sisters
Lost their honour
Rather than the other way around
Those who found
They got away
With crimes against humanity
While all that remains
Is the shame
Stuck on you
Whatever you do

Can't shrug off
The stain we create.

You survived your fate
To find family won't take you in
Woman of sin
Difficult to find work
Not paid if you do
After all

Why pay
When one can say
She is loose
To discard and use
Arid abuse.
When the police and military
Came next time round
It was you they offered
What did it matter
If they soiled you some more?

You are no longer
The mother of your son
Who found out
What you had done
Didn't want to hear what
Had been forced on you
Terrified and disgusted
He, and you, back then
To bear wounds never to heal
Which changed your life
And death
As no one gave you
A piece of cotton
To wrap your lifeless body
Though your soul left
40 long years ago
When you were cornered as you ran

Then it began
Men like giants on you

Till you got used to it
And when you found 'freedom'
In joy and longing

You were reviled
And defiled
By your own.

You are the one
Who dressed up and wore gold
And you sold
Your dreams
To the enemy
But your men folk and homes
Were left alone
For the sacrifice of this
Unsung dilemma.

You are the one
Who was caught
When ten of them
Found you in the dhan khet
Left you half dead
As you jumped in flowing waters
But found yourself still alive
On the other side
As you were pulled out like a
Fish in a net.

Afterwards not able to say
That your faeces dripped constantly
Till the day when you could
Take your own life.

You are the one
Who was stripped bare

When you dared
To tie the sari length around your neck
And when you tried again
Using your thick long braids
Your head was shaved
And like a captive animal
You were starved
To get you to obey
To what they say
Till you had no other way
Out

You are the one
Whose husband shunned you
When you could no longer satisfy him
Of course never yourself
Too scarred inside
And out
Even though your mother-in-law
Said it was not your fault
And ensured you a home.

You are the one
Whose husband cradled you
After his semen dripped
Down your swollen insides and legs
And loved you till
He was killed by local thugs
Greedy over land
And you were turned out
By his family and left to beg.

You are the one
Whose beautiful brown-eyed girl
Has blossomed in a far-away place
In a different time and space
The chosen land
She will never understand

And will never know how
You could bring all to tears
With your sweet lilting voice
Milking ballads of your soul
Or the endless nights of anguish and pain
You felt at giving up
A very part of you.

You are one of countless
Whose story was never told
And never will
As all records were burnt.
And you will never come forward
As your people brutalized you over again.
As your government
Washed its hands
Of you and your sacrifice
And doesn't want to know
What you went through then.
And still are now
If you managed to survive.

In 1971, during the Liberation War of Bangladesh, Pakistani soldiers carried out a brutal rape campaign against Bangladeshi women as a strategy of war. Exact figures are not known, but unofficial estimates put the number of rape victims over 2,00,000. The term given to the rape survivors of 1971 was 'Birangona'. Initially intended to signify a brave woman, this title has effectively become a pejorative label within the context of a conservative society because it is associated with the shame of rape.

After 1971, many rape survivors were not accepted back into their communities; they were ostracized by their families, often refused employment, and did not receive any form of compensation from the newly independent government.

The Pakistani government has still not officially apologized.

GUERRILLA

Bipasha B. Haque

I was taught double standards, crossing lines,
sucking the last raindrops, crumpling the dying narcissus,
doing this—mending that—and I got them all right.
I made them all proud. I ticked all the boxes,
as if I became them, them from top to bottom.
But then I started leaking, bloating, reducing...
I asked what was becoming of me?
They averted my eyes. I knew.
I knew I took the road not taken.
But I needed you. I...I wanted you...no no,
I wished to become your dream.
Your happiness. Your longing. Your sigh.

Your sigh—it lingered in my soul,
I saved teardrops in memoriam of that sigh
and slowly, as if by mischance of heavenly constellations,
by the southern cross, by the melting glaciers,
by this tumultuous time, by these frictions:
frictions that none but Heaven witnesses—
you became my smile.
And that is the time when I went to war.
My rank was that of a kitchen hand or lower,
but still it was a war and I was summoned to fight.

When I came home as a war veteran,
serving the country as a kitchen hand
through all the posthuman warring strategies,
through famine, deluge, through avalanches
and melted glaciers,
through chemical cum biological weapons
and, being a mercenary, being counterfeited,
being gassed and gagged I'd outlived my fellow species.

And above all I kept earning my medals,
O my medals, medals made of onion rings
and garlic, sages, and thymes! I wore them all.
I wore them all upon coming to you—
I had to take short service leave
to brag that I'm proud like Hell in being a kitchen hand.
I'm the kitchen hand by daylight like the daylight
and by night just like the night.

Meanwhile I've kept looking for new frontiers.
As for the blows, when they come left and right
I'll surely survive. I'm the guerrilla of all last frontiers.

SMOKE AND FIRE

Tamoha Siddiqui

'Heh! A cigarette in a woman's hand'
'Allah! No *niqab*[130] no shame!'
'The lady is a little too modern...'
'What does she think of herself?'

Voices rise; a toxic hurricane
discarding and dismissing
you like unwanted danger
a freak of nature

Your femininity is a cage
carefully customized to cater
to 'motherhood' and 'divinity'
enmeshed in clever conspiracy

It leaves no room for you
or your defiant lips
your collarbone your cleavage
your sensual skin your sexuality

There is no room here for you
this show is run by patriarchy
and the sharp whip of gender roles
is quick to try and put you in line. Wh-tch!

But you don't seem worried.
You have your eyes on the horizon
—you have built a fire deep in the forest
and the light, the light can be seen from the sky.

A red *teep*[131] of independence burns on your forehead
and the smoke of your gaze heralds revolution.

AMPHAN[132] CALLS

Mitali Chakravarty

The old Banyan split by
Amphan howls,
grows roots beyond time
into the womb of its Mother,
the Earth.

Born of the ribs of Earth,
Hawwa,[133] Eve
waft into the realms
of Brahmic vision as
Satrupa, an emanation
from a Man-God.

Emblematic of the energy
that gives Life, Prana needs
Rayi's[134] maleness to give matter to the soul,
to the invisible life force.

The old Banyan needs the Earth to grow.

To create Life, Eve, Hawwa, Satrupa became wives
to men in each stream carved by faith—
Age old lores consecrate
the fall of woman,
the greedy allurer of man

And yet in herself, the Woman contains man

Was Amphan—the invisible energy—a Woman?

Did She rage for you and me tearing, searing with madness
for the unspoken wounds which can only heal with phoenix teardrops?

Rise, rise up to Amphan's call—with our souls, let us conquer all

IN THE ABYSS OF NIGHT

Deepti Naval

Actress Deepti Naval talks of how she responded to violences she witnessed with poetry.

The poems in my first book, *Black Wind,*[135] belong to a particular period of my life. The years were 1990 to 1995. Perhaps I was too sensitive during this period. Suffering, madness, pain, abortion, death wish—I was witness to, I encountered them, I suffered their intensity. Women dealing with broken relationships. Lost chances. Riots in the city. Suicidal thoughts. Ephemeral friendship. Disintegration of the body—and of the mind. Which of these was—or can be—most disconcerting?

That time went by, and I moved away from it. I reached a state where I could look back and say, 'Yes, I have lived that...' I no longer squirmed at the thought of what I went through.

Emanating from that period in my life, most of the poems in *Black Wind* were about life in general. But they speak in an unfiltered voice of the sufferings women often put up with—in silence. Without a murmur of protest. Had they raised their voice, who knows, perhaps they would not have attempted suicide. Or go mad.

Black Wind

Anxiety grips me with both hands
Wounds open up and bleed

I gasp for breath and stagger around
Sharp corners of my single bed
A dark belligerent sea rises in anger
The night has a deadly mission, I can see
I will not succumb to its ghoulish lust
Pull the shutters down!
Block all sound;
Clamp it down!
Slam it!
Not in here, it can't get to me!

The telephone rings...no, it stops.
God damn! Why don't anyone speak?
A voice—
Just one human voice
In this shameless, pitiless
Abyss of the night
Gloom deepens to darkness, turns purple
I feel dark inside
They are here, they drive me
Dark shadows in my room
'Go jump!
One leap across the railing—
That's all it takes!'
Rain slashes down my window
Beats it blue!
A dagger pierces the gut and my sanity reels
'One leap! Yes...that's all...I know...'
'Do it! Have the guts! Jump!'
Demons from the sea
Stalk towards me stealthily...
I lurch back, grabble for reason
'...but my life...my art...?'
'Rotten life! Rotten Art! Rotten relationships!
Strip every moment to stark nakedness!
Think hard, debate!

Why should you live? Why?'
Hurled in a corner, I live and relive my life
Closing in on me, inch by deathly inch
Vicious, spiteful beings
Hissing...hissing...

'Your life's a mess! End it!'
'Yes...I...I...'
'A snake pit! That's what the world is! Quit!'
'But I have books...friends...music...'
Laughter hollers! Like the wind's unbeaten track!
'Hypocrisy! Masks! People tearing people!'
'But there's my work...'
'Pressure, competition, failure! An endless struggle!'
'I'll survive'
'Need the killer's instinct! Have it?'
'There's bougainvillea...and long distance calls...'
'Ha!'
'...mountains...movies...monsoons...'
'Escape...escape...escape...'
'Van Gogh's cypresses, and...evenings in the hills'
'You'll never learn!'
'Mustard fields...and motherhood?'
'Bad dreams! Give it up!'
'There are memories, and...letters home!'
'Emptiness! Loneliness! End it now! End it!'
'Making love...'
'Making what? Everyone uses everyone!'
'There is hope...isn't there?'

'It's a four letter word! End it now, you worm!'
'...and faith?'
'Regret! Shame! Guilt!'
'Love'
'Futile...'
'God?'

'Guilt! Guilt!'
'STOP IT......!!!'
A black wind howls through the wet marsh
The sea stands witness to an undefended siege
I will survive this night, its deathly design
I will fight!
The world's a snake pit, so let it be...
I dare the devil to get the better of me!

...Most of the poems in the anthology came out of my deep interest in psychology and aberrations of the sane mind. But, before I go on to those beyond sanity, I must share 'A monologue'. To paint in stark colours the violence against motherhood that many women are still subjected to...

Virgin

A monologue

They wrap me again in cold white sheets
Once again I prepare to die
Strapped down to my destiny
Under blinding white floodlights
I lie bare and vulnerable
Waiting for them to take away from me
The essence of my life.

Unfamiliar faces hover around the blazing disc
Indifferent, businesslike, matter of fact
Crackle of metallic instruments, clinical odours
'Lie...relax...it won't be long.'
Strange hands in pale plastic gloves
Meddle with me
Shave, clean, disinfect my sins
I shut my eyes tight, yet see my life
See with clarity, the phantoms I created!

A warm face bends over mine
'Are you sure you want to go ahead with it?'
Gut knots! No! No! No!
Knuckles twist around metallic rims of cot
Toes curl inward, dig into sheet
Taut knees resist
A fatal thought clutches at the temples
I'm gripped by a sudden desperate hope
Could I still change my mind?
Could I just get up and walk away?
Couldn't there be one reason
Just one reason for me to say 'No'?

Restless eyes search
Lips quiver and turn blue
All nerves stretch to a point of splitting
I try to smile, and a stiff mouth
Cracks into a grin!
'Yes' is the only word I hear in my voice
'It's just a prick, won't hurt...promise.'

A slow sedation cuts me from reality
Everything falls into unreal space
Faces and voices blanch, move in the distance
No one's around anymore
Just me, and my baby, in her blue-blue dress
And fields of white saffron
Endless stretches of ethereal whites
And the two of us in this world, together
Together till eternity, till
Timelessness...

Sounds begin to filter in my dream
I wake to a sense of being hauled
Through dark dizzy space—
Muffled clatter of blunted wheels
Hurled through corridors, butted around corners

One curve stretching into another
And shoved into a room with no windows
Slowly the head reels back to consciousness
And then it hits me—like reality!
Tilted white walls towering over me
Whirling, spinning, falling
Colliding over me...colliding
And I scream!

Scream from the intestines
My knotted up, coiled up centre
I......SCREAM...
A great wail rises from within, hits the ceiling
But no words happen
Only a flood of pain
An open trembling throat, held in
Soundless quiver...
'It's okay...it's over...it's over...'
Voices rush in and *handle* me
Footsteps appear
And disappear into other corridors
I'm left in silence, to face myself
'Yes...it is over...'

Covering my own pool of yellow clotless blood
I lie once again, in cold white sheets
Never so empty, never so still
I'm a virgin again...
I'm a nun...a nun

* * *

The *Silent Scream* section came out of my decision to visit a
mental hospital to study for my role in Amol Palekar's *Ankahee*
(1984). When I was shooting for *Hip Hip Hurray* (1984) for
(ex-husband) Prakash Jha, I came to know that there was a very

big mental institution there—Ranchi Mansik Arogyashala. The Central Institute of Psychiatry was also located there—earlier, it served only the Britishers. The Mansik Arogyashala was for Indians. As I was to play a girl off the rocker in *Ankahee*, I told Amol, 'I can't do the scene—hallucinating, convulsing, and all that—without seeing how some of the patients behave.' He warned me against it, but I went in nevertheless, since I was in Ranchi. I had planned to go there only for two or three days and I spent twenty-three days. After the four hours I spent on the first day, I felt so sapped, so enervated! My God! I thought—just one visit and I'm feeling so drained, so how would it affect an actor who has to spend thirty days of the shoot? What would it do to me as a person? And if an actor has to stay thirty days in that character's state of mind, would she remain unaffected? And, what would it be like for the women left there with no hope of getting out ever?

That was the seed of *Split*, a script I went back to work on later, in the winter of 1993. It was about an actress who gets a script where she has to play a mentally disturbed woman, and how that affects her. She goes to an asylum, spends time in the women's ward, comes to know some of them and imbibes all that into her work. But eventually her own ghosts start popping out of the closet and, in a cathartic moment, she breaks down before the camera.

Yes, it turned out to be a dark script. Nobody wanted to put money on a subject like this, so it got shelved. But what happened is that despite writing that script, there were many images that were floating around in my head.

I took permission and went inside the women's ward. I spent days on the verandah with all the women. I came to know them at close quarters and ended up with a deeper understanding of their minds. Some of the women were not even 'mad', clinically, but if someone came in and wrote, 'her mind is not stable', they could be there for good. Many were dumped there for life simply because no one wanted them back. Some were medically treated and cured yet no one came to take them home. This way they could be excluded from property and totally discarded.

It was a trying time for me—suddenly, I was confronted with so much pain. There were so many faces telling the story of their lives. So, even after the script was shelved, I kept remembering the girls I watched sitting in the verandah every night. And I kept thinking: *this hasn't been woven in...that too got left out....* Those details came out in the form of twenty-two poems.

There was a girl I would watch every night. I would be sitting in the veranda, and she would come out—I could see her trying to deal with herself...

Out Alone

She stands at one end of the veranda,
A naked bulb glows at the other end
Staining the dark floor with dull yellow light.
Beyond the empty ward
Drag echoes of the autumn night.
From pillar to pillar, in severe silence
Skulk slithering shadows.
Out alone in the cold she stands
Night after night
Fighting her demons!
Her body, frail and brittle,
Flaps leaf-like, on two glass feet.
The torched face, broken
Then tacked together, so bluntly
The ragged joints show.
Hounded eyes that do not blink
Frozen in a deathlike glaze.
Her fragile spirit, splintered.
These are not the features
She was born with.
This is the face we gave her.

EDITORS' ACKNOWLEDGEMENTS

The editors of this anthology express their deepest gratitude to Renuka Chatterjee, Ravi Singh, Pragya Singh and the entire team at Speaking Tiger Books for helping us unleash our voices. We extend our heartfelt thanks to all the publishers—Pan Macmillan, BloodAxe Books, Out of Print, Dhauli Books, The University Press Limited (Dhaka), Star Weekend Magazine, and Zubaan Books—for granting permission to reprint chapters and excerpts for this anthology. Special appreciation goes to Shibani Dutta for graciously allowing us to feature her mother's translation and to Deepti Naval for generously sharing her narrative with us. Finally, we are immensely grateful to all our contributors who chipped in for the love of humanity. Thank you all.

PUBLISHER'S ACKNOWLEDGEMENTS

The publishers acknowledge with thanks permission from the authors, publishers and copyright holders to reproduce the following material:

1. 'Satir Puniya' by Sandhya Sinha, excerpted with permission from the Author's estate, from *Sati, a Wife Divine* (translated from the Bengali by Ratnottama Sengupta).

2. 'Sathyavathi: Confronting Caste, Class and Gender' by Vasanth Kannabiran, excerpted from *Sathyavathi: Confronting Caste, Class & Gender*, pub. Women Unlimited, 2015.

3. 'The Witch' by Aruna Chakravarti excerpted from *Suralakshmi Villa*, pub. Pan Macmillan India, 2020.

4. 'The Phone Call' and 'Shadow Play' by Radhia Rameez excerpted from *She*, pub. Life Rattle Press, Toronto, 2023.

5. 'Over and Over Again' by Tisa Muhaddes, excerpted from *Daily Star Weekend*, 2004, and *Lifelines: New Writing from Bangladesh*, ed. Farah Ghuznavi, pub. Zubaan Books, 2012.

6. 'Escaping the Mirror' by Farah Ghuznavi, excerpted from *Woman's Work*, GirlChild Press, USA, 2011; *The Monster Book for Girls*, EXAGGERATED Press, UK, 2011; *Fragments of Riversong*, Daily Star Books, 2013, Bangladesh; and *Out of Print*, India, 2015.

7. 'Fire' by Sucharita Dutta-Asane, excerpted from *Cast Out and Other Stories*, pub. Dhauli Books, 2018, and *Out of Print*.

8. 'Touch Me Not' by S. Bari, excerpted from *Lifelines: New Writing From Bangladesh*, 2012, ed. Farah Ghuznavi, pub. Zubaan Books; and *Star Weekend Magazine*, 2004.

9. 'Claim' by Arundhathi Subramaniam, excerpted from *Where I Live: New and Selected Poems*, pub. Bloodaxe Books, UK, 2009.

10. 'Birangona' by Sadaf Saaz excerpted from *Sari Reams*, pub. University Press Limited, Dhaka, 2013.

11. 'In the Abyss of Night' by Deepti Naval, excerpted from *Black Wind and Other Poems*, pub. MapinLit, Ahmedabad, 2004.

ABOUT THE CONTRIBUTORS

Ankita Banerjee is a writer and poet based in Pune, India. Her works have appeared in *The Bangalore Review, Coldnoon—International Journal of Travel Writing & Travelling Cultures, Eunoia Review, Matter Press, Women's Web, X-R-A-Y, Kitaab, Nine Muses Poetry,* and others. Banerjee's first short fiction series was published by *Juggernaut Books* in 2019.

Anuradha Kumar, from India, is the author of several novels, including *Letters for Paul* (Grantha Corporation, 2006), *It Takes a Murder* (Hachette India, 2013) and two works of historical fiction written under the pseudonym Adity Kay, *Emperor Chandragupta* (Hachette India, 2016) and *Emperor Vikramaditya* (Hachette India, 2019). She also writes for younger readers, and contributes to *Scroll.in, The Economic and Political Weekly, thewire.in, theaerogram.com*, and other places. She was awarded twice (2004, 2010) for her stories by the Commonwealth Foundation, and has received awards from *The Little Magazine* and Hindu-Goodbooks.in. She recently wrote *The Kidnapping of Mark Twain: A Bombay Mystery* (Speaking Tiger, 2024).

Aruna Chakravarti, from India, is a well-known academic, creative writer and translator with numerous published books. Her novels, *The Inheritors* (Penguin India, 2004), *Jorasanko* (HarperCollins India, 2013), *Daughters of Jorasanko* (HarperCollins India, 2016) and *Suralakshmi Villa* (Pan Macmillan India, 2020) have sold widely and received rave reviews. She has also received awards such as the Vaitalik Award, Sahitya Akademi Award and Sarat Puraskar for her translations.

Arundhathi Subramaniam, from India, is a poet, dance critic and freelance arts journalist, and is in charge of an interactive arts forum at Mumbai's National Centre for the Performing Arts. As a poet, she has been published in several journals including the PEN All-India journal,

Poiesis, The Brown Critique, and *Kavya Bharati,* as well as the poetry pages of *The Independent,* and has read her work at several forums. As a journalist, she has written extensively for leading publications in the country, such as *The Times of India* and *The Hindu,* and now writes for several culture portals on the web.

Aysha Baqir founded a pioneering not-for-profit economic development organization, Kaarvan Crafts Foundation in Pakistan, with a mission to alleviate poverty by providing business and marketing training to girls and women in low-income communities. Her novel, *Beyond the Fields,* was published in 2019 by Marshall Cavendish International (Asia). Her writings have been selected for numerous anthologies. Baqir is an Ashoka Fellow, recipient of the Vice Chancellor's Alumni Achievement Award from LUMS, and the Women of Inspiration Award from the Ladies Fund.

Babita Basnet, from Nepal, is a veteran journalist and editor of *Ghatana Ra Bichar,* a popular weekly. She is also executive director of Media Advocacy Group, an NGO that promotes the right to information and gender rights and equity. She has written and edited a number of books, including *In Search of Self Reliance,* which consisted of case studies of survivors of trafficking (UNIFEM, 2004), and the story collection, *Sambandhahin Sambandhaharu* (2015). Basnet received the Celebrating Womanhood Award (2007) from Creative Statements, the Shridhar Journalism National Award (2009) from the Federation of Nepalese Journalists, and the Gender Equality Journalism Award (2016) from the Federation of Nepali Journalists and Motherland Nepal, America.

Bipasha B. Haque, from Bangladesh, writes poetry of life, for life, and by life. She holds a PhD in Educational Psychology from the University of New South Wales and a second Master's degree in English Language Teaching from Warwick University. Haque writes poetry in English, Bangla, and Sylheti. Her poetry has been published in the *Daily Star* and *Prothom Alo.*

Deepti Naval, an award-winning actress from India, debuted in poetry with a selection of poems in Hindi, *Lamha Lamha* (1983). In 2004, she published *Black Wind and Other Poems (MapIn Publishing).* She published her memoir, *A Country called Childhood* in 2023 (Aleph Book Company). Naval has also authored a collection of short stories, *The Mad Tibetan: stories from then and now* (Amaryllis, 2011).

Eli Prue Marma from the Bandarban Hill District in Southeastern Bangladesh belongs to the second-largest indigenous ethnic group, the Marma community, of the Chittagong Hill Tracts. She has an MA in English literature and creative writing from the University of Liberal Arts, Bangladesh. After graduation, she worked at the Accelerator Lab, UNDP Bangladesh. Currently, Marma is an Assistant Teacher at Sakkhoi Commander Para Government Primary School at Thanchi in Bandarban. She loves to write about the people of Bangladesh's hill tracts.

Farah Ahamed's writings have been published in *Ploughshares*, *The White Review*, *The Los Angeles Review of Books*, *The Massachusetts Review*, *World Literature Today*, *The Markaz Review*, and *Asymptote* amongst others. Her short fiction has been shortlisted for the Bridport and Commonwealth prizes. She has been highly commended in the London Short Story Prize, joint winner of the inaugural Gerald Kraak Award, and nominated for The Caine and The Pushcart prizes. She edited *Period Matters: Menstruation in South Asia*. She is a lawyer with a Diploma in Creative Writing from the University of East Anglia and lives between London and Lahore. You can find her work at www. farahahamed.com.

Farah Ghuznavi is a writer, columnist, development worker and writing mentor for the UK-based Write Beyond Borders project. Her work has been published in eleven countries across Asia, Africa, Europe, and North America, including her native Bangladesh. She was Writer-in-Residence with the Commonwealth Writers in 2013. Her stories 'Getting There' and 'Judgement Day' received an award in the Commonwealth Short Story Competition 2010 and placed second in the Oxford University GEF Short Story Competition, respectively. Farah's first short story collection *Fragments of Riversong* was published in 2013 (Daily Star Books), and she also edited *Lifelines*, an anthology of stories on inspiring individuals (Zubaan Books, 2012). Ghuznavi is currently working on a new story collection. She can usually be found procrastinating on Instagram @farahghuznavi.

Dr Hoineilhing Sitlhou, from India, holds a PhD in sociology from the Jawaharlal Nehru University, New Delhi, and is currently working as an assistant professor at the Department of Sociology, University of Hyderabad. She is a recipient of the MN Srinivas Award, 2016 and has published two books *Kuki Women (ed.)*, 2014, and *Deconstructing*

Colonial Ethnography: An Analysis of Missionary Writings in North East India (2017). She has also contributed articles in the *Economic and Political Weekly*, the *Indian Journal of Gender Studies*, the *International Journal on Religion and Spirituality*, *Indian Anthropologist*, *Asian Ethnicity* and chapters in edited books.

Kalpana Kannabiran, a sociologist and legal scholar, is Distinguished Professor at the Council for Social Development in New Delhi. Based in Hyderabad, India, she is a writer, editor, and an independent human rights columnist. She is the author of numerous books, including *Law, Justice and Human Rights in India: Short Reflections* (Orient BlackSwan, 2021), *Violence Studies* (Oxford University Press, 2016) and, with Swethaa S. Ballakrishnen, *Gender Regimes and the Politics of Privacy: A Feminist Reading of Puttaswamy vs. Union of India* (Zubaan Books, 2021). In 2022, she published the translated memoir in English of the eminent lawyer, KG Kannabiran, titled *The Speaking Constitution: A Sisyphean Life in Law* (HarperCollins India).

Mallika Bhaumik's writings have been published in various e-mags and journals. She has two books of poems *Echoes* (Authorspress, 2017) and *How Not to Remember* (Hawakal Publishers, 2019). Her poetry is taught in the Binod Bihari Mahto Koyalanchal University, Dhanbad. Bhaumik lives and writes in Kolkata. Her works have been widely published in reputed e-mags like *Cafe Dissensus, Shot Glass journal, Harbinger Asylum, Mad Swirl, In Parentheses, Madras Courier* to name a few. Bhaumik won the Reuel International Award for the best debut poetry collection in 2018 and was a nominee for the Pushcart Prize for poetry in 2019.

Meenakshi Malhotra's recent works include the coedited *The Gendered Body in South Asia: Negotiation, Resistance, Struggle* (Routledge, 2023). Her writings have featured in journals such as the *Journal of International Women's Studies* and *Indialogs*, and in books including *Making the 'Woman': Discourses of Gender in 18th–19th Century India* (Routledge, 2023), *WGS in India: Crossings* (Routledge, 2019) and *Unveiling Desire* (Rutgers University Press, 2018). Malhotra has contributed to curriculum development at several universities, consulted on school textbooks, served as a short-term Charles Wallace Fellow, been a visiting faculty at Grinnell College, Iowa, and The University of Minnesota at Duluth, and held a Nalanda Studies Fellowship. Malhotra is associate professor in English at Hansraj College, University of Delhi.

Ngurang Reena, a researcher and writer from Arunachal Pradesh, India, works at the Max Weber Stiftung: MW Forum for South Asian Studies in New Delhi. With academic training in political science, international relations, and gender studies, she focuses on feminist issues in India and South Asia. She has taught at the University of Delhi and collaborated with Jawaharlal Nehru University, Freie Universität Berlin, and the University of Wuerzburg. Her recent works explore feminist perspectives in Northeast India, particularly Arunachal Pradesh. Supported by a Zubaan-Sasakawa Peace Foundation Grant, she contributed to *The Inheritance of Words: Writings from Arunachal Pradesh* anthology (edited by Mamang Dai, Zubaan, 2021). Ngurang Reena has also presented at the Sahitya Akademi Writers' Festival, and her work covering cultural and political themes in contemporary India has featured in *The Indian Express*, BBC, TEDx, and other places.

Dr Nishi Pulugurtha is an academic, author, poet, and translator. Her publications include *Out in the Open: Essays on Travel* (Authorspress, 2019); an edited volume of essays on travel, *Across and Beyond*; three volumes of poems, *The Real and the Unreal and Other Poems* (Authorspress, 2021), *Raindrops on the Periwinkle* (Writers Workshop, 2022) and *Looking* (2023). She has co-edited a volume of poems *Voices and Vision: The First IPPL Anthology*; a collection of short stories, *The Window Sill*; a volume of critical essays, *Literary Representations of Pandemics, Epidemics and Pestilence* (ed., Routledge India, 2022), and a volume of essays written during the pandemic, *Lockdown Times* (Virasat Art Publication, 2023).

Radhia Rameez was born and raised in Colombo, Sri Lanka, where she worked as a writer before moving to Canada in 2019. She double majored in Biology for Health Sciences and Professional Writing at the University of Toronto, where she wrote and edited for various campus projects. Radhia still misses the year-round greenery of the tropics but is learning to like (or at least tolerate) the Toronto winters. Her debut book, *She*, was published by Life Rattle Press in 2023.

Sadaf Saaz is a poet, writer, entrepreneur, and women's rights advocate from Bangladesh. She is a festival director and the producer of the annual Dhaka Literary Festival, which she co-founded in 2011. She also runs an arts management company, Jatrik, and a performance space, The Junction. She is a member of the Bangladeshi women's activist organization Naripokkho, and has done research, critiques, advocacy, and activism on violence against women, women's political participation, women's legal rights, women's health and reproductive rights and sexuality. She is the author of a collection of poems, *Sari Reams* (University Press Ltd., Bangladesh, 2013). Saaz's monologues based on Bangladeshi women's stories *Je Kotha Jai Na Bola* (That Which Cannot be Said), have been performed in various locations in Bangladesh.

Sandhya Sinha (India, 1928-2016) resumed her studies seventeen years after marriage, completed her Masters in English, embarked on a teaching career and retired as a senior English teacher from the women's college, Nari Shiksha Niketan. Many of her articles were published in the magazine of the Bangiya Sahitya Samaj in Lucknow, of which Sucheta Kripalani was a founding member. At the age of seventy-five, she embarked on a writing career, having successfully played the roles of mother, social worker, mentor, community leader, and spiritual aspirant.

Dr Sangita Swechcha, a Nepali writer based in England, debuted with the novel *Pakhalieko Siundo*, now published as *Seto Siundo* (2024), with a focus on trafficking in women. Her 2019 short story collection, *Gulafsangako Prem*, was translated as *Rose's Odyssey: Tales of Love and Loss*, and her upcoming novel, *A Quest for Bonding*, delves into women's sexuality, body image, social stigma, and acceptance. She co-edited *The Himalayan Sunrise: Exploring Nepal's Literary Horizon* with Karen Van Drie and curated *A Glimpse Into My Country: An Anthology of International Short Stories* with Andree Roby in 2021. Swechcha established the London branch of Book Hill International Publishers.

Selma Tufail is an academic, writer and artist who has taught in many countries. In 2000, Selma laid the foundation for the very first department of art and design in the United Arab Emirates at Zayed University. The university conferred on her the Outstanding Faculty Member Award. She was also awarded La Cruz de la Orden del Mérito Civil by the King of Spain, Juan Carlos I, for her efforts towards building an academic partnership between Zayed University and Universidad Complutense de Madrid. Tufail teaches at the Community College of San Mateo, California.

Simran Chadha is an associate professor with the department of English, Dyal Singh College, University of Delhi. Her writings are driven by the fault lines of gender and the impact of war on daily life in South Asia. She finds the expression of both these themes in literature from the region both fascinating and transformative. Chadha has also explored adaptations in mainstream Indian cinema and is currently involved in a project on ecocriticism in South Asian literature.

Sohana Manzoor is a Bangladeshi writer and academic. She edited *Our Many Longings: Contemporary Short Fiction from Bangladesh* (Dhauli Books, 2021) a collection of 19 short stories translated from the Bengali to English. Her writings have been featured in numerous journals and anthologies in South and Southeast Asia. Manzoor holds a PhD in English from Southern Illinois University Carbondale and currently teaches English and creative writing at the University of Liberal Arts, Bangladesh.

S. Bari works in public health and currently lives in Switzerland.

Sucharita Dutta-Asane is a writer and independent book editor based out of Pune, India. She edits Red River Story, the prose imprint of Red River, and fiction for *The Bangalore Review*. Her short story collection *Cast Out and Other Stories* was published in 2018 by Dhauli Books and received critical acclaim, including in the Sahitya Akademi journal *Indian Literature*, *Scroll.in* and *The Deccan Herald*. Her fiction and book reviews have been published across national and international print and e-journals. Dutta-Asane is a member of the Advisory Board for the Department of Languages, School of Arts & Humanities at CHRIST (Deemed to be) University, Lavasa, Pune. Dutta-Asane is an independent books editor and was the editor of the international literary journal *Kitaab* (2017-2019). She teaches Writing and Editing at the Symbiosis College of Arts and Commerce and Flame Liberal Arts University, Pune.

Supriya Rakesh is an author, educator, improviser, and researcher with a PhD in Organizational Behaviour. Her short stories have been published in various online platforms. She recently won the Bound's Food Essay contest. She is a Visiting Faculty at TISS, Mumbai. Her stories are often set in urban India, exploring the lives and choices of young adults in a society-in-transition. Rakesh enjoys teaching workshops and courses exploring the intersection between creativity and human development. Her short fiction has been recently published in *Kitaab*, *Dastaan World Magazine*, *Culture Cult* and an anthology of marginalized voices titled

The Other. She is a visiting faculty at the Tata Institute of Social Sciences and the Editor of *ang(st)—the feminist body-zine*. She loves the Mumbai rains, strong cups of cappuccino and stories of unrequited love.

Tamoha Siddiqui is a teacher-researcher and poet from Bangladesh. She is a Fulbright awardee currently housed as a graduate student at Michigan State University. In 2018, she founded a bilingual poetry collective in Dhaka, working as a performer, organizer, and facilitator of local poetry shows and workshops. Siddiqui debuted as a performance poetry artist in America in 2019 through events hosted by *The Poetry Room*, Michigan. Her work has been highlighted in a number of Bangladeshi newspapers and anthologies.

Teresa Rehman is an award-winning journalist based in Northeast India. Her work spans through *India Today, The Telegraph, Tehelka, The Hoot, Reuters*, and others. She is the founding editor-in-chief of *Thumbprint NE (thumbprintmag.in)*. She has written books like *The Mothers of Manipur: Twelve Women Who Made History* (Zubaan Books, 2017), *Bulletproof* (Penguin Random House India, 2019) and has contributed chapters to several anthologies. A recipient of the WASH Media Awards 2009-2010, Teresa also won the Ramnath Goenka Excellence in Journalism Award twice in a row in 2009 and 2010, in the 'Reporting on J&K and the Northeast' category. She also bagged the Laadli Media Award for Gender Sensitivity in 2011, the Sanskriti Award in 2009 for Excellence in Journalism and the Seventh Sarojini Naidu Prize in 2007 for 'Best Reporting on Panchayati Raj' by the Hunger Project. She is known for her persistence in seeking out details and sensitivity. She was featured in the Power List of *Femina* magazine in 2012.

Tisa Coons (Muhaddes) aspires to catch the ordinary moments that make extraordinary people in her stories. Her stories are inspired by the people she has encountered living in Brussels, Dhaka, New York, London, Washington DC, and Nevada. She has been published in a variety of literary anthologies and fiction magazines. She currently resides in northern Nevada with her dog and cat.

Vasanth Kannabiran, a veteran Indian civil rights and women's rights activist, and a writer, teacher, and translator, has written *My Life is a Song: Gaddar's Anthems for the Revolution* (Speaking Tiger, 2021); *Softly Dies a Lake* (Orient BlackSwan, 2020), her English translation of

Akkineni Kutumbarao's autobiographical novel in the Telugu, *Kolleti Jadalu*; *Taken at the Flood: A Memoir of a Political Life* (Women Unlimited, 2019); and *A Grief to Bury: Memories of Love, Work and Loss* (Orient BlackSwan, 2011). She has also written and produced the ballets, Menaka, Ahalya, Gandhari and Rajasimha, which have been performed in several cities.

Hem Bishwakarma is a translation enthusiast. He also writes poetry and reviews.

NOTES

1   'What was she wearing? This display of rape victims' clothes proves truth about assault.' *The News Minute*, January 13, 2018. https://www.thenewsminute.com/features/what-was-she-wearing-display-rape-victims-clothes-proves-truth-about-assault-74706 (Accessed on July 2, 2024)

2   Some segments of an article, 'The Engendering of Hurt: A Feminist Analysis of Hurt Sentiments' previously published by the author, Dr Meenakshi Malhotra in *The State of Hurt: Sentiment, Politics, Censorship* edited by Rina Ramdev et al. (New Delhi, Sage, 2016) were drawn upon in this essay with adequate acknowledgement.

3   Flavia Agnes, 2013. 'No Shortcuts on Rape: Making the Legal System Work,' *Economic and Political Weekly*, 48(2)

4   'Nirbhaya case: Four Indian men executed for 2012 Delhi bus rape and murder,' BBC, March 20, 2020. https://www.bbc.com/news/world-asia-india-51969961.amp (Accessed on July 2, 2024)

5   Roja Mayabrahama. 'Dr Priyanka Reddy case: The brutal rape and murder that left entire nation in shock' *The Hans India*, November 30, 2019 https://www.thehansindia.com/telangana/dr-priyanka-reddy-case-the-brutal-rape-and-murder-that-left-entire-nation-in-shock-585940 (Accessed on July 2, 2024)

6   Agnes, 2013. 'No Shortcuts' *EPW*, 48(2)

7   Economic and Political Weekly 2013, 48(2):12

8   'Speech on the Issue of Girl gang-raped in Delhi: Smt. Sushma Swaraj: 18.12.2012'. Issued by Bharatiya Janata Party on YouTube.com https://www.youtube.com/watch?v=U32KlaW6pV8 (Accessed on July 2, 2024)

9   Abraham, Taisha (2012). 'Sathin Bhanwari Revisited', *Indian Journal of Gender Studies*, Sage, 19(1), 149-157

10 Brinda Karat, 2013. 'Report In, Action Awaited', *Indian Express*, February 2

11 'Don't eat chowmein, it leads to rape, says Haryana khap leader'. *IndiaToday.in* October 18, 2012. https://www.indiatoday.in/india/story/khap-rape-chowmein-118852-2012-10-15 (Accessed on July 2, 2024)

12 Aditi Raja. 'Bilkis Bano speaks: Feel like I can breathe again, this is what justice feels like'. Indian Express, January 9, 2024. https://indianexpress.com/article/cities/ahmedabad/bilkis-bano-speaks-supreme-court-judgment-justice-9100563/ (Accessed on July 2, 2024)

13 Barrington Moore Jr., 1966. *Social Origins of Dictatorship and Democracy: Lord and Peasant in the Making of the Modern World.* Harmondsworth: Penguin.

14 Jasbir K. Puar, 2017. *The Right to Maim: Debility, Capacity, Disability.* Duke University Press.

15 Kalpana Kannabiran (ed.), 2006. *The Violence of Normal Times: Essays on Women's Lived Realities.* New Delhi: Women Unlimited in association with Kali for Women.

16 'Human rights defender and Journalist Siddique Kappan released from jail after two years', February 7, 2023, *FrontlineDefenders. org* https://www.frontlinedefenders.org/en/case/human-rights-defender-and-journalist-siddique-kappan-released-jail-after-two-years#:~:text=Human%20rights%20defender%20and%20journalist%20Siddique%20Kappan%20was%20released%20on,Prevention%20of%20Money%20Laundering%20Act%20. (Accessed on July 2, 2024)

17 Kalpana Kannabiran, 2022. 'Bilkis Bano's lonely battle for justice is a heartfelt cry for India to resurrect its secular values'. Scroll.in. 29 September. https://scroll.in/article/1033703/bilkis-banos-lonely-battle-for-justice-is-a-heartfelt-cry-for-india-to-resurrect-its-secular-values (Accessed on July 2, 2024)

18 Krishnadas Rajagopal, January 8, 2024. 'Bilkis Bano case: Supreme Court quashes early release of 11 lifers'. *The Hindu.* https://www.thehindu.com/news/national/bilkis-bano-case-supreme-court-quashes-gujarats-premature-release-of-convicts/article67718561.ece (Accessed on July 3, 2024)

19 Jill Stauffer, 2015. *Ethical Loneliness: The Injustice of Not Being Heard.* Columbia University Press,

20 Hausing, Kham Khan Suan, June 23, 2023. 'Kuki-Meitei Conflict is More Than Just an Ethnic Clash'. *The Tribune.* https://www.

tribuneindia.com/news/comment/kuki-meitei-conflict-is-more-than-just-an-ethnic-clash-519379 (Accessed on July 2, 2024)

21 Hoineilhing Sitlhou, June 1, 2023. 'How Fake News Created Pretexts to Lynch Kuki-Zo Women in Manipur'. *NewsClick.in* https://www.newsclick.in/how-fake-news-created-pretexts-lynch-kuki-zo-women-manipur?s=08&page=178 (Accessed on July 2, 2024)

22 Mahender Singh Manral, April 30, 2024. 'Manipur chargesheet: Women paraded naked made it to police Gypsy but told no key, left to the mob'. *Indian Express.* (Accessed on July 2, 2024)

23 Makepeace Sitlhou, December 28, 2023. 'When Women Became the Main Spectacle in Manipur's Civil Conflict'. BehanBox.com https://behanbox.com/2023/12/28/when-women-became-the-main-spectacle-in-manipurs-civil-conflict/ (Accessed on July 2, 2024)

24 Josephine Kipgen, August 15, 2023. 'Unpacking Gender-based Violence and Trauma Voyeurism in the Manipur Conflict'. *Hindustan Times.* https://www.hindustantimes.com/opinion/unpacking-gender-based-violence-and-trauma-voyeurism-in-the-manipur-conflict-101692081218348.html (Accessed on July 2, 2024)

25 Sainico Ningthoujam, July 26, 2023. 'In Manipur, Violence against Women, Impunity, and Apathy Show a Familiar Pattern of Events'. *The Wire.* https://thewire.in/women/in-manipur-violence-against-women-impunity-and-apathy-show-a-familiar-pattern-of-events (Accessed on July 2, 2024)

26 Aaisha Sabir, October 8, 2023. '"I have thought of taking my life": A Meitei Woman recalls how she was raped by a mob'. *Scroll. in.* https://scroll.in/article/1057135/i-have-thought-of-taking-my-life-a-meitei-woman-recalls-how-she-was-raped-by-a-mob (Accessed on July 2, 2024)

27 Upendra Baxi, 2006. 'The Gujarat Catastrophe: Notes on Reading Politics as Democidal Rape Culture'. In Kalpana Kannabiran (ed.) *The Violence of Normal Times: Essays on Women's Lived Realities,* New Delhi: Women Unlimited.

28 'Manipur women: "I was treated like an animal"'. *BBC News India.* https://www.youtube.com/watch?v=3NV-TZKmKzI (Accessed on July 2, 2024)

29 Christina Lamb, 2020. *Our Bodies, Their Battlefield: What War Does to Women.* London: Collins.

30   Teresa Rehman, 2017. *The Mothers of Manipur: Twelve Women Who Made History*, Zubaan, New Delhi.

31   Barbara Sutton, 2007. 'Naked Protest: Memories of Bodies and Resistance at the World Social Forum'. *Journal of International Women's Studies*, 8(3), 139-148.

32   Nadine Bloch, December 5, 2012. 'Five reasons to get naked (in protest)'. *Waging Nonviolence*. https://wagingnonviolence. org/2012/12/five-reasons-to-get-naked-in-protest/ (Accessed on July 2, 2024)

33   John Muir, 'The Seneca Falls Convention,' The Library of Congress Digital Collections. https://www.loc.gov/item/today-in-history/july-19/ (Accessed on July 2, 2024)

34   Tawakkol Karman, 'Women and the Arab Spring,' UN Chronicle, December 2016. https://www.un.org/en/chronicle/article/women-and-arab-spring (Accessed on July 2, 2024)

35   T. Rehman, 2017. *The Mothers*. Zubaan, pp XXIII

36   Ngurang Reena, 2022. 'Living through India's race and gender war', The New Indian Express. https://www.newindianexpress. com/opinions/2022/Sep/29/living-through-indias-race-and-gender-war-2503328.html (Accessed on July 2, 2024)

37   To access the data please see: Bhattacharyya, R., & Pulla, V. (2020). *Viewing racism through gendered lenses. Discrimination, Challenge and Response: People of North East India*, 31-55. Palgrave MacMillan.

38   Kikon, Dolly & Karlsoon Bengt G.,2019, *Leaving the Land: Indigenous Migration and Affective Labour in India.* Cambridge University Press.

39   Duncan McDuie-Ra, 2012. *Northeast Migrants in Delhi: Race, Refuge and Retail.* Amsterdam University Press.

40   To read more on this, please see: McDuie-Ra, D. (2012a). 'The North-east Map of Delhi'. Economic and Political Weekly, XLVII (30), 69–77.

41   (i) Renato Rosaldo, 1989. *Culture & Truth*. Beacon Press. (ii) Gupta, Akhil & Ferguson, James 'Beyond "Culture" Space, Identity, and the Politics of Difference,' in Vol. 7, No. 1, 'Space, Identity, and the Politics of Difference' (February 1992), pp. 6-23. (iii) *Border Identities: Nation and State at International Frontiers.* Edited by Thomas M. Wilson and Hastings Donnan, 1998. (Cambridge University Press). (iv) Anderson, Benedict, 1983.

Imagined Communities: Reflections on the Origin and Spread of Nationalism (Verso).

42   Renalto Rosaldo, 1989. *Culture and Truth: The Remaking of Social Analysis*. Beain Press.

43   (i) Borneman, John, 1992a. *Uniting the German Nation: Law, Narrative, and Historicity* in *American Ethnologist*, p. 17. (ii) Michèle Lamont and Virág Molnár, 2002. 'The Study of Boundaries Across the Social Sciences,' *Annual Review of Sociology*. 28:167-95.

44   Berdahl, D., 1999. '(N)Ostalgie' for the present: Memory, longing, and East German things. *Ethnos*, 64(2), 192–211. https://doi.org/1 0.1080/00141844.1999.9981598 (Accessed on July 2, 2024)

45   Joy L. K. Pachuau, 2014. *Being Mizo: Identity and Belonging in Northeast India*. Oxford Academic.

46   Here refers to a person from Mizoram, a state in Northeast India.

47   Professor Berenice is a historian of South Asia and contemporary international relations at King's College London. She writes extensively on Sino-Indian relations and on the strategic borderlands between India, India, Tibet and Burma. She is the author of the book *Shadow States: India, China and the Himalayas* (CUP 2016; awarded the James Fischer Prize 2018 for the best book on Nepal and the Himalayas).

48   'This Booklet for Northeast Students Sparks Ire'. *Hindustan Times*, July 15, 2007. https://www.hindustantimes.com/ delhi-news/booklet-for-northeast-students-sparks-ire/story-WKPR3522wcJ1mqpH7AbDHL.html (Accessed on July 2, 2024)

49   'Press Release: 81 per cent of North East Women Harassed in Delhi'. Jamia Millia Islamia co-conducted survey with the National Commission for Women, 24 January 2013; available at: https://www.jmi.ac.in/upload/publication/pr5_2014January24.pdf (Accessed on July 2, 2024)

50   After the 2012 and 2014 deaths of Loitam Richard and Nido Tania, the legal framework on race-related crimes were investigated. Tragically, Richard and Tania's life gave the impetus for public policy and media debates on the future of such crimes in India. After long agitations and demands from civil society, a robust Bezbaruah committee, headed by M.P. Bezbaruah, was established, led by professionals, experts and community leaders from across Indian society.

51   Ngurang Reena, 2021, 'My Story: A Happy Farewell Night Turned into A Nightmare. They Asked Us, "How Much/What's The Rate?"' *The Logical Indian.* https://thelogicalindian.com/my-story/my-story-ngurang-reena/?infinitescroll=1https://thelogicalindian.com/my-story/my-story-ngurang-reena/?infinitescroll=1   (Accessed on July 2, 2024)

52   *Discrimination, Challenge and Response.* Eds Venkat Pulla, Rituparna Bhattacharyya and Sanjai Bhatt

53   'North East India: People, History and Culture.' NCERT, 2017. https://ncert.nic.in/pdf/publication/otherpublications/tinei101.pdf

54   Duncan McDuie-Ra, 2012. *Northeast Migrants in Delhi: Race, Refuge and Retail.* Amsterdam University Press.

55   J. Angelo Corlett, 1998, 'Analyzing Racism', *Public Affairs Quarterly*, 12, 23-50.

56   (i) P. Bourdieu, & J.-C. Passeron, 1977. *Reproduction in Education, Society, and Culture.* Sage Publications. (ii) Bourdieu, Pierre; translated by Richard Nice, 1984. *Distinction: A Social Critique of the Judgement of Taste.* Harvard University Press.

57   Ratnottama Sengupta, 2006. *Krishna's Cosmos: The Creativity of an Artist, Sculptor & Teacher.* Grantha Corporation.

58   Mehreen Zahra-Malik, October 6, 2016. 'Pakistan parliament passes legislation against "honour killing"' Reuters. https://www.reuters.com/article/us-pakistan-honourkillings-idUSKCN1261OK (Accessed on July 2, 2024)

59   'ANNE BOLEYN: SHE FAILED TO GIVE HENRY VIII A SON AND PAID WITH HER LIFE' From hrp.org.uk https://www.hrp.org.uk/tower-of-london/history-and-stories/anne-boleyn/#gs.aav8n9 (Accessed on July 2, 2024)

60   *Othello, The Moore of Venice.* Shakespeare, William. http://shakespeare.mit.edu/othello/full.html (Accessed on July 2, 2024)

61   Sune Engel Rasmussen, December 27, 2017. ''Honour' killings in Karachi shock Pakistan's largest city'. *The Guardian, UK.* https://www.theguardian.com/world/2017/dec/27/honour-killings-in-karachi-shock-pakistans-largest-city (Accessed on July 2, 2024)

62   'Supreme Court declares it illegal for for khap panchayats to stall marriage between consenting adults'. *The Times of India*, March 27, 2018. https://timesofindia.indiatimes.com/india/supreme-court-declares-it-illegal-for-khap-panchayats-to-stall-marriage-between-

consenting-adults/articleshow/63476839.cms (Accessed on July 2, 2024)

63   'Gotra, lineage segment within an Indian caste that prohibits intermarriage by virtue of the members' descent from a common mythical ancestor, an important factor in determining possible Hindu marriage alliances.' From *The Encyclopedia Britannica*, https://www.britannica.com/topic/gotra (Accessed on July 2, 2024)

64   'Death Sentence commuted in Manoj-Babli case'. The Hindu, March 12, 2011. https://www.thehindu.com/news/national/Death-sentence-commuted-in-Manoj-Babli-case/article14943294.ece (Accessed on July 2, 2024)

65   The Special Marriage Act, 1954, *Indian Kanoon* https://shorturl.at/Hht1T (Accessed on July 2, 2024)

66   'Code of silence in honour killing'. The Times of India, December 9, 2012. https://timesofindia.indiatimes.com/city/kolkata/Code-of-silence-in-honour-killing/articleshow/17540948.cms (Accessed on July 2, 2024)

67   R. Vimal Kumar, December 12, 2017. '"Honour" killing of Dalit youth Shankar in Tamil Nadu: death for six, including father-in-law'. *The Hindu*. https://www.thehindu.com/news/national/tamil-nadu/shankar-murder-case-father-in-law-gets-death-sentence/article21478790.ece (Accessed on July 2, 2024)

68   Swati Shalini, July 25, 2018. 'Case Note on Murder of Nitish Katara'. https://www.myadvo.in/blog/case-note-on-murder-case-of-nitish-katara (Accessed on July 2, 2024)

69   Hemani Bhandari, June 9, 2019. 'Over a year after Ankit Saxena's death, Shehzadi talks about her transformation to a woman in charge of her life'. *The Hindu*. https://www.thehindu.com/news/cities/Delhi/ankit-saxena-murder-shehzadi-opens-up/article27700098.ece (Accessed on July 2, 2024)

70   Sagarika Ghosh, April 21, 2016. 'Rizwanur Rahman died for love, but there can be no love jihad in Bengal, Bengal Muslims say'. *The Times of India*. https://timesofindia.indiatimes.com/elections-2016/west-bengal-elections-2016/Rizwanur-Rahman-died-for-love-but-there-can-be-no-love-jihad-in-Bengal-Bengal-Muslims-say/articleshow/51919137.cms (Accessed on July 2, 2024)

71   Nishikant Karlikar & Pradeep Gupta, December 10, 2019. 'Headless body: Man held for daughter's "honour" killing in

Thane'. *The Times of India*. https://timesofindia.indiatimes.com/city/mumbai/headless-body-man-held-for-daughters-honour-killing/articleshow/72448710.cms (Accessed on July 2, 2024)

72 Piyush Shrivastava, January 31, 2013. 'Police weaken case against man who appeared on Aamir's show Satyamev Jayate'. *India Today*. https://www.indiatoday.in/india/north/story/aamir-khan-satyamev-jayate-show-police-weaken-case-abdul-hakim-152894-2013-01-31 (Accessed on July 2, 2024)

73 'Maruthi Rao, accused of killing dalit son-in-law, found dead'. *The Week*. https://www.theweek.in/news/india/2020/03/08/maruthi-rao-accused-in-killing-dalit-son-in-law-found-dead.html (Accessed on July 2, 2024)

74 *Deccan Herald* (PTI). April 30, 2020. 'Rajasthan: Mother, uncle held for "honour killing" of 16-year-old girl'. https://www.deccanherald.com/india/rajasthan-mother-uncle-held-for-honour-killing-of-16-year-old-girl-831731.html (Accessed on July 2, 2024)

75 'A day after couple hacked to death, girl's brother suspected'. *The Indian Express*, May 29, 2020. https://indianexpress.com/article/india/a-day-after-couple-hacked-to-death-girls-brother-suspected-6432068/ (Accessed on July 2, 2024)

76 Piyush Rai, February 17, 2020. 'Meerut: Girl, 19, shot in her private part, killed by cousin over "love affair"'. *The Times of India*. https://timesofindia.indiatimes.com/city/meerut/girl-19-shot-in-her-private-part-killed-by-cousin-over-love-affair/articleshow/74164988.cms (Accessed on July 2, 2024)

77 Harveer Dabas, December 30, 2019. 'Honour Killing: Dad, Brother Shot Teen Girl, Threw Body In Ganga'. *The Times of India*. https://www.google.com.sg/amp/s/m.timesofindia.com/city/meerut/honour-killing-dad-bro-shot-dead-15-yr-old-girl-in-feb-threw-body-in-ganga/amp_articleshow/73021644.cms (Accessed on July 2, 2024)

78 'Honour Killing: Dad Held for Teen's Murder Near Mandu'. February 16, 2020. *The Times of India*. https://timesofindia.indiatimes.com/city/bhopal/honour-killing-dad-held-for-teens-murder-near-mandu/amp_articleshow/74160065.cms (Accessed on July 2, 2024)

79 (i) Are Knudsen, 2004. 'Licence to Kill: Honor Killings in Pakistan.' Working Paper: Chr Michelsen Institute Development Studies and

Human Rights. (ii) Zehra-Malik, 2016, 'Pakistan parliament passes legislation', Reuters. (Accessed on July 2, 2024)

80   'Taslim Solangi Murder Case'. November 14, 2008. https://www. thenews.com.pk/archive/print/145425-tasleem-solangi-murder-case (Accessed on July 2, 2024)

81   'Cause of Death: Woman', April 6, 1999. http://www. causeofdeathwoman.com/samia-sarwar (Accessed on July 2, 2024)

82   Peter Daou, May 4, 2009. 'Singer Ayman Udas Allegedly Gunned Down by her Brothers for Appearing on TV'. UN Dispatch. https:// www.undispatch.com/singer-ayman-udas-allegedly-gunned-down-by-her-brothers-for-appearing-on-tv/ (Accessed on July 2, 2024)

83   Jon Boone, September 22, 2017. 'She feared no one': the life and death of Qandeel Baloch'. *The Guardian*, UK. https://www. theguardian.com/world/2017/sep/22/qandeel-baloch-feared-no-one-life-and-death (Accessed on July 2, 2024)

84   Haseeb Bhatti, January 2, 2019. 'Girls in 2011 Kohistan video were killed, Supreme Court told'. *The Dawn*, Pakistan. https://www. dawn.com/news/1455038 (Accessed on July 2, 2024)

85   Bryony Jewell, July 28, 2019. 'Husband arrested over honour killing of beauty therapist Samia Shahid is 'planning to return to UK with new British wife'. Daily Mail, UK. https://www.dailymail.co.uk/ news/article-7295007/Husband-arrested-honour-killing-Samia-Shahid-planning-return-UK.html (Accessed on July 2, 2024)

86   Mubasher Bukhari, November 19, 2014. 'Pakistani family sentenced to death over 'honour killing' outside court'. *Reuters*. https:// www.reuters.com/article/uk-pakistan-women-killings/pakistani-family-sentenced-to-death-over-honour-killing-outside-court-idUKKCN0J30SZ20141119 (Accessed on July 2, 2024)

87   Alex Clark, February 14, 2016. 'The case of Saba Qaiser and the film-maker determined to put an end to "honour" killings'. *The Guardian*, UK. https://www.theguardian.com/film/2016/ feb/14/sharmeen-obaid-chinoy-interview-saba-qaiser-honour-killing-documentary-girl-river-oscar-nomination (Accessed on July 2, 2024)

88   Muhammad Bilal, October 6, 2016. 'Pakistan passes anti-honour killings and anti-rape bills'. *Dawn*, Pakistan. https://www.dawn. com/news/1288177 (Accessed on July 2, 2024)

89   Convention on the Elimination of All Forms of Discrimination Against Women, United Nations. https://www.un.org/womenwatch/ daw/cedaw/ (Accessed on July 2, 2024)

90 In Punjab, Pakistan

91 The Hudood Law is part of Sharia Law and enforces punishments mentioned in the Quran and sunnah for zina (extramarital sex), qazf (false accusation of zina), theft, and consumption of alcohol.

92 (i) 'Pakistan: Poor Conditions Rife in Women's Prisons'. Human Rights Watch. https://www.hrw.org/news/2020/09/07/pakistan-poor-conditions-rife-womens-prisons# (ii) Anju Anna John, February 16, 2021. 'Period Poverty in Prisons: Ensuring Menstrual Hygiene and Dignity in India.' *PenalReform.Org* https://www.penalreform.org/blog/period-poverty-in-prisons-ensuring-menstrual-hygiene-and/ (Accessed on July 4, 2024)

93 Niloufer de Mel, 2001. *Women & the Nation's Narrative: Gender and Nationalism in Twentieth Century Sri Lanka*, Rowman & Littlefield Publishers, Inc.

94 Neluka Silva, 2004. *The Gendered Nation: Contemporary Writings from South Asia*, Sage Publications; de Mel, 2001, *Women & the Nation's Narrative*. 57, 102.

95 Amrita Chhachhi, 1991. 'Forced Identities: The State, Communalism, Fundamentalism and Women in India'. In: D. Kandiyoti, (ed) *Women, Islam and the State*. Palgrave Macmillan, London.

96 Neloufer de Mel shows how this idea of 'purity' was legitimised through the construction of the binaries of pure vs impure, chaste vs promiscuous, and so on. The latter half of this binary was attributed to the Burghers and Burgher women. Ref: de Mel, 2002, *Women and the Nation's Narrative*, Kali for Women.

97 Sitralega Maunaguru is a professor at Eastern University, Sri Lanka. She wrote 'Gendering Tamil Nationalism: The Construction of 'Woman' in Projects of Protest and Control', 1995, in Pradeep Jeganathan & Qadri Ismail, eds, *Unmaking the Nation: The Politics of Identity and History in Modern Sri Lanka*. Colombo: Social Scientists' Association (158–175).

98 In this regard, the murder (death) of Ranjini Thirangama, a lecturer at Jaffna University and a strident voice speaking out against state and LTTE oppression, is a case in point.

99 The Indian activist and street theatre director, Safdar Hashmi, was killed when on stage, daring to stage protest theatre.

100 Raka Ray in her study on women-centric protest movements has shown how these often take shape from local problems and are thus

heavily influenced by local cultures and traditions. The 'Mother's Front' in Sri Lanka was similar in this aspect, being born out of a crisis of state. Moreover, when R Premadasa met his end at the hands of a suicide bomber, the perception that folk justice had taken recourse was a strongly prevalent sentiment. Raka Ray, 1999. *Fields of Protest: Women's Movements in India.* University of Minnesota Press; de Mel, 2001.

101	Also see, Mothers de Plaza de Mayo, a human rights organization, for similar movements in Argentina and in Guatemala.

102	Sanmarga's poems articulating sharp socio-political criticism first began to appear in the magazine *Sollatha Seithihal* around 1986. The war in Jaffna between the separatists and the Sri Lankan government had rapidly escalated at the time.

103	It is a well-documented fact that at this point in time, all Tamil in Jaffna were seen as prospective terrorists and treated accordingly.

104	A 'deserter' refers to a soldier absconding from duty. However the situation calls for a military court martial under the State's military law. Thus, this line appears more in keeping with the LTTE's methods.

105	Economic backwardness and the class divide thus engendered was the fundamental problem confronting post-independence governments on the island nation. A socialist revolution was seen as the need of the hour and was the prime cause impelling the student insurgency of 1971. The tragedy in all this is the invisibility of the socialist agenda in what became a brutal civil war with ethnicity as its prime agenda. Sanmarga's poem reminds us of this socialist agenda.

106	This is particularly the case in the labour intensive, agriculture economies of Asia and Africa. Refer to Jyotsana Agnihotri Gupta's *New Reproductive Technologies, Women's Health and Autonomy: Freedom or Dependency?* (Sage, New Delhi, 2000.)

107	*The Mahavamasa* is a post-canonical chronicle of Sri Lanka's history composed in the 5th century and attributed to a monk named Mahanama, about whom little else is known.

108	'Moral Mothers and Stalwart Sons', 1998. Published in *Women and the War Reader,* edited by Ann Lorentzen and Jennifer Turpin, New York University Press.

109	(i) Cathrine Brun, August 2008. 'Birds of Freedom: Young People, the LTTE, and Representations of Gender, Nationalism, and Governance in Northern Sri Lanka.' In *Critical Asian Studies*. (ii) Balasingham, Adele, 2001. *The Will to Freedom: An Inside View of Tamil Resistance*, Mitcham : Fairmax.

110 R. Cheran, 2001. *The Sixth Genre: Memory, History, and the Tamil Diaspora Imagination*, Marga Institute, Colombo.

111 It was after Black July that Sri Lankan Tamils, both young men and women flocked to militant movements afloat on the island. The revenge and rape motive were prime causes.

112 It must be pointed out that the (in)famous suicide bombings, an integral part of the LTTE's war strategy were carried out by the women cadres of the LTTE. This requires tremendous psychological training and physical discipline not to mention the will to revenge a personal wrong even if it entails the annihilation of one's body. The documentary film 'No More Tears Sister' (2005, dir. Helene Klodawsky) bears testimony to the exacting training routine of female cadres.

113 Francine D'Amico, 2007, 'Feminist Perspectives on Woman Warriors', *Peace Review*, 8(3), 379–384.

114 (i) Manoj Mitta, June 12, 2013. 'https://www.indiatoday.in/magazine/nation/story/19961115-rajasthan-court-acquits-all-accused-in-roop-kanwar-murder-case-834069-1996-11-15' *India Today*. (Accessed on July 4, 2024) (ii) https://www.indiatoday.in/magazine/nation/story/19961115-rajasthan-court-acquits-all-accused-in-roop-kanwar-murder-case-834069-1996-11-15 (Accessed on July 2, 2024)

115 'History Behind the Origin and Abolition of Sati System in India'. *Medium*. https://medium.com/@marketing_13585/history-behind-the-origin-and-abolition-of-sati-system-in-india-dc969dee7591 (Accessed on July 2, 2024)

116 Kanwarjit Singh Kang, June 27, 2015. 'Sati "choice" before Maharaja Ranjit Singh's Ranis'. *The Tribune*. https://www.tribuneindia.com/news/archive/features/-sati-choice-before-maharaja-ranjit-s-ranis-99411 (Accessed on July 2, 2024)

117 Poulomi Banerjee, February 20, 2018. 'A wrong sense of honour: The disturbing glorification of jauhar in Padmini's Chittorgarh'. *Hindustan Times*. https://www.hindustantimes.com/india-news/a-wrong-sense-of-honour-the-disturbing-glorification-of-jauhar-in-

padmini-s-chittorgarh/story-JojhRZe4pBCEaeg4zyxCNM.html (Accessed on July 4, 2024)

118 Kanishka Raina, October 29, 2018. 'How Did Sati Get Abolished in India?' *Feminism India.* https://feminisminindia.com/2018/10/29/sati-history-india/ (Accessed on July 2, 2024)

119 Rabindra Nath Choudhury, June 8, 2018. '"Sati" village in Madhya Pradesh adopts distressed women'. https://www.deccanchronicle.com/nation/current-affairs/080618/sati-village-in-madhya-pradesh-adopts-distressed-women.html (Accessed on July 2, 2024)

120 A mandal in Rangareddy district, Telangana, India

121 One of the largest scheduled caste groups in the country, concentrated in the south, engaged mainly in agriculture and leather work.

122 As per the custom of temple dedication prevalent among some Madiga families, the girls so dedicated are called Joginis or Mathangis.

123 US, 1975, dir. Milos Forman.

124 Sylvia Plath, 'Getting There'. From *The Collected Poems.* Edited and with an Introduction by Ted Hughes, Harper Perennial Modern Classics, 2018. P. 248

125 Rainer Maria Rilke, 2005. 'Go to The Limits of Your Longing', *Rilke's Book of Hours: Love Poems to God.* Riverhead Books.

126 'Bangladesh: Indigenous girls target of rape and murder in Chittagong Hill Tracts'. IGWIA.org https://www.iwgia.org/en/bangladesh/3258-bangladesh-indigenous-women.html (Accessed on July 2, 2024)

127 Shohel Chandra Hajang, March 15, 2021. 'Why are we forgetting Lakingme?' *The Daily Star*, Bangladesh. https://www.thedailystar.net/opinion/news/why-are-we-forgetting-lakingme-2060465 (Accessed on July 2, 2024)

128 'What Is Gender-Based Violence?' European Institute for Gender Equality, 29 Feb. 2024, eige.europa.eu/gender-based-violence/what-is-gender-based-violence (Accessed on July 2, 2024)

129 Development, Department for International. 'Gender Violence in Pakistan'. GOV.UK, December 10, 2010, www.gov.uk/government/case-studies/gender-violence-in-pakistan (Accessed on July 2, 2024)

130 Niqab (Urdu): a veil worn by some Muslim women in public, covering the face except the eyes.

131 Teep (Bengali): bindi; a mark (such as a red dot) or piece of jewellery worn on the middle of the forehead especially by Hindu women.

132 Anasuya Basu, May 21, 2020. 'Storm strikes 270-year-old Great Banyan Tree.' *The Telegraph*, Kolkata. https://www.telegraphindia. com/calcutta/cyclone-amphan-storm-strikes-270-year-old-great-banyan-tree/cid/1774880 (Accessed on July 2, 2024)

133 'Hawwa is Eve, created from a being, Hayya, that is Adam...' *Al-Islam.org.* https://www.al-islam.org/hayat-al-qulub-vol-1-allamah-muhammad-baqir-al-majlisi/merits-adam-and-hawwa-eve-reasons-behind And Satrupa is emblematic of the first woman, Manu's wife, in Hindu lore.

134 Shruti Srivastava, July 11, 2017. 'Here's how "Adam" and "Eve" are explained in Vedas'. https://www.speakingtree.in/blog/heres-how-adam-and-eve-are-explained-in-vedas *Speaking Tree*, a *Times of India* publication.

135 Deepti Naval, 'In the Abyss of Night', published in *Black Wind and Other Poems*, Mapin Publishers, 2004.

Additional references for 'Impunity Guaranteed: Brazen Condonations of Violence Against Women' by Kalpana Kannabiran

1. Kannabiran, Kalpana, 2008a. 'Sexual Assault and the Law'. In Kannabiran, K and Singh, R. eds. *Challenging the Rule(s) of Law: Colonialism, Criminology and Human Rights in India*. New Delhi: Sage.

2. Kannabiran, Kalpana, 2008b. 'The Contexts of Criminology in India'. In Kannabiran, K and Singh, R. eds. *Challenging the Rule(s) of Law: Colonialism, Criminology and Human Rights in India*. New Delhi: Sage.

3. Kannabiran, Kalpana, and Reddy, B.S. 2019. *Constitutional Justice is Non-Negotiable. The Hindu.* 9 December.

4. Kannabiran, Kalpana. 2020. '*#I Can't Breathe: Governance by Annihilation and by Hate*'. Livelaw, 3 October. https://www. livelaw.in/columns/i-cant-breathe-governance-by-annihilation-and-by-hate-163925 (Accessed on 1 June 2024.)

5. Sellers, Patricia Viseur. 2002. 'Sexual Violence and Peremptory Norms: The Legal Value of Rape', 34 Case *Western Reserve Journal of International Law* 287.

www.ingramcontent.com/pod-product-compliance
Lightning Source LLC
LaVergne TN
LVHW042346190726

843493LV00005B/943